D0340107

Neo-Baroque

✤

Neo-Baroque

A SIGN OF THE TIMES

✛

OMAR CALABRESE

Translated by Charles Lambert
With a Foreword by UMBERTO ECO

PRINCETON UNIVERSITY PRESS

PRINCETON, NEW JERSEY

Library of Congress Cataloging-in-Publication Data
Calabrese, Omar
[Età neobarocca. English]
Neo-baroque : a sign of the times / Omar Calabrese ; translated by
Charles Lambert ; with a foreword by Umberto Eco.
p.   cm.
Translation of: L'età neobarocca.
Includes bibliographical references and index.
ISBN 0-691-03171-1
1. Arts, Modern—20th century—Themes, motives.
2. Arts, Modern—20th century—Philosophy.   I. Title.
NX456.C3213   1992   700′.9′04—dc20   91-44179

This book has been composed in Linotron Galliard

Printed in the United States of America

1   3   5   7   9   10   8   6   4   2

First published in Italy as *L'età neobarocca* by Editori Laterza, 1987.
Copyright © 1987, Gius. Laterza & Figli Spa, Rome-Bari.

✥ *Contents* ✥

✢ *Foreword* ✢

ALL THE REASONS I am delighted to be writing a foreword to Omar Calabrese's book are reasons for not doing so—with a single exception.

I welcome *Neo-Baroque: A Sign of the Times* because it is written by a friend, by a colleague at the University of Bologna with whom I have research, seminars, and students in common. I welcome the book because it is the work of a fellow semiologist; and also because it is the work of a semiologist who, instead of looking for subjects to analyze with the tools of semiology, begins by finding a subject that needs to be studied, and then applies his semiological knowledge. And when he realizes that semiology is not enough he turns to sociology, the history of culture, the history of ideas, and so on. He might possess this flexibility precisely because he is a semiologist. Whatever the reason, he is not a dogmatic semiologist, and that is why I like him.

Finally, Calabrese analyzes certain phenomena in the mass media not because he is a professor of semiology, but because, in some perverse (and yet healthy) way, he loves them. Or rather, he is conscious of living in a culture in which these phenomena not only exist, but also determine our way of thinking, however isolated we might consider ourselves to be in the ivory towers of the university campus, immune to the charms of Coca-Cola, more attuned to Plato than to Madison Avenue. Calabrese is aware that this is not true, and that even the way in which we, or at least our students, read Plato—if they do—is determined by the existence of "Dallas," even for those who never watch it. And so he tries to incorporate the events around him into his understanding.

For all these reasons I am delighted to write this foreword. According to a certain ethic of instant criticism, however, they ought to prevent me from doing so. Even though we think differently about many issues, we are too close for me to be considered a reliable witness.

But, as I said, I have a genuine reason for writing these few pages. Calabrese himself expresses it at the end of his introduction. It is the fact that someone has suggested a relationship between this book and a somewhat distant work of my own, *Opera aperta: Forma a indeterminazione nelle poetiche contemporanee*, published for the first time in Italy in 1962, but containing reelaborated essays that had already appeared in the period since 1958.

It would hardly be worth talking about this book if Harvard University Press had not decided to translate it as *The Open Work* in 1989. It appears, with a few stylistic corrections, in the form it assumed for the French publication in 1965, with the addition of some essays written in the years immediately after. Essentially, however, it proposes ideas that I had during the 1950s and 1960s. In fact, I only agreed to allow its translation on the condition that someone else (David Robey) write a foreword explaining the cultural environment in which the book appeared and the questions it attempted to answer.

Now, pondering what the differences are between *The Open Work* and *Neo-Baroque: A Sign of the Times* is not simply the subject of a private conversation that I might have with Omar Calabrese in a Faculty Club, over a medium-rare steak and—if the laws of the state permit—a glass of beer. The subject of the conversation would be whether Omar Calabrese (fortunately, younger than I am), if he had written in 1958–1962, would have produced a book similar to *The Open Work* (or, at least, I hope so for his sake); and how closely my book would have resembled *Neo-Baroque: A Sign of the Times* (at least in terms of its presentation of the problem, and the examples chosen) if I had written it now.[1] This is not a private problem, but one that concerns the cultural climate of our century (and possibly even the contraposition between modern and postmodern, although I hesitate to enter such a shadowy and treacherous field).

The situation that faced me at the end of the 1950s was one in which the art of that period seemed to have pushed to an extreme a feature that is characteristic of all art throughout history, a characteristic that the aesthetics of reception and reader-oriented criticism would later reveal more clearly: if any type of message can be interpreted in a way that differs from the intentions of its author, and the author makes an intentional attempt to create an "open" message in the work of art so that it can be interpreted in various ways, this openness then becomes a feature of the aesthetic message. Art during the first half of the century pushed this tendency to the forefront, to such an extent that certain works (especially in so-called post-Webernian music) were offered to their performers (and audience) as a kit of elements that could be assembled in a variety of ways.

When I wrote my book in 1962, however, I had to take into account both a fact and a philosophical assumption. The fact was that openness was a phenomenon found in the avant-garde, but extraneous to messages circulating in the universe of the mass media.[2] The philosophical assumption was that, in all cases and regardless of the liberties the interpreter might take, what I was concerned with was the dialectic between the interpreter's initiative and the structure of the work. More simply, Joyce's *Ulysses* can stimulate *many* interpretations, but not all possible interpretations: some interpretations are worse than others, and in order to decide upon their validity we need to return to the nature of the text, however "open" it might be. In every case, the interpretations had to be of *Ulysses* and not, for example, of the *Odyssey*.[3]

Calabrese is concerned with a problem that is different, for two reasons. Above all he is no longer dealing with two universes, the avant-garde and the mass media, since the distance between these two spheres has been greatly reduced. Nor is he dealing any longer with works and their interpreters, but with processes, flows and interpretative drifts that concern, not single works, but the totality of messages that circulate in the area of communication.

In other words, the "reader" I spoke of in *The Open Work* was confronted by an author who proposed a message, and then had to make his own decisions. Calabrese's "reader," on the other hand, has a remote control device in his hand, which he can use to compose his own message by taking excerpts from the infinite messages that assail him from every direction.

Although I might have simplified the terms of the issue, I believe that this example is the only way of establishing the difference between what Calabrese is dealing with now and what I was concerned with then.

This mutation no longer interests just the two of us. It interests everyone. Even though Calabrese's proposals might not satisfy all of his readers, the problem he is discussing involves profound cultural transformations that have taken place during the last thirty years.

I believe that it is opportune to insist upon the importance of these mutations, and the overwhelming need we have to define them in some way. Since I have not written this book by Calabrese myself, I think it is only fair that I recommend it to the reader, suggesting that he read it with the same interest, the same tension—and in the same questioning spirit—that I have.

UMBERTO ECO

✤ *Preface* ✤

THERE ARE SOME curious people at large in today's cultural world. People who have no fear of committing *lese majesté* when they consider whether a link might exist between the most recent scientific discovery involving cardiac fibrillation and an American soap opera. People who imagine a strange connection between a sophisticated avant-garde novel and a common children's comic strip. People who see a relationship between a futuristic mathematical hypothesis and the characters in a popular film.

My intention in writing this book is to become a member of that group. The nature of what I hope to do is effectively the same: to search for signs of the existence of a contemporary "taste" that links the most disparate objects, from science to mass communications, from art to everyday habits. I can already hear the objections: "How amusing, someone who can't distinguish between Donald Duck and Dante, who's looking for connections when no evidence for them exists." I am therefore obliged to begin with an *excusatio non petita*. It can be summed up by the following two principles.

First, in my descriptions of contemporary cultural phenomena I shall leave their "quality" to one side, if, by "quality," we mean value judgment. The issue here is not to establish which are the finest works of art but simply to examine the existence of a "mentality," or shared perspective of taste. Since value judgments are themselves the product of taste, I prefer to begin with a general definition of that taste rather than with its effects.

Second, it is perfectly legitimate to see connections between objects that are intentionally produced at a distance from one another. If this were not so, one would have to conclude that what is important in the description of phenomena is the intention of their creator, which is not always the case. All of us know far more than we think we know and say far more than

xi

we think we say. The entire culture of an age speaks, to a greater or lesser extent and to a more or less profound degree, in all our work. It is precisely by not producing hierarchies and ghettos among texts that we can discover recurring trends that distinguish "our" mentality (in this case our "taste") from that of other periods. It is only by pursuing unlikely connections that we shall discover—if we allow ourselves the benefit of the doubt—how that mentality and taste might develop.

But what is the prevailing taste—if it exists—of our epoch, apparently so confused, fragmented, and indecipherable? I believe that I have found it, and I should like to propose a name for it: *neo-baroque*. But I should make it clear that this name does not mean that we have "returned" to the baroque. Nor do I think that what I define as "neo-baroque" sums up all the aesthetic production of this society, in either its dominant or its most positive aspects. "Neo-baroque" is simply a "spirit of the age" that pervades many of today's cultural phenomena in all fields of knowledge, making them familiar to each other and, simultaneously, distinguishing them from other cultural phenomena in a more or less recent past. It is by means of this spirit that I am able to associate certain current scientific theories (catastrophe, fractals, dissipative structures, theories of chaos and complexity, and so on) with certain forms of art, literature, philosophy, and even cultural consumption. This does not mean that there is a direct link. It simply means that the *motive* behind them is the same, and that this motive has assumed a specific form in each intellectual field.

It is easy to say what "neo-baroque" consists of: a search for, and valorization of, forms that display a loss of entirety, totality, and system in favor of instability, polydimensionality, and change. This is why a scientific theory concerned with fluctuation and turbulence is related to a science fiction film depicting mutants: both fields share an orientation of taste. The order of chaos had remained undiscovered not because the discovery could not be made, but because nobody was sufficiently interested in doing so. Just like the monster in *Alien*.

But how can we identify which features connect such different phenomena? We can work randomly, using our intuition to make a list and running a considerable risk at each stage. Alternatively, as I shall be doing here, we can begin from the following general principle: If we are able to notice "similarities" and "differences" between phenomena that appear to be extremely distant from each other, this means that there is "something behind them." That, beneath the surface, an underlying form permits comparison and connection. A *form*. An abstract organization of phenomena, which governs their internal system of relationships.

We have thus arrived at the basic principle behind this book, which is not simply a desire to identify the taste of our time, but also to *illustrate it methodically*. Even the table of contents is organized according to a certain criterion: each chapter title refers not only to a formal concept of "neo-baroque," but also to a scientific expression. The reason is clear: the formal concept in question is analogous to a theory in the field of physics or mathematics. This is not affectation on my part. The decision to describe the *form* of cultural phenomena corresponds in fact to the nature of the theories being called into play. They are all theories that refer to spatial criteria. They not only "resemble" the formal concepts, but are also able to explain them. In this way, we achieve another aim: the production of consistent and methodical descriptions.

A desire for consistency and pertinence in descriptions within the human sciences seems to me to be legitimate, quite independently of the result of the present work. An antimethodical breeze, with which I have little sympathy, has recently blown through the world of humanistic thought. But the death of rationality cannot be regarded as a consequence of the decline of certain forms of rationality. On the contrary, their decline can only lead to the search for new forms of rationality that are more adequate for the present. This seems to be increasingly necessary in the human sciences if we want to avoid a sense of having given up our efforts to understand phenomena in the face of a disturbing new "age of chatter." This is why, in the first chapter, the reader will have to put up with a lengthy discussion of method before directly entering the argument. It is also why, of all the general dimensions in which the "neo-baroque" could be examined, I have chosen the most difficult: aesthetics. Almost by definition, aesthetics seems to be the most difficult field to analyze without the aid of intuition. It is, finally, why the themes that have already been mentioned will be flanked by other apparently less pertinent examples: in order to increase the sense of adventure and to illustrate more clearly the risks that are entailed in the field of "improbable links."

A final comment: this book is primarily concerned with the way in which contemporary society expresses its intellectual products, independently of their quality or function. Second, it recognizes that what these products have in common is the spirit in which they are expressed, communicated, and received. If I had to sum up the book in a single phrase I would say that it represents an attempt to identify a "social aesthetics." I would like to thank Paolo Fabbri for having coined this expression, which broadly defines the spirit of my book.

Finally, my dedication and thanks. My dedication goes to my students at Bologna, who have followed the courses on which this book is based for three years, with enthusiasm and, above all, numerous suggestions. I would also like to thank the large number of friends who have participated in the work. First of all, Francesco Casetti, for having read the manuscript so attentively and for having suggested innumerable ideas that I have since adopted as my own. I would equally like to thank Claudio Castellacci, a passionate collector of "neo-baroque" objects (and, as such, my advisor). I shall name no more, to avoid producing the effect of a telephone directory, but they should all be aware that I know and recognize each and every intellectual debt. For the errors and imprecisions contained in this work, I assume full responsibility.

Neo-Baroque

✤

CHAPTER 1

Taste and Method

SOME PRELIMINARY QUESTIONS

Is THERE a character, a quality, a general distinctive sign that we could use to define our epoch? The answer is clearly anything but easy, since the banal simplicity of the question conceals a number of theoretical traps. Let us try to see what they are. The first hidden question: What does "epoch" mean and, above all, how can we define it as "ours"? The second implicit question: Is it acceptable to label historical periods in order to create a general (or, even worse, generic) order? The third presupposition: Why, in any case, should we search for *one* character to define an epoch? Is it acceptable to separate segments of time so sharply from one another, differentiating them according to their homogeneity or lack of it? The fourth, final, and most serious problem: Where does this "character" reside? In human psychology, in public or private behavior, in political or economic history, in social structure, in the form taken by thought, in the arts, in the sciences?

Let us now examine these problems in order, beginning with the question of "epoch." We know that this term, like all equivalent terms used to construct periodization, creates confusion among historians.[1] It is no accident that the term is used with extreme caution, with warnings to readers, for example, that it has been adopted for the sake of convention or simplicity. In effect, the concept of "epoch" or "age" or "period" contrasts with many traditional ways of understanding the flow of events. History would appear to be made up of chains of cause and effect, rather than of sudden, clearly identifiable breaks. To group events together according to categories that separate them from their predecessors and successors even seems paradoxical.[2] It is also true, however, that a more interpretative historiography exists whose first concern is precisely with the recognition of the effects of definition and articulation, rather than with an explanation of causes or origins. This is frequently true of the history of art, literature, music, and every other creative activity. *Before* seeking the prior motivation of a fact or group of facts it is essential to define the *facts* themselves. This is why, for example, we have notions such as "style," "motif," "type," and "taste." These notions succeed events in more compact segments. Their outset is established in a conventional sense and without great importance being attached to it, and their duration is widely variable, on the condition that the "effects" (that is, the objects produced) are sufficiently significant numerically to permit their categorization.

The discussion becomes a little more complicated, however, when we try to attribute a homogeneity and specificity to our own period. From an event-based historical viewpoint it is more difficult to group together phenomena whose coherence is debatable, when compared to a completed historical period whose body of events has been established. Establishing the reciprocal pertinence of events from the perspective of an unknown present and future—which permits nothing but hypothetical forecasts—means running constant risks simply for the pleasure of doing so.[3] Nor is it that easy to establish the pertinence of phenomena when they become confused with many other phenomena that will not be considered pertinent. Nevertheless, a criterion based on common sense does appear to be applicable: taking account of the "emergence" of certain facts compared to the movement of others that fail to provoke "excitement." In other words, in order to establish the relationship and pertinence of certain facts in one "epoch" and not others, we should consider the totality of the culture, as if it were a stock exchange index. There are securities that earn steadily, and have done so for some time: these have no bearing on monthly trends. There are also shares that suddenly rise and fall; it is these other shares that define movement within the market. They do so because of the "excitement" they provoke among traders when compared to the rest of the shares. Even when these shares are in a minority, they are responsible for establishing general trends. It is this feature of "excitement" produced within a cultural system, and among the people who benefit from it, that can provide us with a way of defining an epoch or period.[4]

The second problem stems directly from the first. Is it permissible to use a series of emerging motifs to label an epoch? In the history of taste or style, key words are frequently used to describe periods in an extremely simplified, abstract way. Here are the Middle Ages, with their centuries of obscurantism, ignorance, and superstition. Here is the Renaissance, with its rationality and humanism. And here is the baroque period, involuted, absolutist, and enigmatic. And we can carry on in this way, without ever leaving the field of art history. But simplifications of this type are no help at all in our understanding of cultural history. On the contrary, they flatten it out into a flaccid formalism that has nothing to do with reality. It would thus be an even graver mistake to propose them for an analysis of the present, since it is not yet possible—because of a "lack of good distance"[5]—to distinguish clearly what is important from what is not. In any case, no historical moment can be reduced to a single label for the simple reason that history is produced by the clash of distinct, conflictual, and complex phenomena— phenomena that might even be incommensurable or possess no common ground whatsoever. Having said this, however, it must also be stated that phenomena do form "series" or "families" as a result of shared features. We cannot deny, for example, the existence during the nineteenth-century Restoration period of a series of events on the European scene—in art and literature as much as in economics and politics—that indicate a Continental project to "reestablish order." Although not everything that happened after 1815 forms a coherent part of such a project, it is justifiable to group together the many events that do. Furthermore, since the Restoration was the most widespread and dominant idea, it is quite possible to define a certain period of the century as one of "restoration." It is equally clear, however, that by changing our viewpoint—in terms of social group or focus—we can use something else to classify the "quality" of the epoch, such as the new intellectual spirit of romanticism. The problem, therefore, is simply to define precisely the selected viewpoint and what is pertinent to it, and to establish on which basis the criterion of coherence among the phenomena to be analyzed is to be articulated.

We have now implicitly answered the third question, regarding the uniqueness of an epoch's character. If the character depends on the viewpoint and a system of shared features, it is clear that there exist not *one* character, but many. Furthermore, these characters can exist in a variety of different ways within the same system of shared features or viewpoint. We have just said that society is a complex totality. This means that while we can consider it as a "totality" or "system" (in the manner of a biological system)[6] that represents, micro- or macroscopically, the same features at each stage of its articulation, we can also consider it as something constituted by competing subgroups or subsystems. Some of these emerge successfully, some are defeated, others produce further mutations in spite of defeat, and those that win are destined to a final extinction through exhaustion. In other words, culture can be seen as an organic totality, in which each element has a hierarchically ordered relationship with all the others. We can use Eco's term "encyclopedia" to define this totality.[7] The encyclopedia, however, with regard to each of these elements operates as a general ordering principle, a kind of overall ideal of the organization of knowledge. When we are confronted by individual concrete elements, however, it is difficult to take the *entire* encyclopedia into consideration. Although we might appeal to the postulate of its general organization, we shall only be concerned with a single region, be it large or small. We shall, in other words, be analyzing only one of its "localities."[8] This locality, however, is also organized according to grids of models: these grids constitute the "quality" that unites certain cultural objects locally.[9] At a certain scale, therefore, this quality can be unique, while by changing scale it can be multiplied.

But let us return to the issue of the character of an epoch and to the corollary of our third question: whether it is acceptable to separate historical segments so distinctly from each other. The question brings to mind the conflict between, on the one hand, some of Foucault's basic ideas and, on the other, those of the "microhistorians." To sum up the discussion very briefly, we should recall that one of the most vigorously contested points in Foucault's thought (both in the past and more recently) was his idea of the "episteme."[10] According to Foucault, there are epochs in which a change in mentality is so radical (such as the seventeenth century) that one can justifiably speak of a rupture with the past. This is a strikingly important idea that undermines one of the principles of traditional historiography, that of causality understood as a necessary relationship between a "before" and an "after." It must be recognized, however, that there are also some risks involved in Foucault's concept. The risk, for example, of seeing a *single common denominator* in events, with a consequent twisting of local interpretations according to the logic of the frame in which they are contained.[11] It is obvious, however, that a "logic of culture" exists, even though it might not always be the only one, and in spite of the fact that it would be improper to circumscribe it into portions according to a rigid temporal scheme. We might even say that the feature that has distinguished natural science since Aristotle can also be seen in the history of ideas. Physics, for example, has always conducted its empirical and theoretical research according to the belief that an organizing principle exists in the universe. This can be seen in the concept of *Kulturgeschichte*: as though its logic were unitary. We probably need to reach a compromise. "Characters," "epistemes," and "mentalities" of epochs exist, and they can be recognized as grids of relations among cultural objects. Two points, however, must be made. First, we do not need to trace the precise chronological definition of these grids. Second, they are never unifying features of an epoch, but only of one style of thought and life that enters into a more or less productive conflict with others. In the history of art this principle has on occasion been understood. Two books by Eugenio Battisti and Federico Zeri provide us with examples. Battisti has described the way in which two philosophies fought for supremacy during the same period, with a victor—the Renaissance—and a suppressed loser—the anti-Renaissance.[12] And Zeri has demonstrated in a masterly fashion how a victorious idea in the historical scene, the Renaissance, can render homogeneous less successful ideas, as in the case of what Zeri terms the "pseudo-Renaissance."[13]

These final reflections, however, have brought us to the crux of the matter: the criterion for analyzing those recurrences that permit us to define an epoch's "characters." At this point, it must be admitted, the issue becomes complex. On the one hand, it is fair to express the need for a criterion of method. On the other hand, however, we must reject the homogenization of cultural objects by genre or type (the banalization of method).[14] How can these two needs be reconciled? Let us begin with method. And let us say that we can ensure control over the objects being analyzed only by interdefining the concepts that are being applied. Phenomena never speak for themselves in an evident way. They need to be "provoked." This is equivalent to saying that we need to construct them as theoretical objects, since they have no immediate objectivity.[15] All that exists is the coherence of the perspective from which they are to be questioned, the viewpoint that provokes the response. This is an old problem in the scientific world. The objectivity of the system of chemical elements was established by Lavoisier using, as his criterion, the uniqueness of "weight," the most subjective and conventional of methods.[16] Metaphorically we might say that it is also necessary to "weigh" elements in culture, in order to make them commensurable. Leaving metaphor to one side, these elements constitute a system only when they are related to a system of concepts. Many conceptual systems exist, and the human sciences offer a wide range. It is not my purpose here to suggest that one system might be better than another. I am simply interested in "putting one system to work." Let us see in what way.

If we consider each cultural object as something that can be communicated, we shall immediately see that it becomes part of a communicative chain. It is created by an individual or collective subject, it is produced according to certain mechanisms of production, it manifests itself by means of certain forms and contents, it passes through certain channels, it is received by an individual or collective addressee, it determines certain forms of behavior. The relevant analyses might be carried out for each stage in this series. But this is still insufficient. Further relevant features exist that might be used to examine each polarity of the chain. For example, we might consider the physical existence of the creator in his society, in which case we would be able to reinstate him by using empirical socioeconomic analyses; or we might regard him as an apparatus of production, and thus isolate the professional and decision-making routines involved; or, finally, we might see him as an author and trace his philological and individual history. The same might be said of the receiver: it might be evaluated as the "public," in which case the effects of certain messages can be assessed in a sociological or psychological context; or, alternatively, it might be regarded as an abstract figure, constructed according to a communicative strategy, in which case a pragmatic approach will illustrate the ways in which a text can be called into play. This is also true of the message: it can be seen as determined by other messages, thus leading once again to the production of a philological or textual critique or history; and it might be regarded as a totality of forms and contents, in which case we would apply a semiotic approach.[17]

Let us now come, however, to the body of objects to be examined. The principle that must be rejected is that of homogeneity of genre, type, or art form. For example, this work is not concerned (even though others might be) with verifying the existence of grids of relations of taste or mentality for objects that *are specifically produced to be homogeneous with other objects*. Obviously one can establish the existence of a cinematic, literary, or artistic taste within the confines of a story, an aesthetic, or a critical discipline. But it is far more difficult to seek out the (generally concealed) connections between objects that originate as different, rather than as already belonging to a single cultural series. The progress of ideas almost always derives from the discovery of unexpected relations, unconsidered links, and unimagined grids. A discovery of sense is usually made precisely where previously there reigned not senselessness but an absence of sense. Obviously, to operate in this way involves running risks. It means, for example, making the objects that are being analyzed say more than they actually say. But this risk, fascinating and productive as it is, is not just a question of building castles in the air. We all say more than we know or even imagine that we know. We can never understand all there is to understand in our society's culture, yet the cultural objects that we produce are sometimes capable of expressing implicitly areas of the culture that are quite distant from those that they reveal explicitly. The totality of a culture produces an individual unconscious, a collective unconscious, and even, if we choose to adopt a popular expression, "an unconscious of the work."[18]

The criterion we shall adopt, therefore, is the following. We shall examine widely disparate cultural objects, such as literary, artistic, musical, and architectural works; films, songs, cartoons, and television; scientific and technological theories and philosophical thought. We shall consider these objects insofar as they are phenomena of communication, phenomena that are endowed with an underlying form or structure. My belief is that one can discover certain "deep forms" or common features between disparate objects that have no apparent causal relation. In other words, by considering texts deriving from a number of different fields, we shall notice the actuation of a "relapse" into underlying structures between one text and the next. The con-

cept of "relapse" has been adopted from the work of Severo
Sarduy.[19] In his study of the baroque Sarduy has linked aspects
of science and art, concluding, for example, that the form of
Kepler's discovery of the elliptical orbit of planets is similar to
that underlying the poetry of Góngora, Caravaggio's paintings,
and the architecture of Borromini. In my opinion, analogous
phenomena can be found in every epoch, including our own,
and their repetition might be considered an "epochal trait,"
even bearing in mind all the qualifications expressed above. But
I shall be even more cautious. In spite of Sarduy's clearly structuralist background (Barthes on the one hand and Lacan on the
other), there still appears to be a residual trace of determinism
in his work. Sarduy is secretly convinced, in fact, that the "relapse" has an orientation: that it moves from science to art.
Frankly, there is no evidence for this. It might easily be true
that an important scientific discovery is able, like a kind of
"origin," to revolutionize the mentality of a period.[20] But the
opposite might just as easily be the case: a taste deriving from
art, literature, or mass communication might influence the
body of scientific thought. Establishing before and after, cause
and effect, can on occasion become unintelligible (assuming
we do not think that this is *always* the case). Having discovered
a circle or spiral of reciprocal connections, any single point
might be considered the cause of all successive points, since this
sometimes helps us to put them into perspective, and to situate
them in a conceptual order. In any case, the idea of producing
a formulation of relations (whether the formulation is auda-
cious or not is insignificant) that others can then enrich with
other methods and aims is already interesting. The formulation of a typical "taste" of our epoch, probably conflictual with
other tastes and not necessarily dominant, can be derived from
the characteristics of these connections.

A final warning. We have talked insistently about "taste" and
"forms." It would be as well, then, to make clear that precisely
because of our initial hypotheses, directed essentially toward
the search for a substantially aesthetic "character of the epoch,"

the fundamental point of our research is not only to describe forms, but also to understand what kinds of value judgment they provoke in our society. Each society delineates more or less normative value systems by which it judges itself. Here we shall try to understand one of the recurring value systems in our own society. We shall not base our understanding on sanctions (critical or popular success, the legal system, religion, or politics) but on the *proposal of values* that each text inevitably contains. No work of art exists that does not itself suggest how it should be read and judged, that does not contain some kind of preestablished user's guide. But since we are examining primarily creative or inventive texts, our system of axiological categories will be developed directly from aesthetics, rather than from an ethical, emotional, or physical position.[21] In any case, it takes only a glance to realize that our present society seems to be more widely permeated by a kind of "mass aestheticization" than any previous society.[22]

The Term "Neo-Baroque"

To be perfectly honest, our expressive field already possesses a catchall term that has been widely used to define a contemporary trend: the much abused "postmodern." This term has by now lost its original meaning and has become a slogan or label for a wide variety of different creative operations. The term, in fact, is simultaneously equivocal and generic. Its diffusion is effectively related to three cultural contexts that are frequently confused.

The first, essentially American, use of the term dates from the 1960s, when it referred to literature and cinema. In this context it simply meant that certain literary products existed that did not base themselves on experimentation (conceived as "modernism") but on reelaboration, pastiche, and the deconstruction of the immediately preceding literary (or cinematic) heritage.[23]

The second cultural context is strictly philosophical and re-fers to the well-known work by Jean-François Lyotard, *The Postmodern Condition*,[24] originally no more than a report pre-pared for Quebec's Council of State dealing with advanced Western societies and the development of knowledge within them. The adjective "postmodern" was explicitly picked up by American sociologists during the 1960s, when it was adopted as a concept and reformulated into an original philosophical notion.[25] Lyotard himself writes: "It describes the state of a culture after transformations undergone in the rules governing science, literature, and the arts since the end of the nineteenth century. These transformations will here be related to the crisis in narrations [. . .]. Simplifying to the greatest possible ex-tent, we can consider as "postmodern" our incredulity when faced by metanarrations."[26]

The third and final context is that of architecture and design. In this field the term has achieved success primarily in Italy and the United States. Its starting point was the famous Venice Biennale dedicated to the "Strada Novissima," whose cata-logue, edited by Paolo Portoghesi, was entitled *Postmodern*.[27] In this sector "postmodern" begins to take on a precise ideo-logical meaning, representing the revolt against the principles of functionalism and rationalism that characterized the Modern Movement.

As we can see, although a link between the three cultural contexts clearly exists, it is extremely tenuous. In literature the term "postmodern" signifies antiexperimentalism; in philoso-phy it means casting doubt on a culture founded upon narra-tions that then become prescriptive; in architecture it describes a return to citation from the past, to decoration, and to the sur-face of the object being conceived in a way that contradicts its structure or use. In short, three greatly differing results. They also remain undefined since the most disparate operations have been grouped together beneath the umbrella of overinclusive labels. The practice of citation, for example, has been consid-ered a distinctive feature, but without explaining what type (given that a literature or cinema or art of citation has always existed); or a concern with the surface effect of the work, without any specification being offered; or, finally, a hostility toward "modernism," without realizing that the theoretical framework (Lyotard) certainly did not deny the value of experimentation in the so-called "avant-garde." In this particular context, a very recent book by Lyotard himself, *A Child's Guide to Postmodernism*, examines seven years of postmodern fashions and refuses to accept the commonly held belief in the existence of a look or style of thought either subsequent to or in conflict with modernism.[28] The French philosopher denounces the attempts being made—by self-styled disciples as much as by detractors—to annul, either through praise or criticism, the experimentation that has been carried out in all fields of thought since the beginning of this century. The term "postmodern," in short, continues to be equivocal. For many people, in fact, it has taken the place of a genuine program or manifesto, whereas, according to Lyotard, it was intended to be a criterion for analysis. For many other people it has become a classificatory reference point, under whose banner movements and "-isms" such as the Transavanguardia, neo-expressionism, neo-futurism, and so on have gathered.[29]

But is a generic program (a reaction against modernism) sufficient to define such complex groups of artistic, scientific, and social phenomena as those existing today?[30] And is it enough to declare the end of the avant-garde and experimentalism as the characteristic of so-called postmodern objects? Something more is required from an interpretation. It should at the very least begin with a coherent description of what is being interpreted, and an explanation of the descriptive methods being used. This is why I intend to propose a different label for some of the cultural objects of our epoch (not necessarily those that have been described as "postmodern"). This label is "neo-baroque."

I should immediately like to make it clear that I have no particular affection for this term. It is simply a label like any other.

It does, however, sum up the specific meaning that I intend to give to it. My general thesis is that many important cultural phenomena of our time are distinguished by a specific internal "form" that recalls the baroque.

More than one objection might immediately be raised to the term that has just been suggested. The prefix "neo-," to begin with. Just as the "post-" of "postmodern" brings to mind an "after" or "against" modernism, so "neo-" might induce an idea of repetition, return, or recycling of a specific historical period, that described by the term "baroque." Naturally, the reference to baroque works by analogy, and in many cases I shall try to make the analogy clear. But this does not imply in any sense a hypothetical "recuperation" of the period. Just as the idea of development or progress within a civilization is to be rejected as overdeterministic, so the idea of cycles must be regarded as unacceptably idealistic and metahistorical. "We never step into the same river twice," in other words. What must be made clear, then, is exactly what I mean by "baroque."

In order to do this I should like to draw once more upon one of Sarduy's intuitions. He defines "baroque" not only, or not exactly, as a specific period in the history of culture, but as a general attitude and formal quality of those objects in which the attitude is expressed. In this sense, the baroque might be found in any epoch of our civilization. "Baroque" almost becomes a category of the spirit, in contrast to "classical."[31] Since I do not intend to arrive at a newly metahistorical approach here, however, I should like to translate Sarduy's idea in another way. For example, if we were able to demonstrate the existence in cultural phenomena of underlying forms and of their structural development, and if we were also able to demonstrate that these forms coexist in a state of conflict with others of a different nature and interior stability, we could then say, for example, that we attribute to "baroque" a certain morphological value and to "classical" a second morphological value in opposition to the first. "Baroque" and "classical" would thus no longer be categories of the spirit, but categories of form (of

15

expression or of content). In this sense, any phenomenon would be either classical or baroque, and the same fate would await any age or episteme in which one or the other emerged. This would not exclude the fact that manifestations at any single historical moment maintain their specificity and difference insofar as they are singular cases.

To be perfectly honest, this is not the first time that the term "neo-baroque" has been employed. It was used by Gillo Dorfles, for example, in his work entitled *Baroque in Modern Architecture*, and Dorfles himself took the term from Brinck-mann: even more, in Dorfles's *In Praise of Disharmony*, where, although the term itself is not used, some of the principles that will be developed in the present work are dealt with in some way. In the modern age, in fact, Dorfles identifies the abandonment (or decline) of all characteristics of order and symmetry and glimpses the advent (not always positive, although not necessarily negative either) of disharmony and asymmetry.[32] There are certainly many similarities between the concepts expressed by Dorfles and those developed in this work, such as the rereading in a modern key of certain interpreters (Wölfflin, D'Ors, Anceschi, Focillon). But there are also some profound differences. Dorfles is in favor of attributing a specific historical period to "neo-baroque," a period of the twentieth century that is already in the past, containing movements such as cubism, organicism, or neo-imperialism in architecture. He also claims that "postmodernism" is a later phenomenon. A similar collocation in a sort of implicit history of styles will not be entirely accepted in this work. Nor will the idea (taken up by Focillon and Wölfflin) of a historical "rhythm" or "cyclicity." Classical and baroque will be accepted as formal constants, as will their dominance in one period rather than in another. The principle of their irreversibility, however, will be rejected. In reality history does not reveal—unless it is forced to do so—an alternation of two constants (as Wölfflin and Focillon claim). Nor does it allow us to establish—without the use of unmotivated imaginative leaps—that the classical is the point at which a cultural system reaches perfection and the baroque its degenerate correlative (as Focillon insists).

Another element present in Dorfles that is not considered relevant to this work is his evaluation of the baroque. Like other critics from the 1950s, as well as Sarduy, Dorfles "re-evaluates" the baroque both as a specific epoch and as a formal constant. In our case, it is not a question of judging but of recognizing the reemergence of this constant. Or rather, of understanding or explaining why positive or negative sanctions of taste might exist. Attributing judgment is, it seems to me, consistent with the appearance of homogeneous objects. Aesthetic judgment, in short, is as much a part of the "character of the epoch" as the objects it judges. We have only to think about this to realize how banal it is: as we have already said, every work contains its own instructions for use, even in an aesthetic sense.[33]

CLASSICAL AND BAROQUE

It is obvious that any *formal* consideration of the style of an epoch immediately recalls the numerous theories of art on which formalism has been based. The first mention naturally goes to Heinrich Wölfflin. In his *Fundamental Concepts in the History of Art* Wölfflin explains exactly what is meant by the term "formal": "The present study does not analyze the beauty of a Leonardo or a Dürer, but the element in which that beauty has taken form [. . .] it studies the character of the artistic conception that has been at the base of figurative art for a number of centuries."[34] Beginning from these principles, Wölfflin elaborates his method, which we shall summarize in the following way: (a) each work or series of works is the complex and combined manifestation of certain abstract and elementary "forms"; (b) these elementary forms can be defined as a list of oppositions, since a form is not perceived in itself but only through a system of differences; (c) a "style" thus becomes a specific way of operating with choices made between the poles of basic categories, and usually corresponds to principles of individual, collective, epochal, or even racial coherence. This is why we can define a "historical" style as a totality of the ways in which choices have taken form and been translated into *figures* during a certain period.[35] But, at the same time, there exists an *abstract* style that consists of the logic of both possible choices combined. This is the case of two styles that are simultaneously historical and abstract: classicism and baroque. They take form, for example, in the Renaissance and in what is known as the "historical baroque." In a more general sense, however, we might also say that classical and baroque are totalities of categorial choices that can be found, albeit with different results, throughout the history of art.

I have in a sense "rewritten" Wölfflin's basic idea, which in the course of time has been variously refuted in the name of a presumed "metaphysicism" or "metahistoricism." Perhaps it is time we treated it with the justice it deserves. Other formalists have probably run this risk, but not Wölfflin. On the contrary, if he is to be accused of anything, it would have to be an over-attachment to the idea of the historicity of style. Or rather, to an evolutionary continuity between styles so that, for example, the classical-baroque opposition of "linear"/"pictorial," "surface"/"depth," "open form"/"closed form," "multiplicity"/ "unity," "absolute clarity"/"relative clarity," is conceived as a kind of historical rhythm or cadence.

It would be more pertinent to criticize the conception of another formalist, Henri Focillon, for being excessively evolutionary. Focillon, in fact, compares the system of forms to a biological system (less from a scientific viewpoint than from a philosophical one, in harmony with Kant's arguments on the subject).[36] In his *The Life of Forms*, however, Focillon also distinguishes sharply between historically defined stylistic categories and the formal principles to which, symbolically, we attach the same names.[37] The famous evolutionary "stages" (experimental age, classical age, age of refinement, baroque age) are, in fact, *morphological transformations*, valid within any historical style. We might even deduce from this that the historical "baroque" style possesses a classical period, or that historical "classicism" possesses its own baroque age. What Focillon has spotted, in other words, is an implicit *logic of morphogenesis*. This becomes clear when he considers the four most important elements of form (space, material, spirit, and time). He is primarily concerned with observing changes in individual representations rather than in styles in the general sense of the term. The specifically historic aspect of art is reduced by Focillon to the study of *moments* as clusters of different forms at different evolutionary "stages" and in competition among themselves, and is not recuperated into a history of styles according to a principle of periodization. The fact remains, however, that the logic behind the forms of Focillon is still based upon an idea of cause and effect: the predetermined formal succession of "generation"–"completion"–"perfection"–"degeneration."

Eugene D'Ors, on the other hand, completely denies historicism.[38] His idea of baroque is sometimes frankly metahistorical. The baroque becomes a category of the spirit, formed by constants that D'Ors has named "eons." In this way the notion can be extended to absolutely any historical art movement, independently of period and geographical location. In fact, by transforming Linnaeus's principle of classification, D'Ors treats the baroque as a genus, subdividing it into numerous species. By the end of *The Baroque* he has discovered twenty-two. The weakness of the classification, however, lies precisely in the fact that the different species are named in an inconsistent, almost casual, way. There is, in short, no homogeneity between a "macedonicus," "alexandrinus," "romanus," "buddicus" baroque and, for instance, a "vulgaris" or "officinalis" baroque (unless in fact we resort once more to the historical and geographical dimensions of the phenomenon).[39]

As we can see (and as Luciano Anceschi had already noticed at the end of the 1950s), formalist positions always contain an unresolved contradiction between an abstract conception of

19

style or artistic form and its physical location. The abandonment of historicism in favor of categorization (for example, the opposition between "classical" and "baroque") is important, but it often occurs without the establishment of any criterion for a rigorous interdefinition of concepts. Furthermore, evolutionary and biological demands oblige formalists to make a hazardous return to history. As regards criteria for coherence and the interdefinition of concepts, neither Wölfflin nor Focillon—not to mention D'Ors—is able to construct an articulated "picture." Wölfflin, for example, invents his five formal pairs by starting with the idea of the work of art as an aspect, appearance, or surface under which lie more abstract forms. He fails to explain, however, the interrelationship of concepts such as "linearity," "formal closure," "superficiality," "clarity," and so on. The result is an almost totally unworkable formalism, to which one could constantly counterpose different categorical pairs. Apart from criticizing Focillon's evident determinism, one could also reprove him for a lack of homogeneity for terms of reference such as "space," "material," "spirit," and "time." Then, in the case of D'Ors, one could attack the needless multiplication of subgroups for the genus "baroque." These subgroups become a simple, infinitely extensible list owing to the fact that practically any element of any baroque can be focused upon. Finally, as we have already seen, one must criticize the superimposition of a formal apparatus upon concrete history, demonstrated by the fact that a *philosophy of history* underlies all formalist theories.

The only attempt to solve the problem still seems to be that made by Anceschi.[40] In his various theoretical works, gathered together in *The Idea of the Baroque*, Anceschi follows other authors such as Francastel and Wellek when he suggests that we consider the baroque as a cultural *system* represented by various formal components, but only in the sense of beginning with a *historically* determined description.[41] Only after having constructed theoretically and, at the same time, historically, the borders and characteristics of the baroque can one extend its heuristic function to other periods, movements, and cultural systems. Anceschi in fact had already clearly understood a basic principle of contemporary human sciences: that every phenomenon undergoing analysis is inevitably contructed by the analyst and can thus be transferred beyond its own spatial and temporal position. His controlling principle, however, was the definition and delimitation of the phenomenon in terms of its historical existence. Thus, in order to call a cultural event "baroque," the procedure remained that of comparing it with the historically defined event, even though the comparison might be made by means of formal principles.

Although such a procedure is perfectly correct, it might not be the only possibility. Another equally coherent proposal might be made: that we make formalism "rigorous" by avoiding both the contradiction with historicism and the weakness of casual categorial systems employed in the use of inference. This is the procedure that we shall be using in these pages. It can be summarized very briefly in the following way. *First*: to analyze cultural phenomena as *texts*, independently of a search for extratextual explanations. *Second*: to identify each text's underlying *morphologies*, articulated at varying levels of abstraction. *Third*: to distinguish the identification of these morphologies from that of the *value judgments* to which they have been subjected by different cultures. *Fourth*: to identify the axiological system of these value judgments. *Fifth*: to observe the *duration* and *dynamics* of both the morphologies and the value judgments that influence them. *Sixth*: to define a "taste" or "style" as a tendency to attach value to certain morphologies and to their dynamics, possibly by means of valorizing procedures that possess an identical morphology and dynamics to those of the phenomena being analyzed. As we can see, the historicity of the objects is restricted to an "appearing-in-history," both in terms of surface manifestation (variable within and between epochs) and of the effect produced by morphological dynamics. It is no longer a question of comparing, even formally, a series of distinct moments of historically determined facts. On the con-

21

trary, we must verify the various historical manifestations of morphologies belonging to the same structural plane. History is seen as the place in which difference, rather than continuity, is manifested. An empirical (rather than deductive) analysis of history allows us to rediscover general working models for cultural facts.[42]

CATEGORIES OF VALUE

The clearest difference from traditional formalism lies in the fact that a style or taste is not conceived as a simple sum of forms, but as a tendency to invest value. Values, in other words, are not considered substantially as more or less *present* in this or that phenomenon, but as *attributes* either reflected by each discursive manifestation or derived externally from each valorizing metadiscourse. Furthermore, each value judgment does more than attribute value. By doing so, it brings into play a "polemical" element: the rejection of a competing attribution or competing attributions. The fact that competing value judgments exist can be seen from the term "value," which is inevitably categorial: it indicates a polarity, a difference. Nor is that all. A further "polemical" dimension is constituted by the fact that categories of value do not invest phenomena singly, but in groups. An aesthetic judgment is almost always accompanied by an ethical, emotional, or morphological one, and vice versa. Furthermore, we might even say that each individual, group, or society attributes not only single values, but also correspondences among a variety of valorizing sets of binary oppositions. From a social point of view this is extremely important. The greater or lesser rigidity of these correspondences also indicates the extent and quality of social control of individual behavior, as well as revealing the form of philosophical reflection about society and its nature. It is no accident that in the history of philosophical thought from Plato to the present day we find constant attempts to construct taxonomies of categories of value.

This is clearly not the place to try to summarize this philosophical concern, nor to propose the addition of a further chapter. We should, however, note that every valorizing axiology is always the result of a proposition containing linguistic terms. Values are thus already contained within language, and a coherent semantic and syntactic system can therefore be articulated. Attempts made by many philosophers to propose a "system of categories," such as that of Aristotle or Kant, or the exlusively aesthetic systems of Rosenkranz or Blanché, can effectively be resolved at the level of linguistic analysis.[43] If we take the four most traditional contexts in which judgment is made—the good, the beautiful, the emotional, and the formal—we discover, in fact, that they are all articulated by means of *appreciative* categories, as Aristotle called them.[44] Furthermore, these categories can be expanded by means of the principle of the semiotic square.[45] Emotional and morphological values also rest on apparently *constative* categories (if we continue to adopt Aristotle's terminology), in which appreciation on the part of the discourse's subject does not appear.[46] All valorizing terms, as Robert Blanché has in fact suggested in his *Aesthetic Categories*, derive from a combination of semantic signs produced by the expansion of categories, from the intersection of different categories, and, finally, from contextualization within a discourse.[47]

The theme of values thus possesses a specific semantic dimension. This can be found in types of discourse that we shall call "valorizing discourses." These are concerned not only with the production of a text, but also with its reception: value is in fact preestablished (as we have already said) in every text, just as it is in every metatext. The quality we normally refer to as "taste" is nothing more than the more or less conflicting correspondence of values present in texts and metatexts; the relation of correspondences according to specific "routes" within the

23

category system; and the possibility of *isomorphism* between textual forms and the forms taken by these routes.[48]

Let us see, in a very generic way, how this category system works. We can take the following table as an example:

Category	Judgment Upon	Positive Value	Negative Value
morphological	form	well-formed	deformed
ethical	morality	good	bad
aesthetic	taste	beautiful	ugly
emotional	emotion	euphoric	dysphoric

The names of the categories are in the first column and the objects being judged in the second, while the third and fourth columns contain the two categorial poles. These have a "positive" or "negative" value, although in some cases the term "value" does no more than indicate a position along an axis of opposition connecting two poles. It is also true, however, that an "empty" value can become "full" if another category, that of "appreciation"/"depreciation," is positioned obliquely to those in the table. In this case, the "positive" and "negative" poles become value judgments in their own right. But all this depends on the attribution of value to its object. In other words, "positivity" and "negativity" are not fixed signs at the heads of two columns, but variables. Hence, the table presented here is *one* type of judgment, but not the only one. Let us now address a further consideration. The type of judgment expressed by the table orders, establishes correspondences, and classifies certain binary oppositions according to certain others. Seen as a totality, therefore, it is itself *one* type of axiological system, but not the only one. Other types can establish correspondences between these categorial polarities in a different way, for example, by inverting on occasion the value of single terms. A final observation: The table proposes a list of categories. We have said that these can be related to one another in a variety of ways. But this does not always occur in the same order. The system is constructed by the discourse, a discourse that generally orders categorial terms by starting from one of them. For example, the line "he was beautiful, blond, and of gentle aspect" moves from the aesthetic category to be ratified by means of morphological and emotional categories, to which, some lines later, the ethical category will be added. The discourse, in other words, channels values by starting from a valorizing *perspective*. Different ratifications and perspectives, therefore, simultaneously permit the construction of different types of axiological systems.

We also need to remember that correspondences and perspectives do not only operate according to sets of binary oppositions. Each category can be extended by using the principle of the semiotic square to reveal the possibility of neutralization, complexification, and deixis and, finally, of *suspension*. This occurs when the terms in conflict do not receive "full" valorization compared to the "empty" valorization that, in any case, differentiates them.[49] These final reflections also make us realize how the various typologies produced by constructing axiologies of value clearly reveal the "social" function of such axiologies. It is no coincidence that we can underscore how socially ordered historical phases impose extremely rigid correspondences and perspectives, whereas more doubtful or permissive phases offer a contrasting liberty or laxness in making value judgments. The so-called evolution of customs shows the truth of this general assumption.[50]

What interests us here, however, is that in the construction of axiologies from aesthetic perspectives the mechanism works in the way that has been described above. It is on this basis that we shall be able to contrast, in the following pages, two types of taste: "baroque" and "classical." By "classical" I basically mean the categories of judgments that are strongly oriented toward stably ordered correspondences. By "baroque," on the other hand, I mean those categories that powerfully "excite" the ordering of the system, that destabilize part of the system by creating turbulence and fluctuations within it and thus suspending its ability to decide on values. Evidently this means closing the only historical door left open to us, since the only thing that history allows us to do is verify empirically the appearance of competing classical or baroque forms, and to analyze their figures (since these really are historically determined). It never becomes in any way the *source* of an exclusive classification.

This is the final definition of the procedure that I shall be adopting in this book. The search for the "neo-baroque" will be carried out through the discovery of "figures" (i.e., historical manifestations of phenomena) and the typification of forms (morphological models in transformation). We shall thus acquire a geography of concepts that will demonstrate not only the universality of neo-baroque taste but also its historical specificity.

CHAPTER 2

Rhythm and Repetition

REPLICANTS

THE FILM *Blade Runner* makes use of a metaphor that might be useful in the context of the observations that follow: the metaphor of the "replicant." Replicants are created as robots that are identical to an original—man—with certain improved mechanical features (such as strength). They then become autonomous and even preferable both aesthetically and sentimentally to the original. In effect, the contrast is between "automatons" and "autonomous beings." If we now consider the fictional products of everyday mass communication in the same way, we are confronted by the same concept. These "replicants" (film and television series, remakes, popular fiction, comic strips, cartoons, songs, and so on) are also born from mechanical repetition and a perfecting of the work process. But their own perfection produces, in a more or less involuntary way, an aesthetic: specifically, an aesthetic of repetition.

After having lived through not only idealism but also the historical avant-garde, common sense tells us that repetition and serialism should be regarded as the exact opposite of originality and the artistic. The work of art is necessarily "unrepeatable," to the point of being actually "unsayable" (incapable, that is, of being repeated, even in a discourse based on the work itself).[1] When we read contemporary newspaper reviewing we too often find ourselves reading criticisms of aesthetic objects that "replicate" other objects, which are then considered to be the forerunners of a type or series. At most, a product might be approved of for being "well made." This is permitted by the adoption of a group attitude that promotes serial products to the status of cult objects simply because, in doing so, an aesthetic value is produced that resides not in the work being cultivated but in the position of the consumer. This kind of position seems confused, out of date, and inadequate when confronted by the aesthetic objects produced by our culture. Confused, because the attitude, which is not only idealistic but survives in many other philosophical formulations, tends to superimpose upon each other a variety of accepted meanings of repetition without distinguishing between them. Out of date, because an attitude that idealizes the work of art's uniqueness has undoubtedly been swept away by contemporary practices; since the 1960s invented multiples, modern art movements have delivered a death blow to the myth of the original, and the idea of citation and pastiche is now exalted in many so-called postmodernist creations. Finally, inadequate, because the preconceived notion prevents us from recognizing the birth of a new aesthetic, the aesthetic of repetition.

SOME GENERAL CONCEPTS

Before taking a more specific look at some basic principles in the aesthetics of repetition, it might be useful to pause and consider what the most suitable conceptual framework is for defining what we mean. Above all we need to reconsider the idea of "repetition." We must be careful not to confuse three different notions: (1) the industrial notion of repetition as a way of producing a series from a single matrix; (2) repetition as a structural mechanism for generating texts; (3) repetition as a condition in the public's consumption of communicative products. Let us begin by considering the first two points.

The first type of repetition is synonymous with standardization: it is the mechanism that makes it possible to produce a series of objects (including those of the spirit) from a single prototype. As is well known, it dates back to the 1830s with the beginnings of American industrialization, and comes to an end during the epoch of Taylor and Ford.[2] Among other things, it depends not only on the production and diffusion of replicas of a prototype, but also on the identification of components within the whole that must be produced separately and then assembled according to a specific program. Standardization of goods has always been accompanied by the standardization of intellectual products. This was the fate of newspapers and popular fiction. Toward the end of the nineteenth century Pulitzer and Hearst anticipated Ford. Today electronic means have created the idea of the palimpsest, which is nothing more than an assembly program of entertainment products. It is obvious that serial production derives from a desire to optimize profits. We have only to observe the constantly increasing number of interruptions for advertising during American television serials. But the importance of serialism in terms of social control is equally obvious. Reduction into elementary atomic components makes it possible to recognize fictional products and to regulate "pedagogically" the corresponding systems of value. The ideological judgment of a lack of quality in serial products clearly derives from a refusal to accept a drop in creativity for economic reasons and from a rejection of the resulting social consensus.

A second concept of repetition exists, however, concerning the structure of the product. Let us examine its definition more closely, to avoid running the risk of using the term "repetition" to embrace a series of differing phenomena. The term repetition is in fact adopted not only for further adventures involving the same hero but also for stories that are analogous because they are based on typical scenarios and motifs. This is as true of calques, such as B westerns, as it is of citations and references to standard fragments such as "old Texan village" or "spaceship seen from above." Let us say, then, that the concept of repetition is best articulated by means of the parameters adopted here. Obviously nobody should even begin to talk about repetition without establishing the grid of models according to which the phenomena will be analyzed. It is only by using this grid that these phenomena lose their status as localized individuals and become abstract states of being, which can then be treated as samples.

The first parameter might be the relationship that is created in a text or group of texts between what is perceived as identical and what is perceived as different. We will then have two opposing formulas of repetition, *variations on a unique element* and the *uniqueness of different elements*.[3] Let us look at some examples, restricting ourselves to the world that seems to lend itself most readily to our purpose: that of television serials. In the first category we can place those works whose starting point is a prototype ("Rin Tin Tin," "Lassie," "Colombo") that is repeated in a variety of different situations. In the second category we can place those products that are born as variations on an original but turn out to be identical (for example, "Perry Mason," "Ironside," and "Stavinsky"; "Baretta" and "Kojak"; "Star Trek" and "Battlestar Galactica"; "Dallas" and "Dynasty").

It might be helpful, however, to insert a further parameter into these two groups. This parameter is the way in which the time discontinuity of the story is related to the continuity of narrated time and to the time of the serial. We shall then have two formulas of repetition: *accumulation* and *prosecution*.[4] The first formula describes those episodes that follow one another without calling into question the time scale of the entire series, such as "Lassie" and "Rin Tin Tin." The second formula covers serials in which there is an explicit culmination point, such as "How the West Was Won," "Star Trek," or "The Incredible Hulk," in which time is represented, however slowly, by a group of pioneers moving west, the Hulk's search for an antidote to reverse his terrible mutation, and the search for a planet suitable for a group of surviving earthlings.

But we shall have to add a further parameter, constituted by the level at which repetition and differentiation are established. Let us make a digression. For some time the semiotics of narrative has revealed the existence in all stories of underlying structures, which are more profound and abstract than the surface of what is being narrated. Greimas in particular has shown that narration is developed by generating stories that possess deeper structural levels. There is a discursive level. There is a level of actual narrative structure. There is an even more abstract level that has been defined as "fundamental." It is obvious that the deeper levels are those that reduce complexity to increasingly elementary structures. The fact that these structures are repeated is obvious and even necessitated by the theory itself. But it is quite irrelevant if we want to understand the possible meaning of this repetition. What interests us is the discursive level. And what is repeated is, substantially, a representation of that level. At this stage too, however, we can discover different modes of repetition. A narrowly iconic mode (the hero has blue eyes, the spaceship is seen from above, the policeman speaks with a southern accent); a thematic mode (heroes and villains in the world of economics, as in "Dallas" or "Dynasty," or in crime, as in "Miami Vice"); a superficial, dynamic narrative mode (with typical scenes or recurring narrative motifs, such as the chase, the attack on the stagecoach, the kiss). Types of repetition in these three modes supply us with other categories, such as the *calque*, when there is total repetition, or, alternatively, the *reproduction*, when some modes are omitted. In the first category we might place "Star Trek" and "Battlestar Galactica" and, in the second, "Dallas" and "Dynasty."

We shall be returning to these definitions. For the moment they help to underscore how the categories that have been delineated up to now are homogeneous as far as the two principal problem areas are concerned. The first concerns the question of time. The second belongs to the dialectic between uniqueness and difference. Time comes into play when we realize that, although it is not particularly interesting to describe *what is repeated*, it is extremely relevant to define *the order of repetition*.[5] It is well known that, from the Greek lyrics to the Circus of Prague, repetition is the organizing principle of a poetic, provided that we are able to recognize what its order is. Emile Benveniste has observed that ancient thought possessed terms for defining both a static and a dynamic order of repetition: *rhythm* corresponded to the dynamic and *schema* to the static order.[6] Rhythm and schema were, in effect, almost synonymous and were certainly extremely closely interrelated. The only difference was that schema corresponded to the object's modular instrument of articulation and rhythm to its formular instrument: schema described spatial measure and rhythm described temporal measure. If we wish to express it in musical terms (the field in which it is now considered), rhythm is *the frequency of a periodic wave phenomenon with peaks and troughs repeated at regular intervals*, or, in other words, the *temporal form in which all repeated members are varied in one or more of their attributes*.[7] But if we insist upon the concept of repetition from the point of view of rhythm, we automatically project ourselves toward an aesthetic conception of rhythm, just as the Russian formalists did with poetry. We might in fact define differences at the level of repetition as rhythmic differences, thus concluding, as did Wölfflin, Focillon, and Kubler in the history of art, that variations in rhythm in television serials are aesthetic variations.[8]

The second problem area concerns the dialectic between uniqueness and difference. We must insist upon the fact that we are not interested in *what is repeated*, but in the way that the components of a text are segmented and codified in order to establish a system of invariables, into which everything that does not enter is defined as an independent variable. Structuralist disciplines generally concern themselves with invariables and leave variables to one side.[9] This is a mistake, because the analysis of the relationship between variable and invariable is fundamental to our understanding of the dynamic functioning (and not only the static structure) of a system. Eco is one of the few to have taken this dialectic into consideration, to such an extent that, describing the mechanism behind the invention of a code, he speaks about a reformulation either of the form of expression or of the form of the contents, or of both simultaneously.[10] The constitution of a new style or aesthetic, in other words, is considered as the dynamics of a system as it passes from one state to another, reformulating the relations between its own invariables and the principles according to which those elements that are relevant to the system are regarded as variable. As we can see, from the viewpoint of the dialectic between uniqueness and difference as well, our goal remains to produce an aesthetic definition of a system (in this case, the television serial) in progressive evolution by means of discontinuous states.

At the beginning of this section we mentioned briefly a third group of accepted meanings of repetitiveness, in the sphere of consumption. By repetitive, we generally mean a kind of habitual behavior stimulated by the creation of absolutely equal situations of expectation and offers of satisfaction. It is a type of behavior that Eco has defined as "consolatory," since it reassures the subject by letting him rediscover that which he already knows and to which he is already accustomed.[11] But there are other repetitive forms of behavior in the sphere of consumption. For example, the cult phenomenon of constantly returning to see the same show or film is increasingly common (the most striking example is that of *The Rocky Horror Picture Show*, which has been showing in the same cinema in some cities for years, giving rise to a performance within the performance as the public intervenes directly and in an organized fashion in the showing of the film). A third and final form has been christened "zapping." This term describes an obsessive changing of television channels, receiving in rapid succession a series of different programs and carrying out simultaneous reconstructions of each program as the scene changes. Habit, cult, and cadence are thus three types of repetitive behavior. But each of them has different implications. In the first case we are faced with the kind of behavior described by Propp: the child wants to hear the same fable. In the second case the kind of behavior is not merely consumerist, but also productive, since the consumer adds something of his own to his mode of consumption. In the third case repetitive consumption is adapted to the conditions of environmental perception. It is fragmented, rapid, and recomposed only at the end, exactly like the vision that the consumer has learned to follow (it is no coincidence that "obsessive" behavior is typical of children, who "educate" themselves with afternoon television).

For the sake of simplicity, let us summarize the observations that we have made so far in the form of a table:

Production	Text	Consumption
model	invariable	expectation
standard	serial	consolation
optional	variable	productive consumption

The first column contains the three elements of industrial repetition (production): a model that is used to produce a standard that can then be varied according to certain optionals (themselves forming series). The second column contains the three elements of textual repetition: invariable, serial, and variable. The third column contains the three elements of repetition in the sphere of consumption: the system of expectation generated by a model or invariable, (consolatory) identical repetition, and reoriented repetition (i.e., the taste for varied consumption of the same object).

The problem now becomes that of correlating the three areas of repetition (production, text, consumption) in order to see whether dominant *figures* exist in contemporary repetition, to discover what they are, and, assuming they possess aesthetic value, to establish whether they represent a neo-baroque mentality. In other words, we might discover that the "television factory" that no longer conceals itself as such, a text that exalts the logic of serialism, and a form of consumption that has become a "life-style" are closely linked by superior codes of taste. These codes are no longer proposed as models but have by now become stabilized as behavior patterns in our collective consciousness. We shall begin our analysis by moving out from the repetitive structures within texts generally and, in particular, within the most emblematic of these (the text of the television series). We shall then see whether the variety of models discovered cannot also be found in the other two columns and even whether they might not possess an inner history.

THE ORDER OF REPETITION IN TELEVISION SERIES AND SERIALS

At its origins a television series or serial was the miniaturization of a cinema genre: the adventure film, in its various guises as western, exotic adventure, and swashbuckler. Produced in enormously long series, it was constructed in terms both of the variation of a single theme and of the uniqueness of a number of variables. Since these series were originally produced for children, the dominant model was based upon the presence of a boy protected by an intelligent animal (a dog, a horse, or a monkey) and a heroic father figure, as well as a gruff but kindly uncle figure. Here are some of the identical variables: Rusty, the son of Tarzan, the son of Jungle Jim; Lieutenant Masters, Tarzan, Jim; Sergeant O'Hara, a handful of African natives; Rin Tin Tin, Cheetah, Champion. The structure of each episode is always the same. Each episode contains a complete story, and the series as a whole possesses no story (we never know, for example, where Rusty of "Rin Tin Tin" came from, or what his fate will be). The series can therefore be programmed infinitely, because the time of each episode exists outside history and is identical to itself, and each episode has no recollection of the others. Furthermore, the time narrated is extremely variable. A story can be developed in the space of hours, days, or weeks, since all that counts is the narrative and thematic unity of the functional elements. There need be no proportional relation with a unity of time. From the point of

35

view of the uniqueness/difference relationship, the first series were often calques (a typical case is that of Jungle Jim, an imitation of Tarzan) or, just as frequently, partial calques (from the point at which the iconic mode began to migrate from one series to another, in terms of both actors and physical or moral characteristics). Far more frequent, however, is the case of reproduction, based primarily on the maintenance of certain superficial narrative and thematic elements.[12] At the thematic level, for example, the formulation of the good/evil opposition is always the same. The hero and his associates are entirely on the side of the good and each of them bears specific signs of identification. The antihero, on the other hand, as if to demonstrate his total wickedness, is not only completely evil, but also anonymous. The villains are never portrayed by a fixed group of actors, but are different, without recall, in each episode. In other words, whereas the good is figuratively invariable, the bad changes figure. On a narrative level, the formula for each episode is fairly rigid. If we take "Rin Tin Tin" as a prototype, we discover a clearly repeated dynamic pattern: Rusty accidentally discovers a threat to the fort, whose mascot he is, or to one of its inhabitants. He tries to deal with the threat single-handedly, but is unsuccessful. His dog comes to his aid and manages to control the situation until Lieutenant Masters or Sergeant O'Hara, who were initially unable to deal with the threat themselves, arrives in time to defeat the enemy. The dynamic level is the same throughout the series, even though the figures vary; it remains identical when compared to that in other variants of the genre. For example, the threat might be an Indian attack, a betrayal, bandits, and so on, all of which are variants within the series but identical in that they are commonplace features of the western genre. Furthermore, the superficial narrative level can be found in different series: the same structure might appear in "Tarzan" and "Lassie," even when the figurative elements are utterly different.

A second prototype for television series is represented by "Zorro" and "Ivanhoe." In these cases the origin is unusual, since they are both extremely free adaptations from books. "Zorro" is, in fact, a double adaptation, since he descends not only from the hero created by the American writer J. McCulley in 1919 in his book *The Curse of Capistrano*, but also from the films of Douglas Fairbanks. "Ivanhoe" takes up, modifies, and develops the adventures of Walter Scott's hero. The novelty of this model consists in the fact that, presupposing the existence of the character in a closed and defined encyclopedic place, the plot must also be developed within a finite horizon. While the structure of individual episodes is substantially the same as that of the previous model, the general time of the series changes. In more technical terms, while the entire series is constructed according to a single narrative program that foresees a final solution, each episode is produced according to a working narrative program. The characters have a past and a future: Zorro is secretly a Mexican nobleman and Ivanhoe a knight of King Richard; their enemies have usurped power; their future is the reestablishment of the legitimate order. Thus, although the single episode is autonomous, it is located as a stage in a journey toward a target that is explicitly evoked each time. In this way we begin to have not only an episodic cadence, but also a rhythm of the series as a whole, marked by the oscillation of power relations between heroes and villains and by the *cyclical nature* of this oscillation. Apart from anything else, this makes the thematic mode both more and less rigid: more rigid because the thematic roles become stable (the villains are fixed figures), and less rigid because the good/evil dialectic is better articulated. The iconic mode becomes far more stable, however, since knowledge of the properties of the characters already exists in another place (the book), in which the time of the series and its characters are inevitably recorded. In other words, the system of invariables becomes wider at all levels, and the variables more and more microscopic.

We now come to a third prototype for television series, "Bonanza," the first episodes of which were actually directed by Robert Altman. Altman revealed a great capacity for invention

37

within the western genre. At an iconic level he reproduced all of its classic signs: cowboys, ranches, saloon, village, church, square dancing, herds, Indians, prairies, and so on. He also established a very large number of main characters: the four Cartwrights, two constant female figures, and a dozen supporting characters. The figurative variables thus became very small, but were intended to surprise: the old man of the mountain, the boxer from England, the sharpshooter who had become blind, the Japanese who had still not settled in, and so on. Clearly, in the iconology of "Bonanza" the variables are very independent indeed. Furthermore, the thematic and narrative modes are also liberated from constraints. For example, the roles of hero and villain are constantly being redefined. The screenplays tended to follow type at the beginning, but less so at the end. In the relationship between episode time, series time, and narrated time we can see an important rhythmic innovation. Series time is modified: although the framework is a story, it has no anticipated conclusion or target (at least as a separate possibility, the achievement or failure to achieve a certain purpose). The internal time scale of the series is not translated into plot, but into a mechanism of mutation that modifies the status of characters from one episode to the next, obliging the viewer to keep up with the changing knowledge of the characters. It was impossible to miss a weekly episode without missing something of consequence. Nevertheless, a constraint of continuity existed in which each episode also had a meaning for the casual viewer. This is probably one of the most fascinating characteristics of American television series: the ability to produce both an episodic narrative and a satisfyingly finalized narrative at the same time. In this sense the flexibility of "Bonanza" is archetypal in its ability to create a number of different time levels: a complete story in each episode, the open story of the series, and an intermediate model consisting of an open story lasting for a certain number of episodes. It is a model that has been transmitted to us in an ever more perfect form, above all in saga-series such as "How the West Was Won."

The fourth prototype is "Colombo." In this case we have no overall story acting as a frame for individual episodes, and the series appears to be a case of a variation on a theme. There is a single fixed character and his staff (no more than supporting roles, the most extreme example being the emblematic figure of his wife, who never actually appears on the screen). Colombo is also exactly the same in each episode: raincoat, beat-up car, cigar, and clumsy manner. There is clearly a strongly repetitive iconic element. Other elements, however, such as the hero's adversaries, the situations, and the environmental characteristics of the scenes, vary considerably. The thematic and narrative modes also appear to be fairly standard: perfection/imperfection of the crime, the crime itself, the concealment of evidence, the discovery of the crime, the war of intelligence between the concealer and the discoverer, the criminal's mistake and unmasking. The trick, however, consists in the extremely subtle variation—at an iconic, thematic, and narrative level—at the phase in which Colombo is able to beat his adversary at his own game on the basis of situational elements (such as a hobby or special skill possessed by the criminal). The narrative system is able to contain a very large number of invariables at every level, and even tends to fix the number at its maximum limit. At the same time the number of variables, which is also potentially extremely large, tends toward the maximum in terms of *number*, but toward the minimum in terms of size. The variables concern increasingly tiny elements of the text: the type of poisonous Japanese fish used as the weapon, the allergic properties of a beauty cream that becomes an element in the conflict between two people in the cosmetics industry, the vintage of a port tasted over dinner, and so on. The large number of invariables, on the other hand, also permits a wide range of combinations of components, and a geometric multiplication of possible stories. The "Colombo" stories are specifically articulated according to a taste for variables and combinations. The evidence for this lies in the fact that "Colombo" almost always functions in the same way as examples of oulipomenic literature such as

Queneau's *Exercises de style*: each episode is a variation on a theme produced by a different director (some of whom, such as Cassavetes and Boorman, are famous). Variation on a theme or style: this is the first principle of the neo-baroque aesthetic, since it is based on the general baroque principle of virtuosity. In every art virtuosity consists in the total flight from a central organizing principle, by means of a closely knit network of rules, toward a vast polycentric combination and a system based on its transformations.

But now let us come to a fifth case. "Dallas." Wrongly considered by everyone to be the modern prototype of commercialized repetition, it will, on the contrary, allow us to identify a second principle of the neo-baroque aesthetic. "Dallas" seems to summarize perfectly the last two models analyzed above: on the one hand Altman's technique of producing a dialectic between series time, episode time, and narrated time, on the other hand the "Colombo" technique of the regulated variable. In the case of "Dallas," however, the organization becomes very complex indeed. Let us begin with the uniqueness/ difference relationship. In "Dallas" we have, first of all, an extremely largely number of figurative invariables: places, features of the characters, typical scenarios. The number is so large that any independent variable can become a new invariable in the system after only a couple of episodes. The figurative mode is therefore extraordinarily regulated, but at the expense of the thematic and narrative modes, both of which become extremely elementary. This elementary quality, however, can be transmitted to the various characters, generating an improbably high capacity for combining in different ways. The characters, in fact, are graded according to flexibility. The first generation (that of the parents) is the most immobile and constant, and has a very low number of interrelations. The second generation (that of J.R.) is flexible, but maintains a series of stable characteristics in spite of an ability to have any kind of relationship with all the other characters. The third generation (that of the young people) is highly flexible, and is constantly on the point of becoming either fixed or variable. The different types of potential relationship are marked thematically: family relations, love, money (exactly like the themes of newspaper horoscopes—only health is missing, although even that has been inserted into the most recent series of Ewing family adventures). The recognizable quality of the series is determined by the fact that such a complex system should tend toward disintegration as a result of the multiplicity of internal forces. We thus need to know how and why the system manages to maintain its stability in spite of the ups and down to which its dynamism subjects it. This stability is founded on two main elements: any narrative development affecting any character is always circular, and each partial story (each internal cycle) is developed as if it intersected the map of fixed characters even though the entire map is simultaneously projected upon it.

Let us look at this more closely. Instead of moving a character from one state to another, each series of adventures returns him inevitably to the point on the map at which he started. The circular paths taken by characters might be very long, as in the case of the conflict between J.R. and Sue Ellen, which passes slowly from arguments to betrayal, abandonment, divorce, new relationships, and even, in the second series, remarriage. The ill-fated affair between Lucy and Mitch, on the other hand, is dealt with in a handful of episodes. Sue Ellen's relationship with Cliff Barnes after her divorce lasts just three episodes, exactly the time it takes Cliff's enemy, J.R., to ruin his rival financially. All these stories are repeated cyclically. Furthermore, the characters learn nothing from their experiences. They repeat the same mistakes, stumble into the same traps, and make use of the same strategies. The entire map is projected onto specific planes in a variety of ways. For example, when the war between J.R. and his brother Bobby for control of the business is narrated, there are a number of fixed points, such as the house in Dallas in which is presented, at breakfast and at dusk, the entire family system, both affective and economic, that binds the Ewings to one another and to their allies and adversaries.

41

"Dallas" is also somewhat complex from the point of view of time. Like "Bonanza," although in a more perfected way, series time is potentially finite, however indefinite the actual end might be. There is no specific target at which the serial is aimed, and even when such a target seems to be on the verge of emerging (such as the struggle for control of the Ewing empire), the whole situation could easily change. Nevertheless, "Dallas" is constructed as though it were in a state of historical evolution, according to a complex plot in which, from time to time, a shift can be seen. A second fundamental aspect is that narrated time, episode time, and series time are inversely proportional. Series time is immensely long (at most, the story of three generations), whereas episode time is extremely short (never more than three to four days and generally a single day). This produces a very peculiar narrated time. Whereas in a classic television series scenes are segmented according to a selection of leisurely described focal elements, the continuity of narrated time in "Dallas" inevitably produces a very rapid segmentation of the *measure* (i.e., of the shot). No scene can remain immobile for more than forty-five seconds; no sequence contains more than ten shots; the speed of the characters' speech is from three to five times faster than in ordinary soap operas. The production of a different measure clearly produces a frenetic rhythm, which aids the insertion of commercials into the program. It also is extremely innovative when compared with the rhythm of earlier programs. As a result, "Dallas," which is not particularly adventurous according to the normal criteria for the genre—it does not make use of large narrative leaps that force the viewer into amusing inferential games— acquires a rhythm similar to that of rock and roll from a rhythmic point of view. Furthermore, before leaving the subject of rhythm, it should be added that in "Dallas" we have a series of constructions of continuity. The first is that of the indefinite frame that obliges us to consider changes in the characters in sequence, thus generating our own understanding of the frame. The second is that of the large cycle, the only continuity that permits a reformulation of the map describing interrelations between the characters (for example, it took thirteen episodes to redefine family relations after the death of the head of the family, Jock). The third is that of the small cycle (only a few episodes were needed to show Pamela adopting a child). The fourth is that of the minimal story, concluded in the space of a single episode. Continuity is thus exploited in every possible way: as single occasion, as discontinuity, as norm, and as cult. In each episode these four categories are intertwined, producing an underlying rhythmic effect: each story must always be interrupted and then taken up once again by means of parallel or alternating editing (otherwise the viewer loses track of one of the cycles). This time we are in the presence of a rhythm determined by sequence and editing. And it is this very rhythm that draws attention to itself, rather than narrative inference (when rhythm is used to construct something that remains unsaid). Everything we need to know is supplied explicitly and at once. Once again our satisfaction is based on tiny variable inventions in iconography and plot, rather like disco music, where melody is replaced by a rapid and regular beat and where pleasure is derived, at best, from variations in the introduction, tone of voice, accompaniment, and arrangement. This musical metaphor is quite relevant. The recent television series "Miami Vice" is presented at "rock tempo." The lesson has been learned and applied.

RHYTHMS AND STYLES

From this long and possibly unwise excursion into the example provided by television series and serials three fundamental elements of what I have called the "aesthetic of repetition," itself part of a neo-baroque aesthetic, seem to emerge: organized variation, polycentrism and regulated irregularity, and frantic rhythm. We might say that all three are motivated: from a historical point of view, they are the natural consequences of an

43

accumulation in the number of cultural objects; from a philo-sophical point of view, they are the result of certain ideological necessities; and from a formal point of view, they are compo-nents of a "universal" baroque.

As I said in the first chapter, many people have noted that organized differentiation, polycentrism, and rhythm are consti-tutive elements of baroque taste. Sarduy has underscored the isomorphism that existed in the seventeenth century between artistic and scientific forms around the theme of polycentrism. Kepler's new cosmology, for example, not only destroyed Gali-leo's theory of the centrality of planetary orbits but also in-troduced into culture a taste for elliptical form, provided with real centers and multiple potentials.[13] Wölfflin has spoken of rhythm as a fundamental component of the idea of movement in baroque sculpture and architecture. Cassirer, and then Frye, have identified changes in rhythm as a feature of literary genres (in Frye, for example: the rhythm of recurrence defines the epic, the rhythm of continuity, prose, that of decorum, the theater, and that of assonance, a lyric poem) and the style of an epoch (once again, in Frye: there are epochs with rhythmic relations that are schizomorphic, mystic, synthetic, and so on).[14] Bakhtin goes further: he defines specific rhythmic forms ("chronotypes") as regulators of artistic genres and styles.[15]

In historical terms, the motivation behind a taste for vari-ables, polycentrism, and rhythm is easily explained. We have only to think of the enormous quantity of narrative transmitted by the media each year. In Italy alone it has been calculated that, in a mere five years, private television channels have al-ready consumed ninety years of narrative cinema. Consump-tion has thus made the "replication" of existing products essen-tial. The result of this is a state of production and consumption that can be summed up in the phrase *everything has already been said, everything has already been written*.[16] Faced with the growing awareness of the public, only one way of avoiding sat-uration exists: changing the rules governing both taste and production. As in Kabuki theater, pleasure in the text is produced by a tiny variation, the form of a rhythmic repetition, or a change in the internal structure. A film like *Raiders of the Lost Ark*, with its massive use of quotations, would have been unthinkable a few years ago. Equally unimaginable would have been a book like *The Name of the Rose*, an enormous fresco of semantic, narrative, and figurative invariables in which everything is quotation, and where the presence of the author survives in the combination and insertion of systems of variables adapted to the different types of model reader envisaged by the novel. *The Name of the Rose* seems to be a prototype—if not *the* prototype—of a contemporary neo-baroque aesthetic, not only in this context but also as a result of its techniques of "perverting" the quotation, something we shall be examining in a later chapter. Nor, in any case, am I the first to notice the existence of genuine "poetics" of repetition and variation. The concept that repetition does not necessarily signify an "inferior" or less original aspect of a work has recently been expressed in, for example, studies in aesthetics carried out by the school of Mikel Dufrenne. One of his pupils, René Passeron, has edited a group of studies examining the relationship between creation and repetition. In the field of criticism as well, the magazine *Corps écrit* has studied the link between repetition and variation. Even the School of the Louvre has organized a symposium to analyze the conflict between repetition (formal concept) and imitation (thematic concept).[17] In the field of production, material objects also seem to be moving in the same direction. We have only to think of new methods of automobile production: a small number of structural invariables, known as "basic models," a large number of figurative invariables, a very large number of regulated variables, and, finally, an extremely large number of so-called optionals, those small details that personalize the vehicle.

Furthermore, the love for regulated variables and the love for rhythm come together in the idea of virtuosity, which is increasingly sought after in the world of entertainment and now produced by means of an ever more sophisticated technology. There is no other way to explain films such as *Tron* and *One from the Heart*, which impress us as much for their extraordinarily skillful handling of the visual image as they do for their narrative paucity. Finally, a word for those fields in which rhythm and the aesthetic of variables are most evident: commercials and music videos. Although—precisely because they are so obvious—I have not examined them here, they represent the area in which the characteristics that have been analyzed find their most obsessive expression (frequently with excellent results, it must be said). In conclusion, I shall just say that a possible philosophical explanation also exists for the aesthetic of repetition. An excess of stories, of things that have already been said, and of regularity inevitably produces fragmentation. This was fundamentally Nietzsche's point when he observed that the idea of the eternal return depended on the repetitive nature of history. Boredom, the philosopher observed, often derives from the fact that we are saturated with history. Saturation destroys the idea of harmony and sequentiality and leads us, as Bachelard noted, not only to recognize but also to desire a corpuscular, granular quality both in the sequences of real events and in those of fictional products.[18]

Limit and Excess

LIMIT AND EXCESS: TWO GEOMETRIES

IF WE AGREE with Lotman that culture is an organization of cultural systems (in his case, of an organic and biological nature), it is also possible to conceive of it as a spatial organization. Lotman himself calls an organization of this type "semiospherical"—recalling the biological terms "biosphere" or "ecosphere" and the anthropological "noosphere"—in order to refer specifically to the spatial aspect of the culture system.[1] If, however, we accept this spatial notion of the structure and distribution of knowledge into systems and subsystems, into a total space that is divided into local regions, we shall also have to accept that this space must have some kind of geometry or typology in order for it to be organized. It must, in other words, have a "border."

When used of systems (even of cultural ones), the term "border" should be understood in the abstract sense: as a group of points belonging simultaneously to both the inner and outer space of a configuration. Inside the configuration the border forms part of the system, but limits it. Outside the configuration the border forms part of the exterior, whether or not this too constitutes a system. The exterior, therefore, is distinguished from the border either by opposition (because it is another system) or by deprivation (because it is not a system at all). The existence of a border is guaranteed, in all cases, by the fact that, on the one hand, its points separate and, on the other hand, they cohere to all the other points belonging to the system (which thus includes the points on the border). Not all borders, however, should be considered impenetrable from the outside. Cases of a rigid and absolute closure to whatever does not belong to the system are somewhat rare. We might say that the border articulates and renders gradual relations between the interior and the exterior, between aperture and closure. In this way we can have substantially closed systems in which the border acts as a kind of filter or membrane. Elements outside the system can be introduced on the condition that they are "translated" (in the literal sense of "being carried across") into interior elements by being made into a coherent part of the system (for example, by being adapted to its code). Alternatively, we might have systems that are open in specific areas, allowing a flow between the inside and the outside, and more or less rigidly closed in others.[2]

In the case of substantially closed systems, the very existence of a "perimeter" implies that of a *center*, a center that we might also refer to as an "organizing center." As Arnheim has pointed out, however, the center does not necessarily coincide with the "middle."[3] This means that we shall have to create a new classification, of systems that are either *centric* (in which the center corresponds to the middle) or *acentric* (in which there is either more than one center or, alternatively, a single center situated near the edge of the system). In the case of centric systems, exactly as in geometry, a symmetrically ordered internal organization is produced. In acentric systems, however, the internal organization is asymmetrical, and this generates forces of expansion. It is rather like Lotman's example of geopolitical borders: when a state places its capital near the border, it has either not yet achieved a centralized order or it intends to expand, in which case its present decentralized center is the projection of a future centric center. Let us consider the problem of an asymmetrical organizing center. As we have said, this generates forces of expansion. But this means that these forces begin to press, *from within*, against the very elasticity of the perimeter-border-boundary: they try to upset the totality of points that are common to both interior and exterior by creating tension. This is why, by developing our topographical metaphor, we might say that the border becomes a genuine *limit*. If, however, we accept Bourbaki's topological rather than analytical definition of "limit," we can state that a limit is a border of surrounding values in which all points have the same function.[4] By breaking down the limit we therefore either eliminate the existing border, or we create a new one. Thus any pressure placed on the limit assumes the value of a tension.

Our common language has recorded this situation perfectly in a cultural context rather than a mathematical one, bearing within itself a kind of memory of its spatial nature. Let us take the Latin term *limen*: it means "threshold," that of a house for example, and defines perfectly the opposition between inside and outside, open and closed. The meaning of the term "culmination" is also spatial since it describes the highest point on a curve. The image of "excess" (from the Latin *ex-cedere*, to go beyond) is even clearer. Excess describes the overcoming of a limit in terms of an exit from a closed system. It is always our linguistic use that reveals to us how spatial images are applied to cultural facts. When we speak of an "extreme case," a "limit to tolerance," the "height of patience," or an "excess of evil" we reveal tension, limitation, or the overcoming of the borders of a system of social or cultural norms. The acts that provoke these states are acts that break through the system's borders, or upset them in some way. In this sense, we can also see how a "liminal" or "excessive" act differs from one of stretching the limit. Stretching against the limit tests the elasticity of the border, but without destroying it. Excess escapes by breaking through. It crosses the threshold by making an opening, a breach.

We have said that limit and excess are two types of cultural act. But they are acts that cultures do not always make use of. In certain periods more effort is made to stabilize a centric system than in others. There are cultural epochs and areas in which a taste for establishing "perimetral" norms prevails. At other times a need or desire is felt to break with existing norms.

This is precisely what we have been examining: stretching to the limit and experimenting with excess. The age and cultural characteristics that we have defined as "neo-baroque" clearly belong to the second category.

STRETCHING TO THE LIMIT

Stretching to the limit those rules that make a system homogeneous is a feature that can be seen to some extent in most fields of contemporary knowledge, from art to science, literature to daily behavior, sport to cinema. One of its constant elements is experimentation with the elasticity of the borders of a total system *starting from its most extreme consequences*. In the history of art, for example, the most typical case is that of the late Renaissance and the mannerist and baroque periods, when linear perspective was taken to its "limit" in terms of viewpoint, vanishing point, and distance.[5] The consequence of this was the production of a series of models beyond which perspective destroyed itself, such as trompe-l'oeil, illusionist architectural scenes (*quadratura*), anamorphosis and foreshortening.[6] In the case of perspective we have a system that is already directly geometrical. But other cases can be found in more specifically conceptual systems, such as ideologies, scientific theories, or philosophical ideas. And the mechanism is the same.

Let us take a representative example, as we have done in the other chapters of this book: Michael Crichton's novel *Congo*. Even though the work is highly commercial, it attempts to stretch two distinct systems to the limit: science (which is the subject of the book) and literature (the system to which the book belongs). From the literary point of view it is difficult to classify the work, however much it might declare itself a "genre" novel. It has a science fiction quality: there are scientists and technocrats in search of mysterious diamond beds from which to produce undreamed-of weaponry. There is also an element of the espionage novel: the American agency Erts is intriguing against a sordid consortium of foreign powers. There is a kind of exotic anthropological adventure: a voyage into darkest Africa, the search for a mythical city, the study of a race of "intelligent" gorillas. There is, finally, a detective story: an attempt to discover the culprit of a series of murders like those that took place in the Rue Morgue. There are, in other words, traces of Poe, Conan Doyle, Burroughs, Verne, Fleming, and, obviously, Rider Haggard.[7] But *Congo* is none of these things; or rather, it is all of them at once. The new literary genre, in other words, manages to stretch each preceding genre to the absolute limit by refusing to identify with any of them, and by mixing them all together into a gigantic pastiche. But this pastiche is not simply a work of quotations, as in the literary activity that the Americans have christened "postmodern." It is a preliminary confirmation of the existence of a genre resulting from the recognition of traditional novel types, and followed by the invention of a supergenre (at the limit of its predecessors): a novel of investigation that takes its orientation specifically from already-existing genres.

There is another interesting aspect of Crichton's book, one that is more obvious but equally intriguing: his decision to work with the most advanced scientific theories in such areas of modern research as information theory, anthropology, zoology, geology, volcanology, game theory, and so on. The knowledge he draws upon is anything but imaginary (as we can see from the scientific bibliography at the end of the book). What Crichton does, however, is *take it to the limit*. The most extreme consequences and conditions of use of these theories are simulated. In short, the fantastic is already with us, we have only to push it slightly in the right direction. It is possible to believe in strange hybrids of highly gifted, trained gorillas; after all, we have already produced the Doberman. Talking chimpanzees, such as the famous Arthur, already exist in the United States. As far as accelerated rather than real-time television is concerned, anyone can receive "teletext" programs. Electronic simulation to produce "real" images by means of

fractals is already in use in video games and electronically produced cinema. The American "space wars" program is composed of weapons that belong to the world of science fiction.
And so on. In other words, given the borders of a specific
scientific domain, we have only to examine those limits that
make an advance possible in order to declare, implicitly, the existence of a frontier zone, poised between the "real" and the
"potential."[8]

Congo stretches large areas of meaning to the limit. But in an
era of mass communication we are also familiar with operations
"to the limit" in a formal context—for example, in our way of
representing time and movement by means of communication
technologies. In recent years we have become used to seeing
representations of a time and movement threshold that is
clearly either above or below the perceptible, thus shifting the
limits of our ability to imagine actions. No one is startled any-
more to see the important moments in a football game replayed
in slow motion. On the contrary, fans tend to base their judgment of a referee's decision on the replay, as though it were
possible to observe actions in the same way in reality. Similar
examples can be found in fiction produced for television and
cinema. It is normal by now for us to connect our investigation
of key moments in a scene with a slowing down of its "natural"
speed. We have only to think of the armed conflict at the end of
Butch Cassidy, the decisive duel between good and evil in *For a
Fistful of Dollars*, or the final scene of *The Longest Yard* in which
Burt Reynolds, at the end of a violent football game between
prisoners and wardens, is obsessively slowed down in order to
dramatize his indecision—to flee or to take the ball—in the
sights of a telescopic rifle and with the prison governor's order
to shoot (after having lost the game). We can also consider the
numerous slow-motion love scenes in advertising and soft-core
pornography.

Another example of how we have moved beyond a threshold
in our perception of time can be found in photography. We
have become indifferent to so-called instantaneous techniques.

And yet the "instants" of instantaneous photography are not what they were, but exist distinctly beneath our level of perception. Taking a photograph at a thousandth of a second makes it quite impossible to forecast the final photograph from what is seen through the lens. Nevertheless, having accumulated competence with this kind of technology, we are able to imagine the existence of a time and movement that are beyond our physical capacity of perception. The idea of an increasingly brief instant also leads to a poetic of searching for the *acme* of an action: the decisive pass in football, the dividing point between success and failure in an action, the separation between life and death in a duel, the search for high points in emotion or sexual ecstasy. One might even claim that deeper research into certain fields of representation and their specific time has changed our perception of time itself. Representation and time perception at the lower threshold is linked to an exasperatedly *analytical* stance. What was once considered a unit of time is no longer regarded as such because we are able to divide it into ever smaller units. (Isn't this a "baroque" problem? Just as in the seventeenth century calculus and the calculation of limit were a fundamental problem.) A brief demonstration. If we consider break dancing, we can see that the essence of the dance lies in the dancer's ability to fragment both movement and time into tiny units. When these movements are reunited into a total movement and time we notice that this does not restore continuity, but a linearity that leaves otherwise imperceptible gestures and instants distinct.

A second "natural" time threshold exists, however, which is also taken to the limit: the upper threshold of our speed of perception. A temporality exists that might be termed *synthetic*, in contrast with that described above. It consists of representations that operate with unusual rapidity. The most obvious examples are video games and music videos. If we look at the most recent generations of games and music videos we see that the time in which the action is represented demands extremely accelerated responses if we are to win the game or make sense of the action in the video. That we are dealing with a threshold beyond perception is demonstrated by the fact that the most proficient players and viewers are children, whose reflexes are able to cope with the extraordinarily rapid rhythm of what is being represented. The essentially muscular dexterity of earlier generations is being replaced by a sensory dexterity, based on rapid reactions to stimuli. But it would be limiting to restrict synthetic temporality simply to these products and to their use by young people. Much of the world of mass communications and the behavior it produces is heading toward the destruction or distancing of the upper threshold. Rhythm, analyzed in the previous chapter, is one of its fundamental characteristics, with its ability to schematize a second. Let us take another example from sports broadcasts. Nowadays we accept as normal a speeded-up summary of sporting events. This is not, however, a simply functional procedure (saving time by transmitting greater quantities of information). Speeding up makes it possible to appreciate more successfully the *schema* of an act, its "geometry" (it is no accident that the term has entered soccer and basketball jargon). An analogy can be found at the behavioral level. We have only to think of the practice of so-called zapping created by the existence of a large number of television channels. The spectator is by now accustomed to passing from one program to another, linking them instantaneously, inferring their contents from a few scenes, re-creating a kind of personal palimpsest, And, above all, eliminating "historical" differences between the various images perceived.

Overcoming temporal perception thresholds almost certainly involves changes in our vision of the world. The first significant change, in my opinion, must be sought in a different sense of history from that found in earlier epochs. It is impossible to deny that we live in a period in which all cultural objects are rendered contemporary. Our remote control device, capable of steamrolling into a single level products from a different historical dimension, automatically produces a world in which everything is touching and continuous. University and high school teachers are well aware of this phenomenon, confronted by students who pass with no sense of relativity from Aristotle to Michael Jackson, from Spinoza to the "nouveaux philosophes," as though they were all dialoguing entities.

A second vision of the world derives from our feeling of the verifiability of the real. New audiovisual technologies annul our faith in a personal verification of facts. The illusion of truth is created less by the actual vision of a football game than by its re-vision in television playback. Techniques of representation produce objects that are more real than the real, more truthful than the truth. In this way the distinguishing features of certainty are transformed. They no longer depend upon the security of our own subjective apparatus of control, but are delegated to something that appears to be more objective. Paradoxically, however, the objectivity reached in this way is not a direct experience of the world, but the experience of a conventional representation. St Thomas's doubt has indisputably waned. We no longer believe in miracles if we can touch them. We need to have them told to us in playback.

ECCENTRICITY

Pulsation toward the limit of a system, as we have already seen, might be motivated by the noncentrality of a system's organizing center; or, in other words, by its "eccentricity." Eccentricity, of course, is also an ambivalent term. It has a significance in mathematics (the ratio between the distance of a conic section from a fixed point and from a fixed straight line), physics (the transformation of a plane from a rotary to an alternated movement), and in behavior.[9] An "eccentric" is a person (or subject) who operates at the limits of an ordered system, without, however, threatening its stability; a person who places his or her own "center" of interest or influence toward the periphery or margins of a system. Fashion has ratified such behavior since the nineteenth century, permitting "out-of-the-ordinary," modes of dress, such as that of the dandy.[10] During the baroque period, however, eccentricity was already common (as we can see from the costumes designed for the Sun King's parties in France). These days, eccentricity in dress has practically become the rule, and its presence in the world of fashion is proof of what has just been said. Eccentricity, in this context, exerts pressure on the margins of order without undermining it, since it has already been accounted for by an all-embracing structure of fashion regulations. Eccentricity incorporates casual clothing, haute couture punk, strange decorations on traditional formal wear, a reversal of "uniforms" associated with specific occasions (jeans for ceremonies and dinner jackets for a walk in the park).[11] The example of fashion also confirms a basic feature of eccentricity, its essentially theatrical nature. It is no coincidence that we find eccentricity exhibited as a value in the world of entertainment (music, television, theater, and cinema). Being in the public eye obliges one to seek an individual identity (an identity, that is, with its own center) without, however, becoming socially unacceptable.

An obvious example of this mechanism can be found in the process (apparently ever more eccentric) of naming artistic, musical, and theatrical groups. Giving oneself a name means nothing more or less than inventing an identity within a community.[12] If we look at the names of modern performers, we cannot fail to see the mechanism that produces an image of subjects as objects of theatrical imagination. Here is a brief list of Italian theater groups: Giovanotti Mondani Meccanici, Kollettivo Teatrale Trousses Merletti Cappuccini e Cappelliere, Gruppo oh! Art, Ramazzotti Sisters, Sinestudio per motori generali, Panna Acida, Teatro Momentaneamente Assente, Sosta Palmizi. And in music: Frankie Goes to Hollywood, Level 42, Culture Club, Art of Noise, Shampoo. These are only a very few examples, yet they are sufficient to show how names are being transformed into something far more singular: they have turned into *titles*. The intention is clearly to suggest that the group, theatrical or not, is already a work of art in itself, without making any kind of distinction between art and life, production and execution, ability and performance. But another aspect of eccentricity and activity at the margins of the system exists in the texts themselves, above all in advertising, music, and theater. These kinds of entertainment move ever closer to their own material limits, to such an extent that it is becoming difficult to speak of "advertising," "music," and "theater." Means and languages are influencing each other in a kind of intertextuality at the source, rather than merely as a hypothesis of cultural functioning. A commercial is frequently analogous to a music video, and the two forms can even coincide, as they did with the famous Grace Jones commercial for Citroën, which later became part of her own promotional video. The theater produced by Magazzini Criminali is nothing more than an accumulation of visual effects derived from music, television, advertising, and architecture: a "theater of surfaces" or intertextual conjugations. Eccentricity, therefore, now involves a total shift toward the margin or "skin" of the work, a search for formal and aesthetic aspects instead of a centrality that was once founded on, for example, its ethical or emotional content.

This type of aestheticization is essentially harmless to the system, as long as it is not taken to the limit and beyond by strongly influencing our everyday behavior. We have only to think of the stories of anomalous "feats" performed by anonymous figures in order to enter the *Guinness Book of World Records* or the pages of adventure magazines: crossing America on foot, a month's trekking in the Kashmir, lone sailing expeditions, riding holidays, windsurfing across the ocean, living on Mont Blanc for fifty-two days with food brought from home, riding in a sleigh to the North Pole, participating in cycling races on experimental bicycles designed like cars. This kind of anecdotism of daily life (aesthetic, probably also in a pejorative sense) is increasingly dominant in the modern world, and is subject to a gradual process of industrialization. An example of this is the popularity of television programs in the United States (and in Italy as well: "Jonathan" and "Big Bang") in which these extraordinary "feats" are often presented as expressions of a love of sport, nature, or adventure. In the United States, regulated "eccentric" situations are actually produced to order. War games, using nonlethal arms, are fought by groups of "sportsmen" disguised as marines on pretend battle-grounds. And then there are races using more or less mechani-cal means in difficult conditions, such as Cannonball, a kind of rally in basic survival conditions, or events such as the Camel Trophy and the Paris-Dakar Rally, which often involve real danger. As eccentricity moves toward the limit, it arrives at an increasingly high level of risk.[13] It is revealing that a "Risk Club" now exists in England, the members of which must have performed an extremely dangerous feat, such as diving off Tower Bridge, leaping from heights of three hundred meters with a tiny parachute, or crossing a gorge on a tightrope. The world of sport is exactly the same: everything is geared toward breaking the record and going beyond the limit ("the preced-ing limit").

Excess, and Its Antidotes

Excess, precisely because it goes beyond limits or boundaries, is obviously more destabilizing. Furthermore, any excessive ac-tion, work of art, or individual *wants* to throw doubt upon an existing order, as well as possibly to destroy it or to construct a new order. All societies or systems of ideas, in any case, ac-cuse of excess that which they cannot or do not want to absorb. Each order isolates itself and defines excess by forbidding it. The enemy becomes a cultural enemy: in the word of classical cultures, a "barbarian."[14]

Generally those elements that are accused of excess are exter-nal, and unacceptable, to the system. In baroque epochs, how-ever, an endogenous phenomenon is produced. Centrifugal forces produced within the system move beyond its bounda-ries. The excess is genetically internal. Contemporary culture is experiencing an increasing number of phenomena of endogenous excess, ranging from artistic and media products to political and social behavior. Once more, however, we need to distinguish between various types of excess. For example: excess *represented as content*, excess *in terms of the structure of a representation*, and excess *in terms of the fruition of a representation*.

The first category is composed predominantly of contents representing categories of value, such as the morphological, ethical, emotional, and aesthetic categories to which we have already referred and to which we shall be returning. A fairly obvious example is the rebirth of the "monster," to which we shall be devoting an entire chapter. We shall see that the monster is a constantly destabilizing element because it is either "too much" or "too little" in both quantitative and qualitative terms when compared with a norm.

A second theme that we might consider more generally is that of sexuality. It is widely appreciated that erotic excess is an appropriate way of questioning and disturbing a value system. Nor, after Nietzsche's well-known analysis of the opposition between Dionysiac and Apollonian, would anyone dispute that there is also a sexual basis to the creation of "styles."[15] But what, in a more technical sense, does "excess" consist of? We can give two answers, according to the point of view from which the question is considered. The first answer is based on the dominant norm as a place from which eros is observed. It will thus consider as "excess" not only that which generically evades the norm, but also a kind of inflationary spiral in the quality and quantity of "indecent" objects produced: excess will be seen as a "degeneration" in the dominant value system. The second answer, on the other hand, derives from an opposition to the dominant norm as a place from which eros is observed and considers as "excess" that which produces "scandal," etymologically a "stumbling stone" from the Greek word *skàndalon*. Excessive sexuality, therefore, is not only considered in itself, for what it conveys referentially, but also as a "provocation" to overcome the limits of current social principles. This is shown by the way in which excessive sexuality has always symbolized something else, as we can see from a number of films produced during the last ten or fifteen years. We find sex used to represent joy and liberation in Pasolini's *Decameron– Canterbury Tales–Thousand and One Nights* trilogy, and death in his *Hundred Days of Sodom*. In Bertolucci's *Last Tango in Paris* sex symbolizes imagination. We see sex as accusation, drama, and revolt in East Coast experimental cinema, Fassbinder, and, in his intentions at least, Bellocchio. The same aspect of disturbance and provocation—to the point of vulgarity— can be found in the sexuality expressed by some contemporary rock stars. We have only to think of Michael Jackson or Prince, who combine a violently phallic quality with effeminacy, or the suffused hermaphroditism of David Bowie. We can also see the tendency of certain Californian homosexual groups who produce genuinely "scandalous" performances, such as in the famous *Yankee Robot* video, in which each group member not only sings in a deliberately obscene manner, but also uses his musical instrument as a sexual tool (masturbating with the microphone or keyboard, passing guitar leads between his legs, fellating wind instruments, and so on). The transvestism found in figures such as Boy George is an extreme example of this phenomenon. The same kind of thing can be found among female entertainers, such as the early Madonna, who sang about the explosion of physical love, or the Italian singer Joe Squillo with her song *Violentami sul metrò* ("Rape Me on the Subway"). Another Italian, Renato Zero, is a far less offensive representative of pop music's homosexual trend.

Next to sex we find violence or, more generally, horror. Cinema, theater, and music are once more in the forefront. Apart from the growth in specific genres of horror, with the triumph of Dario Argento in his constant search for increasingly macabre special effects, we can see that a widespread trend toward a cinema, theater, and music "of cruelty" has developed in recent years. The myth, now surpassed, of the Bronx and of representations of "damnable themes" has been invading our screens and stages for some time now, as is shown by titles such as *Warriors, Wanderers, Escape from New York*, and the three episodes of *Mad Max*. It is no coincidence that films of this kind are echoed by sound tracks produced by homogeneous groups, such as The Police, possibly the most typical example of a punk culture that rejects social order by means of a representation (not exaltation) of violence. Italy has very few examples: Kaos Rock, Kandeggina Gang, and, in a clearly ironic vein, Skiantos. A more intellectual violence permeates certain works produced for the theater. A typical example might be Magazzini Criminali's *Genet a Tangeri*, or the video-theater installations of Studio Azzurro. Although these works exhibit a return to a 1950s-style violence, they have a component that is no longer simply ideological (or that has discovered a poetic in ideology), but also aesthetic. We might even entitle these forms of excess-in-content that we have listed as part of the renascent category of an "aesthetic of the ugly."[16] Physical and moral monsters, obscenity, brutality, and violence do not have value in terms of their meaning alone, but also in terms of the forms in which they are expressed. We might even say that transgression on the superficial level of phenomena has become practically fundamental, to the obvious detriment of semantic transgression, which is now regarded as an ideological dimension that is either already surpassed or should be.

We have some evidence for what has just been said in certain recent artistic developments. Let us consider an American painter like Keith Haring. Some of his paintings are excessive accumulations of color and encrusted paint. But this is quite different from the informal—or "political"—gesture that can be found in the work of distantly related artists such as the European Informalists or Action painters. There is no tragic content in the heaped chromatic material of the New York Palladium. There is, on the contrary, an "ugliness" that is not placed in a polemical relationship with the "beautiful" in order to be reassessed. There is an "ugliness" that *is* "beautiful." The same argument can be made for numerous recent "isms," almost all of which appear to be revivals of themes from thirty years ago, and yet are quite different. North American graffiti artists have nothing to do with South American mural painters. "Garbage art" does not derive from Arman, any more than the artists of the so-called Transavanguardia group derive from expressionism, fauvism, Rothko, or Barnett Newman. What has disappeared from these modern works might actually be reference to what is being represented thematically, the significance of the content. The result is essentially an exploration of the "decorative" (and the term is not being used in a negative sense), the surface, the materials, and the formal organization of the work. The excess of which we were speaking is thus transformed from a representation of excess into an excess of representation, a kind of formal "too much." It is, of course, no coincidence that the form of works by these contemporary artists demands an enormous expenditure in terms of material.

Cases of monumentalism and giganticism can also be found: Christo's packaging of the Aurelian walls in Rome or of part of the Australian desert; the transformation into sculpture of an entire hill in Arnaldo Pomodoro's project for the Urbino cemetery; Daniel Buren's plan for the square in front of the Palais Royal in Paris, previously a parking lot.[17] We have clearly arrived at the second of our initial categories, that of an excess of representation, which we can explain as a need produced by a representation of excess. Depicting an excess in terms of content, in fact, transforms the actual structure of its container because it requires an excess in spatial terms as well. One of the formal constants in neo-baroque containers is excess, especially in popular culture. We have only to consider the ever-increasing size of public events. In the world of sport, for example, the Olympic Games and the World Cup have reached extraordinary organizational dimensions, the most triumphant example being the 1984 Los Angeles Olympics. Events such as the Live Aid concert or the March for Peace, with simultaneous broadcasts in the world's major cities, are another sign of an attempt to produce a "universal container" by means of the communications industry. The "Beaubourg effect" is also producing results throughout the Western world, both in museum organization and in the phenomenon of temporary exhibitions. A brief list: the "grande Louvre" project in Paris, with Pei's celebrated glass pyramid; the Musée d'Orsay and Musée de la Villette, also in the French capital; great traveling exhibitions passing between Europe and America (the impressionists in London, Paris, and Los Angeles; seventeenth-century Emilian painting in Bologna, Washington, and New York; Donatello in Chicago, Detroit, and Florence; Viennese Liberty in Venice, Vienna, and Paris; the voyages of the Thyssen collection from Lugano and of Soviet collections); Fiat's projects involving Palazzo Grassi in Venice. Even the world of industry is succumbing to the temptation of spectacle, as the fin de siècle taste for universal expositions raises its head once again, with approximately twelve million visitors to Tsukuba in Japan in 1985, and almost fifteen million a year later in Vancouver.[18]

But the content that is represented and the representation of content also provide us with signs of excess in terms of behavior. The kind of reaction required by such texts and the form they take is, effectively, "abnormal" in its demands for uncontrolled cult worship. From this viewpoint there is very little difference between the criminality of British soccer fans at the 1985 European Cup Final between Liverpool and Juventus in Belgium's Heysel Stadium and the mass delirium of music fans at rock concerts. We might place in the same category the spectators of *The Rocky Horror Picture Show*, whose ritual behavior in cinemas in London and New York (for almost ten years) and Paris and Milan (for six) involves the imitation of the characters and scenes represented on film in a "performance of fruition." Another example might be the increasingly common "marathon entertainments"; "all-nighters" in which four films are shown consecutively, or endless dance competitions. A more "tranquil" version of excessive behavior is the exhibition of one's private life by treating it as theater. In this sense we might regard as complementary the search for a so-called look, amply encouraged by the latest trends in fashion, and the wave of "courtly" festivities, once the prerogative of a hereditary aristocracy and now revived by the most varied new aristocracies. A few examples: the party organized by the Rothschilds in Paris in 1985 to celebrate the reopening of the Musée des Arts Décoratives, during which two hundred guests consumed a magnificent dinner in a room within the building while thousands of guests "of the second rank" watched the goings-on from above, as in a fresco by Tiepolo; the Agnellis' opening bash for the *Futurismo e Futurismi* exhibition in Venice, held on the yacht the *Orient Express*; the display of Venetian high society that surrounds the minister of foreign affairs, Gianni De Michelis; the magnificent weddings of Prince Charles and Lady Diana, the heirs of the great families, and Pippo Baudo and Katia Ricciarelli. It is no coincidence that new professions have sprung up around these events, such as "party architect," "dish designer," and "fireworks architect."

Another characteristic, alongside that of quantitative excess, is that of qualitative excess, or virtuosity. Once again, we can find this characteristic at every level. Virtuosity is treated as a theme in a film about Diaghilev, Peter Brook's *Meetings with Remarkable Men*, or the television series "Fame." But the thematic treatment of virtuosity itself demands a virtuosity of form, as we can clearly see from films such as *Raiders of the Lost Ark*, or Fellini's most recent works: the masterly ecclesiastical fashion parade in *Roma*, or *E la nave va*. And isn't virtuosity by now the reigning feature of practically all performances, even in the visual arts, which have progressed from hyperrealism to such recent works as the overperfect quotation of Fleming primitives by the American Murray, the slightly twisted reproduction of mannerist still-life theories by the Neapolitan Cantone, Scolari's metaphysical representation, and the "signed fakes" by the Forgers' Collective of Cremona? Virtuosity can also be found in certain aspects of daily life, such as cult movie-going, the revival of strange hobbies, and the collecting of extraordinary objects, all of which imply an almost maniacal "pleasure derived from hyperspecialization." And it must be stressed that these forms of real behavior are always induced by the texts insofar as they are written into them. A couple of examples: in *Fame* (the film this time, not the television series) two students from the performing arts school in which the story is set attend a showing of *The Rocky Horror Picture Show* in which other young people derive pleasure from acting out what they see; and in *Gremlins* Spielberg's little monsters, having occupied the city, watch Walt Disney's *Snow White and the Seven Dwarves* in exactly the same manner.

In conclusion, we might consider the fact that even though the neo-baroque excesses of our epoch involve not only content but also form and discursive structure, not to mention the way in which texts are received, they do not necessarily produce social unacceptability. Only in certain cases, almost always relating to content, are the boundaries of the system (generally ethical) exceeded, with a consequent rejection by the system. In other cases—particularly in those relating to form and structure—the knocking down of boundaries does not lead to destruction or exclusion, but to a *shifting of the limit*. When confronted by an "acceptable" excess, the limit is simply moved (perhaps to a considerable distance) in order to absorb it, in an accommodation that might involve conflict. There are also intermediate cases, in which excesses of content are absorbed into the system. This occurs for a number of reasons. First, because the system becomes more elastic at its borders, isolating certain phenomena in ghettos around its edges. Second, because the entire system becomes more elastic (as principles such as "tolerance," "permissiveness," "libertarianism," and so on arise). Third, because the system is able to integrate the excess by distorting its objective, thus rendering what appears to be excessive substantially normal. This final principle is, in effect, a regulating constant in all social systems (whether political, religious, or of taste). It consists in the creation of antidotes or antibodies to the excess, even in those cases where excess func-

tioned at the outset. This also explains the inevitably inflationary character of any movement that operates at the limits of a
system. As it exceeds these limits, its activity becomes increasingly exaggerated and exasperated.

With these final observations we are now able to introduce a
criterion of differentiation between the various neo-baroque
operations intended to operate upon limit and excess. First of
all, let us take the following schema:

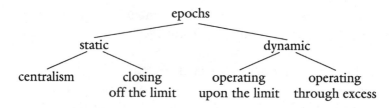

We might say that whereas static epochs favor their systemic
center, or annul the possibility of trespass by closing off the
boundaries of the system, dynamic epochs operate upon the periphery and the boundary. In this sense limit and excess become
opposing categories, the former producing innovation or expansion of the system, and the latter revolution or crisis. In our
case, however, we are faced with a more complex situation.
Neo-baroque taste appears to favor a *double* or *mixed* tendency,
either by exchanging the terms of this opposition or by annulling them. For example: it adopts a limit and yet makes it seem
excessive by trespassing on a purely formal level; or, alternatively, it produces excess and yet refers to it as a limit in order
to render acceptable a revolution in terms of content; or, finally, it confuses or renders indistinguishable the two procedures. Unlike a *genuinely* dynamic epoch (by which I mean
"revolutionary"), neo-baroque taste is represented as though in
perennial suspension, stimulated but not inclined to upset categories of value. This is why certain avant-garde activities do not
belong within the neo-baroque. Dadaism is excessive and aims
at the crisis of the system. Neo-dadaism, on the other hand, can
even be regarded as "acceptable" if it appears to be excessive

and yet merely operates upon the limit. In the same way, the kind of student movement that occurred in Italy in 1986 is excessive and yet, by presenting itself as an operation at the limit, seeks social acceptability. As a result, our criteria of judgment are suspended, blocked, out of scale.

CHAPTER 4

Detail and Fragment

THE PART AND THE WHOLE

Our philosophical tradition is well aware of the dialectic that exists between the idea of the "whole," totality, or entirety, and the idea of the "part," portion, or fraction. Without returning to the heart of the debate, it is enough for our purposes to stress that from a linguistic viewpoint the part/whole pair is a typical example of interdefining terms.[1] One cannot be explained without the other. The two terms are related by reciprocity, implication, and presupposition. We might also add that their relationship is not exhausted by a simple opposition of terms, but can be further "unwound" or expanded until it reaches its greatest possible explication. This occurs when the potential link between the two opposing poles is itself defined according to a concrete viewpoint or criterion of pertinence. The idea of the whole, or totality, or system, in fact, already presupposes the idea of the part, the element, the fragment, the detail, the portion, and so on. Such a presupposition, however, becomes meaningful when the pair is interpreted in an "oriented" way according to a criterion of observation. For example, we can interpret a system/element dialectic by making the pair pertinent according to a notion of *con-sistency*, that is, of a simultaneous functioning of both parts. Alternatively, we can interpret a fraction/entirety opposition by adopting the notion of *integrity*, that is, of a behavior on the part of both elements produced by pressure placed on the entirety. Or, finally, we can base our interpretation of the global/local pair on the idea of *collocation* of parts within the whole.

The terms "detail" and "fragment" can also be examined in terms of their specific relationships with *certain* ideas of the "whole" and the "part." They are, in fact, synonyms "oriented" toward the "part" end of the polarity and thus opposed to certain specific concepts of an equally oriented "whole." As we shall see, however, respective interpretations within the category are themselves placed in reciprocal opposition. Thus "detail" and "fragment" become interdefining terms: corresponding in relation to the "part" pole, and opposing in relation to the interpretation of the part/whole category.

This rapid theoretical introduction is needed in order to show how, at even the most basic semantic level, it is possible to articulate a genuine system of lexical differences. This will become useful when we begin to analyze not so much verbal terms as analytical procedures intended to produce meaning. These procedures can then be directed toward "details" and "fragments" in the sense of interpretive tools or aesthetic effects. This will become particularly relevant when the critical or creative practices in question deal with the visual arts. From a critical point of view, in fact, the analysis of a work by means of details or fragments is not only widespread, but even materially evident (we have only to think of how many details we are shown by art history, or of the number of fragments employed in archaeology). From a creative point of view, a large number of contemporary artists produce works based on, or composed of, details or fragments. Finally, new technologies provide us with new way of conceiving the idea of detail and fragment, above all in the field of mass communication. In conclusion, observing the criterion or criteria of relevance based on procedures involving details and fragments allows us to say something about a certain epochal taste for the construction of textual strategies, in both a descriptive and a creative context. The first criterion of pertinence on which the notion of the divisibility of a work or of any object whatsoever is based, and which is presupposed by the very possibility of naming something as a detail or fragment, is constituted by the difference between at least two types of divisibility: the cut and the rupture. In the pages that follow I shall try to show that these two concepts not only are opposed to each other, but correspond to different effective acts, signifying practices, epistemological procedures, and even separate aesthetics. This is obviously true in the general or abstract sense, since the polarities of a category are never pure, but appear in the form of mixed and extremely combined objects. As a kind of shorthand, I shall refer to the first procedure as the *assassin's practice* and to the second as the *detective's practice*, since it would even be possible to exemplify them according to the thematic roles in that most classic of genres, the detective story. The analogies and differences between the two practices will be illustrated by means of three sections:

a. etymology, which we shall consider as a kind of lexical memory of the path taken by meaning;

b. the status of certain human sciences, which we shall reconsider as metadiscursive practices;

c. the status of two aesthetics, which we shall observe as an act of valorization of the two procedures analyzed in the preceding points.

We shall conclude by observing, in the context of a categorial opposition that is really far more traditional than it might appear, whether a particular *mode* of realizing such an opposition has appeared in contemporary taste, or whether there exists an orientation capable of shifting the balance in one direction or the other.

The Etymology of Detail

"Detail" derives from the Renaissance French (and obviously, in its turn, from Latin) *dè-tail*, to cut from. It thus presupposes a subject that "cuts" an object. This is confirmed by the existence of the reflexive verb "to cut oneself" (*se tailler*), as well as another Italian term in the same lexical family, *ri-taglio*, meaning clipping, or offcut, which indicates the existence of something cut from a previously existing whole. The word clearly represents an entire plan of action, an action that will change the relationship between the subject and object of the cut. The preposition "from" implies a state preceding that of the cut, as well as the provenance of the cut element from an originally integral whole. Furthermore, the verb "to cut" focuses attention on the action of the subject inducing us to consider the fact that the preceding whole and the successive part are concomitant in the action. Finally, the act of cutting underscores the fact that the detail is created by the subject and, therefore, that its configuration depends upon the viewpoint of the "detailer," who generally explains the significance of the detail, explains the subjective reasons behind it and its function.

A second reflection concerns the value to be attributed to the prefix "de-." This particle not only indicates an anterior state and origin, but also illustrates the nature of the operation. The detail is, in short, "de-fined," that is, made perceptible from within the whole by the action of the cut. Only the existence of the whole and the action of the cut permit the "de-finition" of the detail, that is, the gesture of drawing a motivated attention to an element compared to that which surrounds it. In other words, we approach the detail after having previously approached the whole; and we perceive the form of the detail while it remains in a perceptible relationship with the whole (while it is made of the same material, while its outer edges conform to the lines dividing it from the whole, and so on). There are thus at least two qualitative thresholds above and below which no details are produced. The lower threshold is represented by an essentially perceptive limit: for example, the grain of the material approached, the texture of the whole, the eidetic consistency, none of which can be divided *ad infinitum*. The upper threshold, on the other hand, is represented by the size of the detail and the way in which it is focalized, which presupposes a certain quantitative relationship with the whole: when the detail of a picture is almost as large as the picture itself, it is, effectively, no longer a detail.

There is another mechanism implicit in the cutting out of details, which is revealed by the way in which a *discourse* that deals with details is constructed. Since the production of details depends on the specific action of a subject upon an object, and from the fact that both the whole and the part are present simultaneously, this discourse anticipates the appearance of enunciation marks, that is, of the *I-here-now* element in the production of the discourse.[2] In some cases this is obvious, such as when we see a zoom used in a film or on television: the appearance of an enunciated space and of a subject manifested by the approaching "eye" is quite clear. The use of a slow-motion camera is equally evident. In this case too we suddenly become aware of the existence of a subject-eye slowing down what is seen, as well as of the time of the enunciation.

A final point needs to be made about the nature or, rather, the function of the action of cutting out. When we "read" any kind of whole by means of details, it is clear that our purpose is to "see more" within the "whole" under analysis, to the point of discovering elements that are imperceptible "at first sight." The specific function of the detail is consequently to *re-constitute* the system of which the detail forms a part, by discovering laws and particular aspects that were previously regarded as irrelevant to a description of the work. This can be proved by the fact that forms of *excess of detail* exist in which the detail actually becomes the system. In this case the coordinates of the system by means of which the detail belongs to the whole have been lost. The whole might even have disappeared entirely.

THE ETYMOLOGY OF FRAGMENT

The etymology of "fragment" is quite different. It derives from the Latin *frangere*, to break. Two other terms signifying parts of a whole—"fraction" and "fracture"—come from the same source. We should note that the diversity of the three terms depends on their temporal relationship to one another in terms of the breakage: the fragment is successive, the fraction is the dividing act, and the fracture is a not necessarily definitive potential for breakage.

The idea of the fragment presupposes an object rather than a subject of the verb "to be broken." This is revealed by the fact that the reflexive verb is intransitive but not passive. Unlike the detail, the fragment, despite having formed part of a previous whole, does not need to take the presence of that whole into account in order to be defined. On the contrary: the whole is *in absentia*. From a discursive viewpoint, in fact, the act of breaking forms part of a historical discourse, rather than a discourse of enunciation. The fragment is presented to the viewer as it is, rather than as the product of an act performed by a subject. We might say that it is determined by accident, and not by a subjective cause. Another way in which a fragment differs from a detail is that the edges of a fragment are not "de-fined" but "interrupted." It does not possess clean edges but is jagged like a coastline. We might even say that the opposition between accidental and causal that differentiates the fragment from the detail can be translated, in the former case, into fractal geometry, and, in the latter, into traditional, regular plane geometry.[3]

In effect, however, the geometry of the fragment is that of a breakage in which the boundary lines are produced by forces (e.g., physical forces) responsible for the "accident" that has isolated the fragment from the "whole" to which it belonged. An analysis of the fragment's irregular boundary line will enable us not to *re-constitute*, as was the case with the detail, but to hypothetically *re-construct* the part's relationship with the whole. The fragment, considered as part of a system, *is then explained according to it*. The detail, on the other hand, while being considered in the same way, *explains the system in a new way*.

For these reasons the fragment is not situated in a discourse by leaving traces of enunciation. A discourse involving, or based on, a fragment does not express a subject, time, or space of enunciation (unless it is examined in detail). Its thresholds are therefore purely quantitative: a microscopic threshold (below which an object is no longer recognized as a fragment but simply as "dust") and a macroscopic threshold (above which we perceive it as nothing but a whole with a piece missing). For example, a small uncolored, untreated, unworked piece of stone is merely dust if our intention is to reconstruct the form of a temple. In the same way, a statue that lacks only the little toe of the left foot is not a fragment but an incomplete whole.

Finally, for the fragment too there exists a form of excess that changes its nature: the fragment itself becomes a system whenever the assumption that it belongs to a system is renounced.[4]

Concerning Certain Human Sciences

As I promised, we shall now try to transfer the observations that have been made up to this point onto a more general plane. We can immediately recognize analytical procedures in the field of the human sciences that can be classified according to a semantics of the detail or fragment. In other words, forms of analysis exist that adopt either the detail or the fragment as tools in strategies of research into, and description and explanation of, phenomena. The categorical opposition that has just been revealed lexically continues to function in the same way. We are thus able to contrapose an epistemology of the detail and an epistemology of the fragment.

In a very general sense, we might say that an analysis of phenomena "by detail" operates substantially by means of deduction and hypothesis. The detail is regarded as a portion of a whole which allows us, through closer examination, to reinterpret the global system from which it has been temporarily extracted. Certain disciplines in the field of the human and pure sciences are almost naturally adapted to analysis of this kind. Structuralism, for example, in linguistics, semiotics, and anthropology is based on the concept of a phenomenon as a detail of a structured system.[5] This phenomenon, which permits close reading, is, on the one hand, explained by the system (or structure) and, on the other hand, allows us to validate or reformulate the structure. An identical principle operates for the phenomenon in itself. It displays general systemic rules since it is a system in its own right (endowed, that is, with a structure). Thus, its details will, on the one hand, allow us to validate its own structure and, on the other, are themselves open to analysis, given the structured nature of the whole. But the same principle applies to disciplines that were not conceived in structuralist terms. In the history of art, for example, iconology works in the same way. It is based on a theory of levels of meaning, involving a pre-iconographical, an iconographical, and an iconological analysis. The first is concerned with the "motifs," or naturally recognizable figures, of the work; in the second, the combination of motifs leads to the recognition of a theme; in the third, the symbolic content and attitude of the work in a given environment are examined.[6] But this is nothing more than an observation of portions of the work according to a system based on moving closer and closer to a part in order to reinterpret a whole. The work is considered as a system endowed with a more or less concealed content, in which each portion is intended to contribute to an overall meaning and has sense at different levels according to a system of relationships that integrate these portions with one another.

An analytical practice based on the examination of phenomena as fragments, on the other hand, is substantially inductive or abductive.[7] A fragment is generally a present portion that refers back to a system that is hypothetically absent. Analytical research based on fragments has more the air of an investigation than an analysis. It is no accident that in those disciplines that lend themselves most naturally to analysis "by fragment" one frequently has the impression of suspense, an adventurous progress toward a solution, initially hypothesized and finally confirmed. There is another side to linguistics, previously referred to as a science that lent itself to detail analysis. There exists, for example, the "fragmentary" semiotics based on Peirce's notion of *abduction*, which, in its present-day form at least, seems to be closer to detection than deduction. It is no coincidence that numerous Peirce-based semiologists have devoted a volume, *The Sign of the Three*, to the investigations of the great fictional detectives Sherlock Holmes and Auguste Dupin.[8] And Carlo Ginzburg has attempted to define the existence of a "conjectural model" of knowledge that arose toward the end of the nineteenth century in three important thinkers from different fields: Peirce in logic and semiotics, Freud in psychoanalysis, and Giovanni Morelli in the history of art.[9] We have already spoken of semiotics. As far as psychoanalysis is concerned, Freudian practice effectively regards the narrated dream as a clue. The dream forms part of an unknowable whole composed of the personality of the patient, a whole that can be reconstructed only by starting from the fragment represented by the dream itself.[10] We are confronted by the same principle in art. Acts of attribution regard the temporarily anonymous work as a fragment of a system whose integrity must be reconstructed (by establishing to whom the work belongs or even, if the object is itself a fragment, to which work it belongs). Or we might consider the way in which small particulars belonging to the work might be literally extracted from it, and analyzed as "fossil guides": these particulars effectively reveal more clearly than the work as a whole can do, another more fundamental integrity based on its belonging to an author, a style, or an epoch. A certain branch of art crticism seems to be attracted by the ideology of the fragment: the kind of criticism, for example, that privileges certain portions of the text, praising only those portions and annulling the globality of the text.[11]

It is clear, however, that "fragmentary" criticism has had its greatest development in the field of history. It is no accident that archaeology operates by means of hypotheses and reconstructions based precisely on existing fragments of past works. It has no choice, since time has destroyed the whole and left nothing but parts. The name of Carlo Ginzburg, mentioned above, might remind us that so-called microhistory functions ideally by means of fragments. A view of history that is not based upon the centrality of great historical moments favors micro-events for two reasons: they make it possible to check the fact being examined; and they express more clearly than any macro-event the "spirit" of an epoch, which is assumed to be more or less the same in every section and level of a given society at a given time.[12]

A Schema of Relationships

On the basis of the preceding notes, it now seems clear that the use of the detail or fragment in analytical procedures presupposes that the relationship between the portion and the system to which it belongs possesses value. "Returning" from the part to the whole implies a different evaluation of both the element and the entirety. When the whole, or system, is a work of art, this evaluation actually becomes an aesthetic. In the case of the detail, in fact, there is a tendency to overvalue the element insofar as it allows us to rethink the system: the detail is, so to speak, "exceptionalized." In the case of the fragment, on the other hand, the element is regarded as an accident, from which one then reconstructs the whole: the fragment will be conducted back to its hypothetical "normality" within a hypothesized system.

The opposition between exceptionality and normality thus allows us to categorize details and fragments in a new way. Let us look more closely at this opposition, in order to expand and articulate it. To do this, we must first schematize it by means of a consistent terminology. We shall adopt a scientific metaphor. In topology, we can regard as a system any curve controlled by the parameters of its values on the axes and ordinates, and that respects a function. The curve, in turn, is constituted by a series of points. These points are said to be "regular" when they only obey the law of the function represented by the curve. They are said to be "singular" when they obey not only this function but also another function simultaneously. More technically we shall refer to these points as "triples" or "*n*-ples."[13] Regular and singular points can be represented as follows:

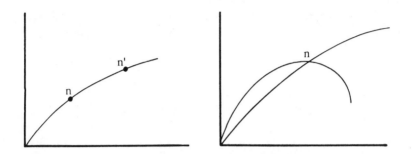

We shall now consider regularity and singularity, not as technical mathematical terms but as metaphors for cultural phenomena (phenomena at the limit, aesthetic phenomena, and so on). This operation is permissible because, in linguistic use, we do it all the time. Thus, from a common lexical viewpoint, we can regard the terms "singular" and "regular" as opposites. At this point, by adopting the procedure of extension envisaged by the "semiotic square," we can also articulate the relationship between the two opposing polarities, by discovering their contradictors, subcontraries, and deixes.[14] We thus obtain the following schema:

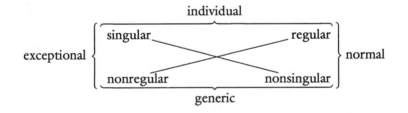

Let us consider the individual terms. "Singular" and "regular" are the two principal oppositions. Their contradictors are "nonregular" and "nonsingular," and these terms are themselves related as subcontraries. The most interesting extension of the square is that of the combinations. Singularity united to regularity produces "individual," thus revealing the individualizing aspect of singularity and, at the same time, the characteristic of nonevasion of the norm, which is typical of regularity. The opposing combination unites nonsingularity to nonregularity: these two aspects are, in a sense, neutralized and the phenomenon under analysis can be recognized as being neither singular nor regular. We thus have a kind of indistinctness that I propose we call "generic." The combination along the axis of the deixes relates singularity and nonregularity: the phenomenon being analyzed is not only singular, but its singularity makes us lose sight of any residue of regularity it preserves. I propose that we use the term "exceptional" in this case, since it takes into account singularity while, at the same time, allowing for the fact that it is produced by nonregularity (poetic license, for example, which is singular in terms of variation from a linguistic norm, yet takes place by making use of grammatical exceptions). Finally, the opposing deixis denies singularity and affirms regularity. I propose that we call this "normal," since this will make it possible to consider both the absence of variations from the norm and the insistence upon its being respected.

This schema effectively helps us to describe the analytical operations carried out by means of strategies based on the detail and the fragment. Detail-based analysis consists in shifting a phenomenon from the individual to the exceptional, or rather, from the regular pole to the exceptional pole. Such a procedure effectively treats as exceptional a portion of the phenomenon that would otherwise have seemed normal. A fragment-based strategy is quite different. The fragment is originally presented as singular, possibly because of its geometry. The analyst, however, attempts to return to the normality of the system to which the fragment originally belonged. In its initial state the fragment is an "emergency" that is annulled by its restoration to the whole.

TWO OPPOSING AESTHETICS
AND NUMEROUS MIXED PHENOMENA

I have already suggested that strategies based on the detail and the fragment produce aesthetic positions. The reason for this is simple. Whenever an analytical practice is used to evaluate a work (of "art," or otherwise), value is automatically invested in that work. Obviously, this value concerns the work, but the criterion behind it also depends on the basic strategy adopted. In order to appreciate this argument more clearly, let us reconsider the expansion schema we have created for the category singular/regular. The combination that produces "exceptional" or "normal" is not necessarily endowed with aesthetic value in itself. It becomes so only if the various terms are themselves invested with value, almost as though they became inserted into implicit propositions that asserted the approval or disapproval of an individual or collective subject. Certain interpretive poetics work in this way. For example, the avant-garde movements of this century have contributed to the enormous valorization of the "exceptional" in preference to the "normal." We have only to think of the principle of "deviation from the norm" enunciated by Shklovsky and by the Russian formalists, on which the aesthetic function of language is based.[15] Other poetics (sometimes defined as "classicist") have, on the contrary, insisted upon the valorization of norms and canons of beauty. We have evidence of this in the explicitly contraposed titles and contents of two classic texts dealing with the "formal" historiography of architecture: John Summerson's *The Classical Language of Architecture* and Bruno Zevi's *The Modern Language of Architecture*.[16] The former interprets the various "grammars" of historical classicism as a series of adjustments to a norm, the rationalism of Greco-Roman antiquity. The latter interprets modernity (in every period, not just our own) as a deviation from dogma, the rule, and formulaic repetition.[17]

But recognizing the existence of these two aesthetics, that of the exceptional and that of the normal, still does not explain how they become aesthetics based on the detail and the fragment. At this point we need to introduce a further principle: that any category whatsoever can be imbued with value (in our case, by aesthetic valorization); this includes categories that are combined with each other, that can *form* an aesthetic, and that can be valorized by means of simultaneous or successive operations. Let us see. We have said that two aesthetics, of the normal and of the exceptional, exist. These can reveal themselves in many different ways. One of these is *also* the analysis of phenomena starting from their elements. In this way the part/whole category can be invested with value whenever one decides, for example, that "small is beautiful," in contraposition to a more global idea of beauty. We have also seen, however, that this same category can reveal either detail or fragment at its "part" polarity. This new category—detail/fragment—can then, in turn, be invested with aesthetic value. It can produce, for example, poetics that—in their entirety—favor the exceptional nature of the work, the fabrication of its parts, the emergence of a detail, or the creation of a fragment (the work as fragment, or parts of the work as fragments).

Once again, however, these generalizations appear to me to be generic and banal: fluctuating models of valorizing interpretation. Two further considerations need to be made in order to produce more specific definitions. First, that each valorization can be made in two ways, either as an *investment of value at source* (the moment of the work's production, at which its underlying poetics are indicated) or as *investment of value at consumption* (the moment of the work's fruition, at which the act of reception itself constitutes a poetic).[18] Second, that each investment of value emerges as "taste" when the general model of valorizing interpretation becomes excessive or exaggerated. We thus obtain four types of phenomena of taste: a poetic of production of details; a poetic of production of fragments; a poetic of reception of details; a poetic of reception of fragments. All four types are further characterized by the fact that details tend to become increasingly autonomous in their relation with wholes, and that fragments tend to emphasize their breaking away from the whole, with no sign of any desire to recombine. In this sense, simple models of valorizing interpretation, directed toward classicist or anticlassicist preferences, become the specific form of a new taste in which all these preferences are incorporated. In my opinion, this is yet another manifestation of that which we have been calling "neo-baroque," as we shall see more clearly at the end of this chapter.

Let us test these hypotheses on some concrete phenomena. We shall begin with the production of increasingly autonomous and complete details. We can find numerous recent examples in the field of mass communications, particularly that of cinema and television. We have only to think of the extreme formal valorization of certain types of "detailing" provided by technological innovations. The most important of these seems to me to be the "temporal detail" produced by slow motion. This technique has moved from serving an analytical function (observing a pass in a football game, for example) to fulfilling an aestheticizing role. The aesthetic aspect consists in the obsessive search for the acme of a dramatic action: the goal or foul in soccer, the shot and death cry in a murder, the embrace after running toward each other of a couple in love, the climax in a sex scene, and so on. But the attempt to isolate these acmes has a consequence: the time of the decisive action is meticulously decomposed by the slow-motion camera and, as such, is represented within a normal time scale. In this way, however, each slowed-down sequence occupies a greater amount of space in the flow of normal time, which is thus reduced within the standard time scales of mass media products. Some recent films are exemplary in this context. *Nine and a Half Weeks* and *Flashdance*, for example, tended to multiply temporary details for a specifically aesthetic effect. The same function can be seen in

Robert Aldrich's *The Last Yard*, where the decision to narrate a dramatic game of American football almost imposed the formal choice (unless the choice of theme was determined by the pleasure of the form?). A variant of temporal detail produced by means of slow-motion effects is that of narrative detail. In this case too we are faced by an analytical approach that transforms narrated time in its search for a cadence of events that resembles real time more closely. We have only to think of soap operas. Time is again dilated, but at the level of narrative content rather than formal representation. Nevertheless, detail once more proceeds toward autonomization, as the plot advances by means of miniscule details. Finally, other manifestations of detail exist that we might sometimes describe as spatial. These too can be divided into details of form and of content. The first example: an increase in the number of close-ups. Once again, in the field of mass communication, we see increasing emphasis being given to something that can be defined as a pornographic effect. A feature of pornography is the attention it pays to scandalous details. This is also becoming frequent in soft-core "art" films: *Nine and a Half Weeks* once again, the work of Tinto Brass, some recent films with Stefania Sandrelli, and *Betty Blue*, based on the sexual activity of the duo Betty-Beineix. This pornographic effect, however, is not concerned only with sex, but also with other equally scandalous procedures of detailing, such as those concerning violence. Action films and newspaper and television journalism both proceed in the same way, by searching out details that become increasingly more autonomous than the entirety to which they belong. Brian De Palma's ruthless editing makes him the master of such cinema. Two films successfully anticipated this trend, exploiting its narrative potential in a masterly way. The first was Antonioni's *Blow Up*, in which the detail of a crime accidentally uncovered by a photographer becomes the central element in the plot, and the eventual moral of the film is the impossibility of reconstructing the whole. It is hardly surprising that the second example should be De Palma's homage to Antonioni, *Blow Out*, in which the detail becomes a sound and the moral remains the same.

In a more specifically artistic context we can find analogous procedures. If we look at some works by conceptual artists of the 1960s, for instance, we discover the autonomization of detail. Giulio Paolini provides us with at least one perfect example. Consider his *Giovane che guarda Lorenzo Lotto* (*Young Man Looking at Lorenzo Lotto*) and his subsequent *Controfigura* (*Stand-in*), dated, respectively, 1967 and 1981. As is well known, both works are quotations from a painting by Lotto. They are produced by means of operations involving detail: in the former, by means of the title, which invites us to consider the portrait purely in terms of the position of the young man and hence the fact that he is *obliged* to look at the artist; in the latter, by means of an unfocused form that the title invites us to consider as the autonomous nucleus of the painting (the "deterioration" of the form is considered in itself, and as the "other," in its relation to the first painting). In the exhibition *Arte allo specchio* (Art Reflected), organized by Maurizio Calvesi for the Venice Biennale of 1984, we could see other examples of the autonomization of detail, all based on citation.[19] Tano Festa, for instance, isolated elements from the work of Michelangelo and Van Eyck. The Argentine Osvaldo Romberg presented "analytical" works based on the *Large Odalisque* by Ingres. The French artist Jean-Michel Alberola isolated details of works by Titian, Tintoretto, and Veronese in a painting composed of seven panels entitled *Actaeon fecit*.

An aesthetics of the fragment at source also belongs both to the world of mass communication and to that of art. In the context of the media it can be found in the by now extremely common practice of creating container-objects, which no longer contain finished products but, predominantly, fragments of other works. Sunday variety shows on most Italian television networks all have this characteristic, even though it is always corrected by the fact that the fragmentation possesses a moment of final recomposition: the program-container itself, its direction and presentation. In this case it might be said that we are confronted by a traditional model: the fragment is conducted back to its appropriate whole. Yet this is not the case, since the whole belongs to a completely different logic from that of the fragments, and the recomposition is based on a pretext. A case of recomposition in which this use of pretext is transformed into ironic virtuosity is the film *Dead Men Don't Wear Plaid*, in which a thriller is created from fragments of famous detective films from the past. At this stage, however, we are dealing more with a collage effect, differing from cubist and dadaist procedures by virtue of the fact that the game implies a receptive pleasure on the part of the spectator, who is led to recognize the original fragments. This kind of pleasure is carried to an extreme by Peter Greenaway, who in *The Draughtsman's Contract* and, even more obviously, *Two Zeds and a Nought* emphasizes and simultaneously conceals his use of citation. A final example might be the curious and masterly film by David Byrne *True Stories*. Here the ideology of the fragment has actually become the constitutive element. Byrne has based his film on a collection of newspaper clippings describing scenes from American life with no links between them. The film brings them together. But it does so by following a fragmentary principle, given that there is no semblance of frame or plot to unite them, apart from the voice and face of the narrator (Byrne himself). The film makes leaps, or "intervals," as Dorfles would define them, from one pole of America to the other, and deals with a variety of disparate social themes. Their unification (assuming it exists) lies in the juxtaposition of the parts, and from the pleasure to be derived from a description possessing no unitary quality.

There are many more examples in this sector in the field of art, and, once more, they almost all involve the practice of citation. This is not irrelevant if we hope to understand the exact nature of a poetic of the fragment. Why on earth do so many artists—from Claudio Parmiggiani and the Poiriers to Michelangelo Pistoletto and the ever-present Giulio Paoloni, from the Belgian Didier Vermeiren to the Czech Jiri Anderle—make such explicit use of fragments from earlier works? I prefer not to accept Maurizio Calvesi's evaluation, implicit in the name he gives to these artists, that they are "anachronists." I can see no sign of nostalgia for the past in the recent works of the painters mentioned above. Citation, in this case, has a quite different function from that adopted by the artists referred to in the preceding paragraph. We are confronted here by the voluntary fragmentation of past art works *in order to extract material*. If we consider for a moment how extremely difficult it is for the contemporary artist to produce works by renewing his expressive means, and assuming the impossibility of discovering "new" plastic material, we realize that these fragments of the past *themselves* begin to become a hypothetical artist's palette. The art of the past, in other words, is nothing more than a storehouse of materials, rendered contemporary and, even more significantly, imposing the need for fragmentation. Only by fragmenting that which has already been made can one annul its effect; only by rendering the fragment autonomous from the whole of which it formed a part can the operation be carried out. The fragment thus becomes a "de-archaeologized" material. It maintains the fractal form required by the situation, but, rather than being reconducted to its hypothetical whole, its by now autonomous form is retained.

As we have just said, the fragment has its own form, its own geometry. The valorization of its appearance is also part of the aesthetic of the fragment, and it is no coincidence that many contemporary writers have experimented with the form. First mention, naturally, goes to the Roland Barthes of *Fragments of an Amorous Discourse*. This is what the author has to say about it in *Roland Barthes by Roland Barthes*: "To write by fragments: the fragments are then so many stones on the perimeter of a circle: I spread myself around: my whole little universe in crumbs; at the center, what?"[20] The aesthetic of the fragment, in other words, is a spreading around, an evasion of the center, or order, of the discourse. It is hardly surprising that Barthes adopts as his motto a phrase by Gide: "Incoherence is preferable to a distorting order." The fragment as a creative material thus responds to a need for both form and content: form, in that it expresses the chaos, rhythm, casualness, and intervals of writing; content, in that it avoids the order produced by connections and keeps at bay "the monster of totality."

Since Barthes, fragmentary writing of this type has become an increasingly common creative gesture. It can be found in a variety of manifestations, all of which were foreseen by the French critic: diaries in the manner of Gide, aphorisms, scattered thoughts. The phenomenon has even reached a mass audience with the constant publication, particularly in Italy, of nonbooks produced by second-tier essayists and figures from the world of entertainment, such as Maurizio Costanzo, Roberto D'Agostino, Nino Frassica, Pino Caruso, and so on. In these cases the fragment has been vulgarized to the point of becoming a kind of "one-liner." In other cases, however, the fragment has reacquired what is probably its most authentic and original role: in poetry. Italy's most important poets have begun to use the poetic fragment once again. The list ranges from ex-members of the Novissimo group, such as Antonio Porta and Nanni Balestrini, to less classifiable writers, such as Andrea Zanzotto, Giovanni Raboni, and Giovanni Giudici. In all these cases fragmentary expression has the same flavor as that found in the visual arts: fragmentation not only in order to rediscover a "palette" of words and phrases but also to recuperate the poetic quality inherent in the annulment of order and regular geometries. The fragment becomes autonomous. The sense of totality of the fragmentary work, however, is different than before. It stresses irregularity and asystematicness, and gives the appearance of "being in pieces." In conclusion, a suspension of fragmentariness inhibits a tendency toward the normal, leaving the exceptional intact; the autonomy of the detail, on the other hand, makes the normal hyperexceptional. The aesthetic system deriving from the detail is in a state of perpetual excitement.

In an opposite position to these aesthetics of source we find the two aesthetics of consumption. An aesthetic linked to detail might be called a "hi-fi aesthetic" since it is concerned with valorizing the pleasure to be obtained from the perfect technical reproduction of a work. The detail, in fact, as an isolated portion of the work, is always a reproduction. Hence to insist on the pleasure of detail means insisting on the quality of its reproduction, since it is this that will allow the consumer of the work to perceive the portion more clearly. Certain instruments are created specifically to satisfy the pleasure obtained from detail—for example, hi-fi stereos, personal cassette players, professional recording equipment, video recorders, compact discs, flat-screen televisions, eidophor systems, high-definition television, headphones, slow-motion and pause controls on video recorders, zoom lenses, photographic enlargers, stereo television, and so on. This process is evolving extremely rapidly, with technologically superior equipment being introduced every few months. This aspect of technology is inevitably accompanied by mutations in perceptive behavior and taste. Enjoyment is already seen (to the extent of being "inscribed" into the work) in the context of attention to detail and close contact with the work. Sometimes, as we have already noticed, this is transmuted into narrative terms, as in the scene in *Blade Runner* in which we discover that one of the characters is a replicant by means of the increasingly blown-up detail of a photograph; or as in the previously mentioned *Blow Up* and *Blow Out*; or even in certain popular television series (Lieutenant Colombo works exclusively with details, Lieutenant Koester solves a case by recognizing the detail of a musical performance). Even our appreciation of art is influenced by an aesthetic of detail. There can be no other explanation for the proliferation of specialized publishing houses, producing more and more books containing images of details; or the success of exhibitions on art restoration, showing quantities of material based on detail (x-rays, photographs of the grain of paintings, tiny images of lacunae, and so on).

In the same way, we can recognize an aesthetic of reception based on the fragment. It consists in an accidental rupture in the continuity and integrity of a work, and in the pleasure obtained from the portions that have been made autonomous as a result. An obvious example is the practice of "zapping" with our television remote control device. An act that might otherwise be defined as neurotic can be transformed into a genuinely aesthetic program of consumption. Our attitude toward acquiring anthologies is identical: "anthology," in this context, describes any kind of compilation, from music, literature, and cinema to television and photography. Our pleasure in these cases lies in the *extraction* of fragments from their original context, and in their recomposition within a frame based on the notion of multiplicity or "variety." In each case, we are dealing with a loss of contextual value, and with a taste for the uncertain and fortuitous nature of the work thus produced. New values are acquired from the *isolation* of fragments and from their re-situation in another context. Sometimes this receptive pleasure coincides with that felt at source: in architecture, for example, when a fragment (of the past, or of a citation from the past) is literally situated in a neutral construction, which acts as a background to the fragment, throwing it into relief. Architects such as Carlo Scarpa and Franco Albini have transformed this practice into a genuine style of construction, consisting of an underscoring of the *irregular* by means of the neutralization of background and context. This is a perfect metaphor for the pleasure to be obtained from the fragment: the cancellation of a systemic and contextual memory.

In conclusion, we can observe that, in spite of the differences between them, both detail and fragment participate in the same "spirit of our time," the loss of totality. In the neo-baroque the distinctions that have been made obviously continue to apply. Nevertheless, the acceleration and exaggeration of their characteristics make them *nuances* of a general option that is, *in every case*, that of the decline or fall of totality. This is another possible explanation (one of many) for the dwindling power of "strong" ideological systems. We are not simply dealing with a decay of models in the face of modernism (or postmodernism). The fact is that detail and fragmentation of systems become autonomous facts; valorized independently, they make us "lose sight" of our larger general frames of reference.

CHAPTER 5

Instability and Metamorphosis

MONSTERS

Let us begin with a simple observation. In recent years we have witnessed, and continue to witness, the creation of fantastic universes pulsating with monsters. Cinema, television, literature, advertising, and music are providing us with an impressively wide-ranging gallery of examples. We have seen the reptiles of two television series of "Visitors"; the protean being of Carpenter's *The Thing*; the antagonist of *Conan the Barbarian*, who transforms himself into a gigantic snake; the evil Alien and its female counterpart in *Aliens*; the enormous worms of *Dune*; the green-skinned monster into which the protagonist is transformed in "The Incredible Hulk"; the extraterrestrial populations of various episodes of *Star Wars* and "Star Trek"; the ironic hero of *An American Werewolf in London* and his parody in *Thriller*, Michael Jackson's video for the song of the same name and directed, as was the film, by John Landis; the specters of *Ghostbusters*; the apparitions of *Poltergeist*; the devils in Dario Argento's *Demoni*, the (almost) beneficent monsters of *Close Encounters of the Third Kind*, *E.T.*, and *Gremlins*; the mini-alien of *Liquid Sky*; the cartoon robot-man of the Italian comic strip "Rankxerox"; and the list has only just begun. This observation is already enough to suggest that there might be a superficial relationship with the baroque, and with other periods which have produced a similar range of "monsters": the late Roman epoch, the late Middle Ages, the romantic era, and the period of expressionism. These are all epochs in which the monster represented not so much the supernatural or fantastic as the "marvellous," a quality that depends on the rarity and casualness of its appearance in nature and the hidden and mysterious teleology of its form.

This is, in effect, the most interesting point. When we look at the etymology of the word "monster" we find two basic meanings. First, the idea of spectacle, since the monster *demonstrates* itself as something outside the norm ("monstrum"). Second, the idea of mystery, due to the fact that its existence brings to mind the idea of admonition, concealed by nature, which we must divine ("monitum"). All the great prototypes of the monster in classical mythology, such as the minotaur or sphinx, are both marvellous and enigmatic. They challenge us in the two mutually reflecting areas that make up human experience: the realm of the "objective" (the world that lies outside us) and that of the "subjective" (our spirit). They challenge, in short, both the regularity of nature and that other form of regularity, human intelligence, as it adapts to nature.

The central principle of teratology, or the science of monsters, derives from this: it is based on the study of irregularity and is concerned with *excess*. From ancient times to the present day, monsters have always been excessive in their dimensions (giants, centaurs, cyclops, dwarves, gnomes, pigmies) or in the number of limbs or parts (Gastropods, Sciopods, Blemmyes). Natural perfection is based on a mean, and anything that oversteps its limits is "imperfect" and monstrous.[1] But anything that oversteps the limits of the mean of spiritual perfection is also regarded as imperfect or monstrous. Perfection and the mean, particularly in certain periods of taste, have been considered almost synonymous, as Jean Paulhan ironically revealed when he said that "nothing resembles mediocrity so much as perfection."[2] The enigma of the monster, and of its *spiritual excess*, derive from this. This final characteristic makes the monster not only abnormal, but also, in most cases, negative: a being for which a judgment of physical or morphological excess is transformed into a judgment of spiritual excess. This is why a teratology of "positive" science becomes a moral discipline based on socially acceptable value systems.[3]

Highly normalized societies usually establish a system of correspondences between different categories of value. Let us, for example, consider these four categories: ethics, aesthetics, morphology, and emotion.[4] The first two categories are appreciative, in the sense that they contain judgments that attribute either praise or blame. The second two categories are constative, since they contain judgments that concern reality. We can see, however, that a rigid correspondence exists between both the positive and negative terms of all four categories, particularly during more "ordered" periods. The appreciative categories inform the constative ones, and these, in turn, provide the former with their content. For example, whatever is physically well formed is also good, beautiful, and provokes euphoria; whatever is good must also be well formed, beautiful, and provoke euphoria; whatever is beautiful will also be well formed, good, and euphoric; and whatever is euphoric is also well formed, good, and beautiful. And vice versa, as we can see in the following table, which has already been discussed in the first chapter of this book:

Category	Judgment Upon	Positive Value	Negative Value
morphological	form	well-formed	deformed
ethical	morality	good	evil
aesthetic	taste	beautiful	ugly
emotional	emotion	euphoric	dysphoric

We should notice, however, that it is often possible to deviate from correspondences of this type. There are in fact groups or entire societies who sometimes propose different systems or, more simply, neutralize the systems of correspondence that already exist. If we return to monsters we shall find that, according to the "most-ordered" system of correspondence, we are dealing with beings that are essentially deformed and, therefore, evil, ugly, and dysphoric. Changes in our correspondence system can, however, take place: someone might begin to say that the monster is perfectly well formed and thus beautiful, but also dysphoric and thus essentially evil. The prototype: Dorian Gray. Catholic morality has sometimes proposed such a mutation of viewpoint. Someone else might insist that deformity and dysphoria are bearers of beauty and goodness. Many romantic works obey this rule. Hence we begin to see a series of combinations of values, capable of defining the different attitudes held by groups, individuals, and societies in the formal, ethical, aesthetic, and emotional judgments they make about a phenomenon. It is obvious that the blunt and simple propositions stated above are expressed in ever-less-general categories. For example, the notion of being well formed can be expressed by means of symmetry, height, fair coloring, blond hair, slenderness, and so on. Whatever is the opposite of this is defined by society as "deformed." A change occurs when the "deformed," socially corresponding to the evil, ugly, and dysphoric, is suddenly associated with the good, beautiful, or euphoric. When changes of this nature become stabilized in a society, they establish a new realm of correspondences. In this way a general dialectic of collective values in different epochs is produced.

Having dealt with this premise, we can return to contemporary monsters, in order to consider whether or not they are associated with some change in our system of correspondence. Our answer must be positive: there is a specific character to modern teratology. Rather than corresponding to categories of value, our new monsters *suspend*, *annul*, and *neutralize* them. They are presented as unstable forms that belong to no precise point in the schema. They are thus forms that possess no specific form, but are searching for one. This makes us reflect on the need to add a new chapter to our history of teratology; a chapter on the "natural" instability and formlessness of contemporary monsters. And since, as we have seen, teratology is a basic social science, a chapter on the "natural" instability and formlessness of our society.

FORMLESS FORMS

In order to produce a basic classification system for our new monsters, we need to establish some descriptive criteria. The choice of a name, for example. How should we "baptize" the form of E.T., of Yoda in *Star Wars*, of the monster in *Alien*, of the being in *The Thing*? I say "baptize" because, whenever a new form fails to correspond to what we know, our only way of fixing it, and of rendering it perceptible and communicable, is to give it a name. This name might begin with "like . . . ." It is usually our verbal language that allows us to stabilize any form at all. Yet it is obvious that we are quite incapable of inventing a name for modern monsters other than "monster." This immediately distinguishes them from monsters of the past, given that the many teratological catalogues of the past contain lists of properties to be attributed to monsters: bat's wings, lion's head, lynx's body, reptile's tail, bird of prey's claw. The monster, in short, was a sum of properties that were generally inaccessible to one another but were, nevertheless, recognizable.

Do not imagine that cinema producers have failed to ask themselves the same questions. At least one contemporary monster perfectly, and consciously, reflects the problem: the alien in Carpenter's *The Thing*. At a certain point during the first half of the film, the doctor on the American Antarctic expedition who found the creature discovers its secret. The thing has no autonomous form; its cells imitate those of any being that happens to pass by, to the point of absorbing them and then transforming itself into that being. When we see the thing, we might be seeing a dog, a member of the expedition, and so on. Or, alternatively, we might witness an amorphous mass in a state of transformation and metamorphosis. The doctor actually explains the concept by means of a computer program in which we see a schematic theater of action across which symbols of the real and parasitic cells both move. Whenever a cell reaches the predator, it is captured, absorbed, and transformed. Yet the thing itself has no form at all.

A somewhat analogous mechanism can be found in another very different recent film: *Zelig* by Woody Allen.[5] *Zelig* is a figure from the 1930s endowed with a natural peculiarity: he does not, or appears not to, possess a personality and appearance of his own. Rather, he transforms himself physically and spiritually by imitating the people and surroundings closest to him. Thus we see him in a brown shirt next to Adolf Hitler at a Nazi rally, as a Jew among Jews, and as a black musician in a jazz band. We witness a crescendo of situations in which Zelig becomes slim, fat, rich, poor, oil magnate, athlete, politician, German, Italian, American, and even psychoanalyst when he is obliged to undergo analysis during an attempt made to "cure" him. The film, in short, depicts a human chameleon. But *Zelig* the film also has a chameleon-like character. Woody Allen has constructed a perfect montage in which we see films being transformed into another film. The base film is in black and white, with a slight sepia tint characteristic of 1930s films. New film is integrated into these genuine documentaries in such a way as to become indistinguishable from them. Even the ground noise, cuts, and speed of cinema from the period are reproduced. Some documentary inserts are in color and contain interviews with such famous figures of contemporary American culture as Susan Sontag and Bruno Bettelheim. In the midst of interviews with imaginary characters belonging to the invented story, however, they contribute to our inability to distinguish between the genuine and false sociology proposed by the film. Even the interviews are chameleon-like. They imitate two such different films as Warren Beatty's *Reds*, interrupted by interviews with people speaking about the personality of the journalist John Reed, and Alain Resnais's *Mon oncle d'Amérique*, containing the biologist Henri Laborit's reflections on mice. The theme, and its expression, are once again focused upon formlessness and instability. One of the characters in *Zelig*, Dr. Eudora Fletcher, explains it perfectly: "Ever since he was a child Zelig had a completely *unstable* character. In order to feel accepted he began to transform himself into anything that he felt was normal and recognized by everyone."

Carpenter also revealed his awareness of the dynamic mechanism he was constructing, as we can see from a not insignificant detail of the film. As is well known, the film is a remake of *The Thing from Another World*, produced in 1950 by Christian Nyby and Howard Hawks. In the original film, however, the thing was humanoid in form, even though we discover that it has the biological structure of a vegetable and that it feeds on blood. Carpenter's transformation is so radical that he must have considered the matter at length, possibly searching for the most effective way of representing the linguistic phenomenon of the creature's name. Out of all the words that were available to him he chose the one that, more than any other, describes something that is undefined, "the thing," removing even those specifications that, in the original, contributed to maintaining an air of vagueness rather than of absolute uncertainty. From a figurative viewpoint as well, the formlessness of the thing produces a phenomenon of suspension and neutralization, since we are dealing with a being that is neither "well formed" nor "deformed." Other curious features stem from this, concerning those categories related to form. From the ethical viewpoint, the expedition members do not consider the thing either good or evil, but simply as a predator whose prey (the men) attempts to get away, possibly by transforming itself into predator (the hero MacReary) of the prey (the monster), in a process that in scientific terms would be described as a "hysteretic loop." We could thus claim that the ethical category is effectively suspended. Something else occurs in the emotional category. Since we are dealing with a horror film, someone might object that the monster is clearly dysphoric. But this is not the case, since passion is also in a state of constant suspension. There is dysphoria only when the monster is in action. The rest of the time the spectator and the characters in the story are in a state of *waiting*, of suspension or, in the more expressive literary and

97

cinematographic term, suspense. This is revealed by the fact that the story has no conclusion. We do not know whether the monster has been eliminated, whether our heroes will survive, or whether there will be another episode. From the physical, ethical, and emotional viewpoints, then, Carpenter's film distances itself from its predecessor. Ethically, Nyby and Hawks presented only one character (the scientist on the base) who believed the thing to be a superior being. Emotionally, the film preferred to make the spectator euphoric by declaring the thing dysphoric and having the hero eliminate it by means of a trap.

The final viewpoint is that of aesthetics. Although it is not actually suspended, this category is also rendered complex. While, on the one hand, the monstrous nature of the thing is expressed by means of "ugly" elements (tentacles, sliminess, unpleasant noises, localized deformities), some marvellous special effects are used in its realization. Something similar can be found in another famous monster in contemporary cinema: the creature in *Alien*. Once again we have a formless form, which sometimes resembles a gigantic mantis, sometimes a mechanical robot, and sometimes a dragon. On the whole, however, the monster remains mysterious, since it is never seen in its entirety, nor for sufficient time to enable the spectator to stabilize perception. It is true that, ethically, this formlessness is associated with evil; but only by those characters who tend toward its "preservation" (even though Sigourney Weaver indisputably inclines us to align ourselves with the "well formed–beautiful–euphoric–good" system of correspondences). It is, however (once again!), the spaceship scientist who insists that the monster must not be killed since it is itself a "perfect killing machine." Emotionally, the discourse is identical to that of the preceding film. Aesthetically, too, we find the familiar sliminess, unpleasant noises, and reduction of human beings to fleshy lumps. Nevertheless, an Oscar was awarded to the creator of the monster, Carlo Rambaldi, and to his designers, including the well-known illustrator Giger, whose paintings of ambiguously polymorphous and polysexual monsters have been published with the title *Necronomicon*.

With the mention of Gramaldi we have inadvertently arrived in the realm of the most popular of all contemporary monsters: E.T., the Jedi, the Gremlins. They only appear to be monsters in a manner of speaking; they are more like puppets or cuddly toys. Nevertheless, they obey all of the principles described above. Let us look at them more closely. In a series of interviews given between 1981 and 1983, Rambaldi stated that the original idea for both the aliens of *Close Encounters of the Third Kind* and E.T. came from his earlier experience as an artist, as well as from the inspiration provided by his Himalayan cat. Let us begin with the cat. Rambaldi has repeatedly shown that E.T., at least as far as his head is concerned, derives from a cat that has been reduced in two ways. The first reduction is a simplification of the cat's form by means of an almost caricatured profile. The second is the elimination of certain feline features, such as the ears, fur, whiskers, and teeth. We can thus conclude that the morphology of E.T. is less the result of a deformation than of a "loss of form." Another aspect confirms this impression. Rambaldi has always said that the original prototype of the alien had a bottom resembling that of a baby's, in order to allow both adults and children to identify more easily. Spielberg, however, made him modify this feature, since he preferred a less recognizable bottom, a "cross" between a reptile and Donald Duck. Now let us consider the artistic aspect. Rambaldi always declares that as an artist he divided his time between painting and sculpture. This information is interesting when we remember that as a painter, he was essentially a neorealist, whereas his sculptures were far less formal. He was concerned with producing objects from rough materials that, immobile, had no significance but that, when provided with movement, began to "express" things like "anguish," "anxiety," "joy," and "emotion." If we consider E.T. in the light of these comments, we can see that Rambaldi has amply exploited this effect in his puppet. Rambaldi himself has written that he had refused to exhibit E.T. in an exhibition devoted to his special effects in Los Angeles for two reasons. The first was that the immobile puppet might fail to arouse emotion. The second was that children, becoming used to his static existence, might no longer want the story to continue.

Let us now translate these comments in the light of our categories. To begin with, E.T.'s derivation from the informal is clear. In other words, the character is created explicitly as *formlessness*. This formlessness is also revealed by the fear that presenting E.T. statically might produce a stabilized and stereotyped perception. E.T. has to be *dynamic* (dynamism is actually considered to guarantee the production of *emotions* in the spectator). There is a further proof of the formlessness of Rambaldi's extraterrestrial, and it can be seen in the film itself. On at least three occasions E.T. behaves like a chameleon. The first moment is when he sees the child in the cornfield at the beginning of the film. The second is when the children hide him from their mother by placing him in the middle of a mountain of toys in their wardrobe, and the woman is unable to distinguish him. The third time is at Halloween, when the children take him disguised around the streets of the town and everyone assumes that he is a child in fancy dress (a scene that allows Spielberg to reverse the rules delightfully: E.T. "recognizes" a child dressed up as Yoda as a member of his own race). If necessary, there is a final proof of the formlessness of E.T. and his colleagues. In a fascinating essay entitled "The syntax of the alien" Renato Giovannoli has shown how the canonical form of our new monsters, including those in video games, is elastic, rubbery, and mutable.[6] It is a kind of octopus-figure, capable of swelling up, stretching, shrinking, and changing itself as it chooses; and also of exploding (as we can see in a number of video games) in situations of extreme crisis.

But what do Spielberg and Rambaldi do with the physical formlessness of their little monsters? Something absolutely extraordinary, which differentiates them from the kind of ethical, aesthetic, and emotional suspense that is maintained in *Alien* and *The Thing*. The formless form of the alien, in fact, not only remains suspended in terms of its correspondence with other categories. On the contrary, it is actually judged as good, euphoric, and beautiful. Not by everyone, however: like all inventors of forms, its value is recognized only by a chosen few, while the rest remain in a state of conflict. Parents (at least at the beginning), adults generally, and the government all refuse to recognize the ethical, aesthetic, and euphoric value of E.T., and even the child, at first, is as afraid of the alien as the alien is of him. The formless form, in short, *provokes* a bimodal behavior in the society in which it is inserted. In this sense, *Gremlins* is a genuine extension of *E.T.*, since it takes the aesthetic of formlessness to its extreme. As you will remember, the puppet-animals are born from a "stable" form, that of cuddly toys, totally acceptable to everyone since they represent euphoria, charm, and nauseating sweetness. But human distraction and stupidity make it impossible for the Gremlins to maintain their form, and they change into ugly, wicked, dysphoric, and deformed creatures. The truth of the matter, however, *for those who are able to understand*, is that they are transformed into splendid, euphoria-producing creatures, perfectly well formed in terms of their nature as "little monsters" rather than real monsters and, in their way, "good" (since they punish the most hated members of the Midwestern community, such as the wicked proprietor of the local bank). Certain scenes in the film do anything but provoke fear or disgust, and must be regarded as minor masterpieces in the history of cinema: the poker game, for example, in which the ringleader is represented as Humphrey Bogart; the scene in which the Gremlins watch *Snow White and the Seven Dwarves* at the local cinema; the final duel in the toy shop; the Gremlin rock band. In these scenes Spielberg's ability to play with categories of value, their bimodality and instability, seems to me to reach new heights. But not in the sense that the creatures are "beautiful." On the contrary: value judgment is transferred from the form in itself to its dynamism, and to its ability to construct uncertainty, complexity, and variability of attitude.

It is strange, then, that almost all critics regard the products of Spielberg, Lucas, and company as "conformist." That there is some basis for this judgment cannot be denied. But the conformism of Spielberg and Lucas is simply one level, and possibly the most superficial, of their cinema. Beneath it there is a skin of a very different nature indeed: a second skin that rejects, or at least casts doubt upon, ordered correspondences, and upon the traditional, rigid categories of value within our society. We have said since the beginning that contemporary teratology is not only different from that of the past, but also encourages us to envisage a new, and final, chapter regarding the relationship between monsters and the surrounding culture. Our way of thinking about monsters, in fact, conceals our ways of thinking about categories of value. In the cases that we have examined it seems obvious that we are no longer faced with a classical deformed-evil-ugly-dysphoric system of correspondence. Nor, however, is it what might be termed the "anticlassical" system (deformed-good-beautiful-euphoric), nor even one of the characteristic systems that can be found in certain discourses of "genre" (comic, for example: deformed-ugly-good-euphoric). We have to recognize the appearance of new poetics linked to uncertainty and the nondefinition of forms and values, to games that play with the boundaries of existing categories.

OTHER KINDS OF INSTABILITY: VIDEO GAMES

We have referred in passing to the existence of monsters in video games. But if we are following the principle of a poetic based on instability, we should really define the video games themselves as "monsters," particularly those that belong to the subgenre known as "war games." Nothing is so governed by the principle of dynamics of form and the bimodality of structure as these games. Let us try to analyze some of their characteristics.

In one of the most famous recent electronic games, *Defender*, by Williams, a genuinely filmic series of credits appears on the screen. The word *Williams* is composed in three dimensions, along with the phrase "Williams presents." The image changes to form the word "Defender," and this is followed by another change of image as an illustration of the characters and interpreters appears (the player's spaceship, his various enemies and their properties, along with their names and the points received as a result of their elimination). It is clear that the game is intended to resemble an action film. There is a subject who takes responsibility for the successive text, as if to say: "I am here to tell you that. . . ." This text is destined for us, outside the screen in a theatrical space.[7] It is presented, therefore, as a tale told by someone, yet the story is in the third person with a protagonist (the spaceship) whose voyage and adventures we watch. It is not a coincidence that, as spectators, we observe the exterior of the spaceship, of its enemies, and of the world being narrated. Other features of the game, however, contradict this "position." A command panel, for example, projects us inside the game by transforming us into "pilots" of the spaceship. But these two spaces (the subjective space in which we are pilots, and the objective space of the game) coincide only partially on the screen, so that our perception constantly oscillates between the two positions. From a strictly narrative viewpoint, as well, the existence of these two contradictory spaces renders the narration unstable. On the one hand we maneuver the game by projecting ourselves into the role of narrator: the story is determined by the moves we make. On the other hand we maneuver the spaceship or, in other words, one of the characters subjected to events within the story, and narrated by the story. The game-narration thus becomes a kind of journey that the player completes not only materially—in terms of the concrete skills demanded by the game—but also theoretically—by showing the narrative skill required to enjoy the game from outside, as spectacle, and from within, as adventure. All of this depends on the different geometrical structures, within a single video space, of the two regions in which the narrator-actor is situated. Only certain games, which simulate a subjective and three-dimensional vision of space, are able to resolve the instability of these two coinciding geometries.

Nor is this the only form of instability in video games dealing with heroes. Many others exist, both on a strictly figurative level and in terms of the relationship between game and player. In most video games, in fact, there are at least three elements of instability. The first consists in the characters of the protagonists themselves. The "enemies" of the spaceship, for example, are frequently endowed with the ability to transform themselves and to progressively increase their offensive capacity, thus becoming highly unpredictable. The second consists, once again, in a spatial conflict. The only space that we can control is that represented on the screen. But the "enemy" also belongs to an external (and invisible) space, which is assumed to be a continuation of the internal space. Continuity, maybe; but one that the player cannot predict, a continuity that is promised but not maintained. Hence any enemy action coming from this "external" space is a surprise.[8] The third consists in the relation between game and player. Unlike a pinball machine or certain "fantasy" video games where, in theory, a player could continue to play forever, in "heroic" games the player is constantly on the brink of death. In other words, in terms of both technical difficulty and narrative representation the player lives on the edge of the abyss, awaiting an ineluctable destiny, whose arrival he seeks to postpone, in which the death of the hero finally coincides with the end of the game.[9]

OTHER INSTABILITIES: FIGURES, STRUCTURES, BIMODAL BEHAVIORS

We have spoken up to now of two significant examples of instability. One of these is constituted by a theme, and the other by an object that not only includes instability as a theme and that itself behaves unstably, but also provokes instability in the actions of those who use it. Before continuing, I should like to consider this observation more closely. We do, in fact, need to stress that the phenomenon of instability appears in "neo-baroque" objects on at least three levels. One, that of the themes and figures *represented*. Two, that of the textual structures that *contain the representations*. Three, that of the relation between figures and texts, and the *way in which these are received*. The three levels can be more or less concurrent. One thing, however, appears to be clear: although figures, textual structures, and patterns of consumption cannot be divided without analysis, they usually coincide in neo-baroque objects. In other words, if instability is represented, it inevitably follows that its representation is also unstable, and that the user's guide for these representations (programs for use, rather than effective uses) will indicate unstable uses.

The examples that we have considered up to now seem to be fairly relevant to the subject at hand. We might, however, briefly examine some more samples, in a kind of annotated list. Cinema, television, and video-game monsters might make us think that only the media are influenced by a poetic of formlessness and instability. But this is not quite true. Let us take some examples, to begin with, from recent literature, in particular, three novels whose style might appear in other respects very different and yet in which the principle of metamorphosis is constantly at work: *If One Winter's Night a Traveler* by Italo Calvino, *The Name of the Rose* by Umberto Eco, and *Duluth* by Gore Vidal.[10] As confirmation of their neo-baroque nature, all three books are discussed elsewhere in this work. Let us begin with Calvino. As you will remember, the novel consists of a series of tales, involving different environments, characters, and periods. These tales interconnect without, however, reaching a conclusion. The *emboîtement* is permitted by the fact that all the tales are, in fact, different manifestations of the same underlying structure. Furthermore, even though the representations change, the tale remains perfectly homogeneous. Each narrated tale is situated in a different segment of the same nar-

105

rative program. As a corollary of this, each tale is the potential figurative metamorphosis of each of the others. This is expressed in the novel by making the narrative metamorphosis of one tale actually take place within another. Furthermore, all these tales are placed in the framework of a further tale, effectively of the same rank and yet elevated to the superior rank of "container."

The case of Eco is slightly different. Here, too, as Carlo Ossola has noted, we are confronted with a process of metamorphoses.[11] In this novel, however, the theoretical basis is more specific. Instead of beginning from Calvino's hypothesis (taken from the semiotics of Greimas) of the structural equivalence of all stories sharing the same matrix,[12] Eco starts from the idea that structures and figures can be transported into a "new" story. This story will then become a combination of more or less preexisting encyclopedic material. Eco creates a "montage" of a large number of texts (narrative, figurative, philosophical, scientific, and so on) at a variety of explicative levels. These texts are then encased in a new text in which they are homogenized at a figurative level as well, by being translated and deformed to suit their new role.

Our third example is that of Vidal. Despite being of "lower" literary quality (which is not, however, the issue here), his novel seems to unite both of the metamorphic principles considered above. *Duluth* tells the story of an imaginary city, after which the novel is named, that covers practically the whole of the United States. This megalopolis provides the setting for a series of events involving groups of characters who represent the literary metamorphosis of prototypes found in American television soap operas. Up to this point we are dealing with the kind of technique used by Eco, except that Vidal introduces into the coherence of the basic framework the apparent (and only figurative) incoherence of Calvino. In *Duluth*, in fact, characters can pass from one story to another, interacting even when they belong to different epochs and plots, and transferring their "novelistic" memory (the representation, that is, in

106

which they are found) to other, concurrent sets of events. There also exists a level of enunciation (the author identified with the name on the cover who addresses his readers) that bounces constantly in and out of the novel, to the point of making it literally impossible to identify its appearance as such—a level that, in the work of Eco, functioned merely as an ingenious way of framing or encasing a number of different narrative voices before reaching that of Adso of Melk, and, in Calvino, as a false distinction between tale-frame and framed tales.

An approximate typology might be derived from these three morphological mechanisms. In Calvino we have a genuine *translation* of narrative motifs. In Eco we witness the principle of their *transferability*, due to the journey they make from their sources to their "new" destination, by means of their hypercodification in the "encyclopedia"—the knowledge that is held in common in a society. Finally, in Vidal, translation and transference live side by side. But at this point we are considering only the figurative level, at which narrative motifs are rendered unstable insofar as they pass from one place to another, *modifying themselves during the journey*. The second level is that of the narrative machine. In Calvino this machine is unstable because of the simple fact that, being obliged to demonstrate the principle of translation, the narration itself moves in leaps and bounds. It thus becomes the task of the reader to reconduct this narration to normality by means of the intelligibility of the text. In Eco we are confronted with an apparent continuity. The reader, however, is constantly being offered an inverse challenge because the text is threaded by tracks that lead toward the multiplicity of its sources—tracks that might or might not be recognized by the reader, and that frequently lead to deliberate confusion (given that the quotations are often false, as we shall see in the chapter of this book devoted to mechanisms of "perversion"). In Vidal, finally, we arrive at total discontinuity. The text becomes a kind of practically formless "mass" produced by leaps in motif, style, quotation, and surface structure, in which it is almost impossible to reunite these different elements. The third level, finally, is that of the reader's behavior, not as such, but in terms of the text's expectations. We have already touched on this implicitly in the preceding lines. In Calvino's novel we find a reader challenged to rediscover a unity that has been concealed by variety and, simultaneously, invited to enjoy the conflict between the two planes. Eco offers a contrary challenge: to rediscover difference in homogeneity, and to find pleasure in the excavation work required to do so, with all the traps that this involves. The principle, as we shall see in the next chapter, is that of constantly confusing the authenticity and falsity of the "finds" that are employed by the text. In the novel of Vidal, finally, the reader is invited to take pleasure in the sense of vertigo, and in the inability to make decisions about the roles and characteristics of the protagonists that this provokes. The reader, in other words, is practically asked to abandon himself in delirium to the metamorphoses and instability of what is narrated.

Analogous examples can be found in the figurative arts, once again at the three different levels that have just been indicated. Let us take an emblematic case in architecture, that of the American group Site. Beginning at the end of the 1970s Site has constructed a series of stores for the department store Bell's, scattered throughout the United States, the most important being in Richmond. The essential feature of these buildings is that they are based on a simple parallelepiped, like most "normal" industrial constructions. The building's exterior, however, is treated in an unusual way, as though it were a kind of "skin" that has undergone some catastrophic transformations. The buildings appear to have been the victim of some kind of destructive force: bad weather, a cyclone, an earthquake, and so on. For example, a facade has been made to resemble sheets of paper, crinkled up in one corner as a result of moisture. Alternatively, the parallelepiped has not been "placed" on the site, but rather twisted on its axis as if part of it had sunk into the earth. In another case, corners of the building have been raised to resemble ruins, with blocks of bricks that seem to have fallen from the cornices and an absence of paint at the points from which blocks are presumed to have fallen, almost as if the building had been damaged by the elements. Finally, the parking lot in front of one of the stores has been covered by a gray powder of cement which totally or partially covers a number of cars, giving the impression of post-catastrophe neglect. As we can see, we are in the presence of an architectural instability, or rather, of a representation of instability.

Another example comes from contemporary art. In 1981 Salvador Dalí produced six drawings entitled *Catastrophe*, depicting a flat but elastic geometrical space with one or more internal folds. From the dedication ("to René Thom") we understand that Dalí is dealing with some of the so-called elementary catastrophes, the seven geometrical models elaborated by the French mathematician to describe various forms of structural dynamism. In this case, a scientific model representing instability becomes the "figure" of a work of art. Most significantly, the figure is itself manipulated, since Dalí does not restrict himself to reproducing the canonical figures of the models, but elaborates them. As a result, they are no longer immediately recognizable and thus become unstable in terms of perception. A structure, in other words, becomes the artistic figure or motif. Furthermore, the unstable way in which the structure is presented is determined by the structure itself.

If we move onto a more structural level, we can find a number of multimedia works in which a series of forms, ranging from photography and architecture to theater and television, become the containers into which other material is inserted. These examples have one thing in common: it is the structure of the work that operates upon the instability of its appearance. Let us take the example of an Italian photographer, Carlo Fabre. Fabre has recently made use of material that produces only temporary images to take photographs of stable and "normal" photographic figures. The image gradually disappears, rather like tomb paintings exposed to the light without due precautions having been taken. An analogous case is that of the painter Filippo Panseca, who, almost as though he wished to represent the brevity of life, has begun to produce "limited-life" paintings, in which the short duration of aesthetic life is represented by canvases with fading colors. As a result, we have works that begin to disappear, like the frescoes of Leonardo, which, owing to the experimental nature of the pigments adopted, are unable to resist the passing of time. A certain structurally programmed instability has also been used experimentally in computer graphics, in the work of Giovanotti Mondani Meccanici, for example. Here we see a program in which the figures, treated by means of a fractal technique, are no longer projected representations of objects reduced to simple geometrical (three-dimensional) objects. This program actually treats the surface of the screen, without reference to any "reality" even though the images might seem extremely "real." This eidomatic program can now operate upon the screen surface in two or more ways; thus a "realistic" image can be transformed, according to a rhythm imposed by modifying individual parts of the screen, into a different "realistic" image. The screen itself reveals the dynamics of this image transformation, which appears to be dominated by a kind of internal "proteanism." A somewhat similar case can be found in the experimental performance of the Florentine theater group Krypton. In this performance, significantly entitled *Metamorfosi*, a number of experimental techniques, such as lasers, computer graphics, holography, and so on, transform the architecture in certain places (e.g., the main square of Linz, the square of Brunelleschi's church of the SS. Annunziata in Florence, and so on). Here too we have a dynamic based on figures. In this case, however, it is focused primarily on the programmed instability of the textual apparatus, rather than on the figures produced by it.

In conclusion, we can look at the final level of instability: pragmatic instability. The most convincing examples obviously appear at the level of entertainment, as it is in this field that a reader can be "rendered" unstable in the most concrete manner. Consider a hard rock concert, from The Police to the more violent punks that succeeded them. Interaction with the public is sought in a peremptory way by means of belligerent actions: verbal provocation, spitting, objects thrown into the crowd, and so on. The atmosphere is not unlike that of futurist and dadaist evenings during the second decade of this century, even though these could clearly not be regarded as baroque phenomena. The same thing occurs in certain forms of "avant-garde" theater, such as that of Leopoldo Mastelloni, who leaves the stage to slap his public, or of the French mime Yves Lebreton, who finishes his show by throwing paper balls into the audience, or of Pier'Alli's *Morte della geometria* (*Death of Geometry*), based on a text by Giuliano Scabia, in which spectators are "provoked" into perceptive reactions by insistent lights directed into their eyes from the stage. But theatrical forms based on spectator "involvement" are generally rather old: they derive either from the experimental years of the 1960s (like Living Theatre) or from the earlier concept of "total theater" developed in Germany during the 1920s. In the figurative arts the phenomenon has not been seen since the performance artists of the 1970s (type: the perverse behavior of Ketty La Rocca, Gino De Dominicis, Wolf Vostell, or John Cage; model: the mongol or stud bull presented at the Venice Biennale or the butchered horse exhibited slightly more recently by Magazzini Criminali).[13] It can still be seen, however, in the *presentation* and organization of exhibitions by critics and architects. There is, in short, an element of "behaviorism" in the work of critics such as Achille Bonito Oliva and exhibition designers such as Luciano Damiani. It can even be found in the way in which certain museums, such as the Picasso Museum and the Musée d'Orsay in Paris or Sterling's Stadtmuseum in Stuttgart, structure their exhibitions.[14] Nevertheless, behavioral ambivalence on the part of the public has been sought most actively of all in the cinema, by means of the massive increase in films devoted to horror and suspense. The eighteenth-century formula of

mixing pleasure and pain is rendered banal by a cinema of special effects in which the spectator is left suspended. Stephen
King makes this quite clear in his trailer for *Maximum Over-
drive*. Dario Argento is less explicit in *Demoni* when he sets his
horror film in a cinema.

SCIENTIFIC THEORIES OF INSTABILITY

Some of the examples described in the preceding pages, such as
the chameleon-like nature of Zelig or the amorphism of the
"thing," bear an extraordinary resemblance to certain scientific
theories that have been developed during the last few years, as
well as to areas of applied research that have also "exploded"
recently. I am referring to the so-called catastrophe theory, famous above all thanks to the previously cited René Thom, and
also, among other things, to the analysis of animal chameleonism in ethology.[15] Before illustrating the resemblances these
bear to our cultural objects, however, it would be well to specify the sense in which these scientific fields are associated with
the humanistic areas with which we have been concerned up to
this point. I should say immediately that theories or scientific
analyses of instability or metamorphosis interest us from at
least two different points of view. The first is probably the
more obvious: if we accept the idea that any cultural elaboration at all, whether scientific or humanistic, reveals a conceptual inner dimension, we are bound to say that all cultural objects have an abstract "form" or "structure" independent of
their manifestation or application. In this sense, a work of art
and a chemical formula can easily share a "model" of internal
articulation. This is a different way of discussing the phenomenon described by Sarduy as "relapse," since it avoids the risk of
having to establish a causal nexus between two or more cultural
areas.[16] Hence we shall not say that a scientific theory provokes
changes in taste, or vice versa. We shall, however, say that a
theory and a change in aesthetic taste can both belong to the
same intellectual "environment" or "mentality," and can share

with it an abstract structure, *even though the individual authors of works, theories, or analyses are unaware of the adjacent fields*. We all, in fact, know more than we are aware of knowing, and can express it quite independently of any conscious desire to do so.[17] In conclusion, the scientific fields to be examined here can be associated with the cultural objects that we have already indicated by a kind of "similarity" in the form of their conceptual expression.

But there is also a second aspect. As a result of their inevitably schematic internal nature, scientific models, and above all theoretical ones, can possess a further capacity: not only are they able to "express" a taste equivalent to that of other cultural objects, but they can also "describe" or even "explain" it.[18] In other words, alongside the notion of "resemblance," scientific models can be used as theories of the models themselves: they are self-explanatory beings. This is clearly true for the "catastrophe theory," which can thus be used as an explanation or intrinsic description of itself and of other objects associated with it.[19]

Let us look more closely at "catastrophe theory." Very roughly we can say that its basic core is the following: each phenomenon has a structural internal morphology; this morphology is stable for the simple reason that, even when it changes, the phenomenon remains the same; in the first place, however, there exist phenomena that are not at all stable and, in the second place, even stable morphologies are subject to transformation, or are capable of undergoing changes during their lifetime. Since the advent of evolutionism and behaviorism, these changes have usually been explained by considering them as a series of different *states*, related to one another by cause and effect. In short, the diversity of two connected morphologies in a system is always explained in terms of *continuity*. Thom and other mathematicians, however, have tried to provide different models for describing mutations in form. Above all, Thom has produced a *dynamic* theory of morphologies; in the course of time a stable form actuates a sort of journey that results in the form undergoing disturbance. When the form is not changed by this disturbance, it remains stable. When, however, it changes as a result of this disturbance, it means that the form has crossed a "catastrophic" threshold that has modified its structure. But how does this happen? It happens because a number of competing forms, separated by "thresholds," can exist in the same flexible space. If a form reaches the edge of one of these forms on its journey, it "tumbles" into the zone of attraction of one or more conflicting forms, and then stabilizes itself according to the new model. For example, if we consider the transformation from tadpole to frog, we must no longer say that the frog passes uninterruptedly from tadpole-state to frog-state, but that tadpole-form and frog-form coexist on an elastic geometrical plane, and that the tadpole-form, during its historic journey, reaches the frog-form threshold, tumbles over, and stabilizes. We might represent this process as a passage between two stable states represented by zones in this plane:[20]

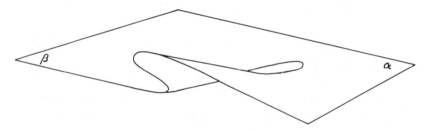

The first form is maintained in all places on the right, and the second in all places on the left. In the middle is a fold. When our form arrives at the edge of the fold, it suddenly tumbles from state A to state B. In geometry this "suddenly" is conveyed by the term "catastrophically" and indicates the entire series of points at which this brusque formal shift can occur. The binary model represented above is only one of seven possible models, and mutation can take place not simply between two forms, but also between more than two. We must say, in conclusion, that the acquisition of a form depends on a conflict during which a subject, in Thom's words, "chooses its own future."

Another aspect of catastrophe theory, merely touched on rather than analyzed profoundly in this discussion, also tells us something that is extremely relevant to the cases that we have examined in the preceding paragraphs: the existence of "formless forms," morphologies, that is, that are not of forms, but of entities in search of their form.[21] These have a very special status: they are not endowed with structural stability, but assume the appearance of any stable attractor that appears within their field of action. If there is more than one attractor, they are able to assume the characteristics of each of them. In short, a formless form can become a "formed" form only by means of the attraction exercised upon it by a stable form. The most obvious examples of formless forms are totally bimodal forms, such as Necker's cube:[22]

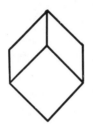

Here it is impossible to decide whether we are looking at an empty cube with a visible inner edge or a full cube with its outer edge facing in our direction. A similar "formlessness" in terms of perception can be found in the figures produced by artists such as Magritte or Escher, above all in the latter's work, where the impossibility of deciding which is the dominant stable form gives rise to paradoxes in perception. As we can see, given that catastrophic models are genuine representations, they too follow the fate of the representations they model. At the same time, they supply them with a structural description (and even, since they are geometrical, an "intuitive" one).

Certain morphogenetic phenomena, such as those in the field of ethology mentioned above, can also be described in terms of catastrophe theory. In a work that has rapidly become a classic, the zoologist Leonard Cloudsley-Thompson offers us a fascinating panorama of hunting and flight phenomena in the animal world.[23] In very many circumstances, and quite independently of genus or species, animals transform themselves in order to capture or avoid the enemy. Some cases, such as that of the chameleon, are well known. Others, less famous, are just as extraordinary and frequently far more complex. There are creatures, for example, that blend in with the environment. Partridges change their color with the season; some spiders create webs with more than one center in order to distract the predator's attention from the body of the prey; many insects disguise themselves as leaves or excrement; there is even a worm capable of opening its posterior to resemble a flower. Then there are animals that imitate other animals. A certain type of spider carries dead ants on its back so that, seen from above, it resembles an ant itself; another insect assumes the form of a tiny alligator; others have the same appearance as the face of a monkey. Nor is this all: some animals transform parts of their own bodies. There are small prairie vertebrates with what look like false eyes and a mouth on their backs in order to distract the attacker and gain enough time to flee, preferring a wound to death; others invert their upper and lower parts by an appropriate use of color so that the enemy is unable to determine the position of the body in shadow. But predators also disguise themselves in order to trick their prey. There are snakes of the crotalid family who pretend to have two heads, so that their victims are unable to decide where to strike. Certain cats blend in with their environment and leave false scent trails. Another zoologist, Desmond Morris, tells us that chameleonism can also be found in the sphere of human sexuality (where human beings and animals are clearly very closely related).[24] Transformation, in fact, is the rule in both seduction and attraction. Mandrils provide us with a perfect example. The faces of the males imitate the form of their genitals, while the females belonging to a certain subspecies bear the form of the vagina on their breast. Morris skillfully documents the fact that something similar can be found in human beings, when certain bodily positions echo the form of the woman's posterior or the man's penis.

These ethological examples are also nothing more than competing forms, which become effective phenomena when a disturbance occurs that "provokes" them (sexuality, hunting). These examples effectively represent morphological instability. Although they clearly exist in nature without reference to periods of "taste," the fact that scientists select these phenomena rather than others, out of the myriad of natural facts that have yet to be studied, is itself an indication of taste. Furthermore, even though the research we are dealing with is empirical, experimental, and conducted in the field, it is nevertheless born from the fact that hypotheses capable of distinguishing this type of fact from all other possible types are being elaborated at this precise moment. The *discreteness* of certain things from others in the natural continuum depends on establishing fixed ways of seeing the world, which make it more or less meaningful. And certain aspects of the world can be recognized only because there exists a certain taste in the world of research and discovery, rather than another.

CHAPTER 6

Disorder and Chaos

THE ORDER OF DISORDER

IT MIGHT BE SAID that since the origins of philosophical and scientific thought, and throughout Western history, two series of notions have been contraposed: that of order, regularity, cause, cosmos, finiteness, and so on; and that of disorder, irregularity, randomness, chaos, indefiniteness, and so on.[1] These two series are contraposed because they reveal two different orientations toward the same problem, that of describing, interpreting, and explaining phenomena that have already occurred (in order to establish their cause), or that of foreseeing those that have not yet taken place (in order to establish the possibility of their occurrence). The first series of notions encourages us to believe that it is possible to define the origin of, and to predict, phenomena. The second series, on the other hand, is intended to justify their unpredictable and unintelligible nature. However, these qualities of unpredictability and unintelligibility can, in turn, be interpreted in a multiplicity of different ways. This is why our notions of disorder, irregularity, randomness, chaos, and indefiniteness can be defined in so many different ways. At least three of these definitions might be regarded as "classical" within the history of Western thought. The first might be termed the idea of the "beginning and end" of phenomena. It consists in the notion of order as a principle of regularity that is superimposed upon an indistinct original or, inversely, as a condition that tends toward final dissolution and the absolute equiprobability of phenomena. All pre-Socratic philosophy imagined that the order of the cosmos derived from an original chaos. Inversely, modern information

118

theory accustomed us during the 1940s and 1950s to the concept of "entropy," the equiprobable state of elements in an information system to which that system inevitably tends. The second position is more deterministic. It consists in the notion that any phenomenon is sustained by a necessary order. Only an insufficiency of information prevents us, in certain cases, from perceiving this order: it is thus defined as "irregular" for our convenience. In this case, too, we are dealing with a concept that is simultaneously ancient and modern. It can be found in Aristotelian physics as easily as in pre-Newtonian mechanics, positivism, or Marxist dogmatism. The third position is more relativistic and indistinct, as well as the most contemporary. It consists in the notion that the principles underlying irregularity, randomness, chaos, and indefiniteness rely on the fact that the description of a phenomenon (and thus its eventual interpretation and explanation) depend on the system of reference into which it is inserted. An aspect of an event that is not perceptible *according to a certain description*—based, that is, on certain concepts of relevance—will be defined as random, variable, irregular, and so on.[2] If the concepts of relevance are changed, this randomness can disappear.

In the context of the human sciences, as in that of the natural sciences, the contraposition of these two series of concepts has been further complicated by another factor. Scientific disciplines (including those humanistic disciplines that, modeling themselves on the natural sciences, have aspired to "scientific" status) have almost always produced *unified theories of order* and, as a corollary, *unified theories of disorder.* They have done so in the following way: on the one hand, scientific disciplines have regarded their aim as oriented toward the discovery of a universal order of things. On the other hand, they have regarded it as oriented toward the discovery of the internal order of a local system of specific reference. Disorder has become, on the one hand, the outer edge of a unique order, with the implicit risk of moving that order farther and farther out (or even of eliminating it); and, on the other hand, the local occurrence of nonrelevance in the specific order analyzed by each discipline.[3]

In the last ten years, as a result of combined pressure from some scientific discoveries and philosophical theories, the series composed of disorder-randomness-chaos-irregularity-indefiniteness has undergone a radical transformation in science and in the science of culture—above all in science, where the idea that phenomena do not all necessarily follow a single natural order is increasingly influential, as is the principle that phenomena with a simple systemic appearance can be susceptible to such complex dynamics that they are completely transformed. The turbulence of these quite inexplicable dynamics can actually reach the point of becoming the specific principle behind their transformation, requiring *ad hoc* instruments in order to be described, interpreted, or explained. These dynamics, found in certain phenomena with a tendency toward maximum complexity, have now taken the name of *chaos* and constitute the principle of studies of "disorder" (chaos theory), a disorder that, before receiving this denomination in 1975 by James Yorke and Tien Yien Li, had no name at all.[4] This radical change has occurred, secondly, in the science of culture. The quality that certain idealist critics proclaimed as the "ineffability" or "unsayableness" of some cultural phenomena (such as creative phenomena) has now been translated into a "principle of complexity." From philosophers such as Niklas Luhmann to current aesthetologists, people have begun to proclaim the principle of the relativity of *explanations* and an orientation toward the *challenge of complexity*.[5] It was, in effect, a short step to make. A desire to refute the idealistic ineffability of art, while maintaining a belief in its explicability, inevitably led to the concept of a "complexity" ingrained in all aesthetic phenomena. The alliance of ideas and philosophical concepts such as "deconstructionism" and "weak thought," recent protagonists on the contemporary cultural scene, might lie in this "spirit of the time."[6] A final point must be made for the sake of completeness. Complex or "disordered" phenomena are analyzed in science by means of differing and competing theories, according to whether stress is placed on the systemic aspect of the objects being examined, on their superficial form, or, finally, on their structural morphology. This is why the preceding chapter, as well as the two following chapters, are devoted to the same aim: tracing the articulation of simultaneously analogous and diverse concepts of complexity in science and culture.[7] In the previous chapter we examined complexity in morphological structure. In this chapter and the next we shall be looking at the formal complexity of surfaces. In the chapter after that we shall be examining systemic complexity.

THE BEAUTY OF FRACTALS

In one of the most successful books of "new" mathematics in recent years, *Fractal Objects*, Benoit Mandelbrot makes an observation that interests us greatly. When talking about the purpose of his book, Mandelbrot says: "At worst, even if certain applications [of the theory] are shown to have no contact with reality, the reader will, nevertheless, have discovered numerous old, beautiful, and difficult scientific problems, and *a mathematics that is beautiful in itself*."[8] The italics are mine and are intended to underscore the fact that "an aesthetics of mathematics" exists. This notion is familiar by now and is sometimes expressed by the term "elegance" (to describe, for example, a demonstration). In the book by Mandelbrot, however, the notion acquires a different value from the one it has in the history of the discipline. Earlier in the same work the author says: "In certain applications, I shall simply be naming concepts that have already been expressed by earlier researchers, an activity that runs the risk of having no more than an aesthetic, and possibly even cosmetic, interest."[9] But the cosmetic interest to which Mandelbrot refers possesses something new: it is not the classical principle that I have just referred to as "elegance," consisting in the rapidity with which a concept is formulated, its deductive proof, or its simplifying rationality. In our case, the fascination of mathematics derives from the *form* of laws that have been rediscovered or conceived, a form that is decidedly "baroque."

Let us explain very crudely what a "fractal object" is. In an intuitive sense, "fractal" means anything whose form is extremely irregular, interrupted, or jagged, at whatever scale we choose to examine it. A "fractal object" is therefore a physical object (natural or artificial) that intuitively reveals a fractal form. Such objects are very common in nature: the jaggedness of a coastline, the profile of a snowflake, the distribution of holes in a piece of Gruyère, the form of the craters of the moon, a river network. And the list could continue. The form of these natural objects has usually been considered random, incapable of being predicted, described, or calculated. The notions on which traditional Euclidean geometry was based, in fact, appeared to be insufficient (or, more importantly, *inadequate*, as we shall see later) for such a purpose. How do we measure a jagged coastline in order to reproduce it on a map? By simplifying or approximating its contours into rectilinear segments *according to a certain scale*, which is that of an aerial view at a suitable distance for the task at hand. But methods such as these can never provide us with a "real" measurement of a jagged coast. It is easy to show that for each scale chosen, a smaller scale exists (a closer view) in which the jaggedness increases the value of the distance between two points when compared with the approximation stabilized by the scale itself. The fact that common geometrical instruments only allow an approximate measurement of fractal objects, however, does not mean that more precise instruments cannot exist. On the contrary, natural phenomena such as those listed above reveal to us that nature would appear to require them. But this means that we can imagine the existence of "*ad hoc* geometries," able to offer more precise descriptions of the complexity of these phenomena: geometries, in other words, that are founded on the nature of physical phenomena. Mathematicians are, not surprisingly, divided on this point. On the one hand, we find the people responsible for the notion that we have just been examining. On the other hand, we see those who insist upon a necessary separation between mathematics and natural, concrete phenomena. The former group obviously includes Benoit Mandelbrot, "inventor" (or rather, as we shall see, "reformulator") of a geometrical theory able to describe fractal objects.[10]

The idea of reexamining a series of geometrical principles and, in particular, the concept of *dimension* has in fact been around since 1877 (June 20, in a letter from Cantor to Dedekind).[11] In the years immediately following Cantor's famous letter, other mathematicians—such as Peano, von Koch, and Hausdorff—became aware of theoretical, rather than natural, phenomena that contradicted the idea of dimension.[12] These phenomena were universally described as "mathematical monsters" or "chimeras." They were geometrical figures that did not respond to general topological rules—for example, very special curves, such as those discovered by Peano, that functioned as intermediary figures between straight lines and planes. Other figures occupied a medial position between the dimension of the point and of the line, or between that of surface and volume. But this means that our definition of "dimension" had to be corrected. We are accustomed to thinking of dimension in terms of units: zero dimension for a point, one for a line, two for surface, and three for volume. In a case of geometrical "monstrosity," however, dimensions correspond to fractions, and not to wholes. They are, in fact, fractal dimensions. It is only now, with the scientific acceptance of what seemed to be no more than mathematical games, that the notion of fractal dimension has entered the scientific limelight. The results obtained in hydrology, botany, anatomy, information theory, and other areas[13] have changed our perception of fractals, which have now actually reached the threshold of aesthetics and mass communications. Three properties of fractal objects—whether natural or constructed—recently seem to have received an aesthetic valorization.

The first is their *random* character; not in the vaguely disquieting or metaphysical sense that this term acquires when it is used to justify the impossibility of prediction in terms of a phenonemon, but in the scientific sense of *pseudo-aleatoriness* or *primary randomness*. In other words, randomness as defined in the calculation of probability, and artificially inserted into any simulated system. In information theory this type of operation is called *randomization*. To randomize a collection of objects, for example, means to replace their original order with another order that, in spite of being chosen at random, is ordered and statistically forecast.

The second is their *scalar* character. This term refers to the fact that, although fractal objects have an irregular structure or form, this is repeated more or less equally in the whole as well as in the parts of the object, whatever scale is used to analyze it.

The third is their *teragonic* character. This means that fractal objects always have a "monstrous" polygonal form, with a very large number of sides. A "teragon" is, in fact, a polygon of this type. The Greek etymology of its name suggests both monster (*teras*) and the numerical prefix (*tera*) that now stands for 10^{12} in the decimal system, and is the last existing verbal prefix for "expressing" a power of ten.

As we can see, all three characters belong to the same aesthetic area, which was also examined in the previous chapter devoted to monsters. Fractals are special monsters. They are monsters at a very high level of figurative fragmentation; they are endowed with a scalar rhythm and repetitiveness, despite being irregular; their form is random, but only as the equiprobable variable of an ordered system. It might be said, then, that the forms—jagged, random, and of a fractal dimension—of certain objects undergo the same process of valorization that was noted in the previous chapter and explained in the Introduction. In certain periods, these objects are treated unfavorably, whereas in others they are regarded as "beautiful." It is no accident that mathematicians from the end of the nineteenth century to the present have regarded chimerical entities and "monsters" in a negative light, whereas, exactly at this very moment, two German mathematicians, Heinz-Otto Peitgen and Peter H. Richter, have organized an exhibition of fractal objects, obtained by means of computers and colored with an appropriate chromatic system, entitled The Beauty of Fractals, which has traveled around Europe.[14]

FRACTAL DIMENSIONS IN CULTURE

Up to now we have spoken of *fractal configurations*, and shown how they *exist* in natural or artificial objects, from the viewpoint, for example, of their figurative contours. We have also pointed out that these configurations can undergo valorization according to taste and epoch. The frequency of fractal objects in our age allows us to define this type of substantial cultural production as "neo-baroque." However, we might at this point develop our metaphor by suggesting the existence of "fractal dimensions" throughout the process of cultural production-consumption, and not merely in certain specific objects. After all, if we accept the initial hypothesis of a culture's "form," it is extremely probable that this "form" might assume an appearance analogous to the figurative irregularity of some of the objects contained by the particular culture.

It occurs to me that a fashion for talking about cultural "dimension" existed during the period around 1968. A very famous book by Herbert Marcuse was entitled *One-Dimensional Man*, and denounced the fact that all totalitarian powers—and, primarily, capitalism—tended to construct both a "one-dimensional society" and "one-dimensional thought."[15] Marcuse contrasted the one-dimensionality of the technocratic West with the "liberating catastrophe" of critical thought's multiple dimensions. The metaphorical use of the term "dimension," however, remained Euclidean. The single dimension of power and the plural dimensions of liberation were metaphors derived from whole numbers. Would it, however, be possible to imagine fractal dimensions in culture? What would they be like?

125

Let us reconsider for a moment the scientific terms of the question. The birth of fractal geometry is linked to many different areas of research into chaotic phenomena. Essentially it might be said that their main shared interest is examining the cause, operation, and predictability of *turbulence*. This term describes the (chaotic) appearance of any cyclical phenomenon in which normal regularity is replaced by chaos *within a certain threshold of complexity* (for example, the accelerated rhythm of the cycle). Mathematicians and physicists have named such phenomena "tendency lines toward chaos" or "transition lines of chaos."[16] Hence it is not merely the jagged appearance of form that establishes the chaotic nature of an object, but also the appearance of turbulence. In order to develop our cultural metaphor, we must conclude that any communicative phenomenon (i.e., any cultural phenomenon) that possesses either an irregular geometry or turbulence in its flow *is a chaotic phenomenon*. This does not refer only to the object, therefore, but also to its process of production and consumption.

In effect, as we shall see in the following paragraphs, we can easily identify in contemporary culture examples of fractal objects, turbulence or intermittence at the source, and deliberate chaos at the moment of reception or consumption. Fractal objects, irregular communicative productions, and turbulent flows constitute the horizon of an aesthetic that is itself irregular and based on a fractal dimension.

CHAOS AS ART

I have just mentioned the German exhibition The Beauty of Fractals. On that occasion, in spite of the caution expressed by Herbert Franke and the skepticism of another creator of fractal images (the American Bob Devaney), we witnessed the deliberate production of scalar abstract figures with an explicitly aesthetic function.[17] Other researchers, in fact, have also begun to speak of the "beauty of fractals," almost as though this were a characteristic shared with similar configurations.[18] This is clearly an unacceptable viewpoint: as we have repeated since the beginning of the book, an object *becomes* aesthetic after an act of valorization by an individual or collective subject. Nevertheless, it is also true that fractal figures possess at least one characteristic that makes them suitable for valorization: the marvellous. In the computer figures produced by artists such as Peitgen, Richter, Franke, Devaney, and, in Italy, Daniele Marini, fractal objects constitute a sophisticated, technological version of the ancient kaleidoscope, an object that is, almost by definition, surprising. This is only true, however, in certain periods. In other epochs a kaleidoscopic quality in visual production is considered nothing more than a fairground phenomenon.

There are, however, many other cases of artists searching for jagged objects as material for their art. This is a frequent occurrence in contemporary sculpture (if we are permitted to call it that). Another example might be Keith Haring's objects encrusted with multicolored paint; or the large murals in tormented materials by Marco Gastini; or the terracottas of Corrado Morelli; or the fragments of self-portraits (on acrylic surfaces) by Carlo Alfano.

More frequently, however, artists orient themselves toward an intermittence in the production of the message. This is the case, above all, in works that make use of screens (television, computer, and cinema screens).[19] For example, in the installations of the Milan group Studio Azzurro, we sometimes find a chaotic use of the film camera. The same effect, using different materials, appears in the computer elaborations of Giovanotti Mondani Meccanici, in which the adoption of fractals makes it possible to produce a continuous formation and dissolution of "realistic" images. Intermittence at the source can also be found in the field of music. Much avant-garde music, ranging from the important Milan school of Demetrio Stratos to the experiments of Franco Battiato, or even the high avant-garde of composers such as Daniele Lombardi, Franco Cardini, and Beppe

Chiari, has introduced the "disruptive" dimension of noise. The origins of this procedure naturally date back to the futurist Russolo and, more recently, John Cage.

In a considerably lighter form, however, analogous operations can also be seen in popular culture. Television signatures, for example, exploit abstraction processes involving images in transition toward chaos more and more frequently. An effect of chaos, or at least of intermittence, is produced by the insertion of commercials into programs on private television channels, interrupting broadcasts and encouraging viewers to regard television as a fragmented dimension. Fractals themselves are by now commonly used in cinema for the creation (paradoxically) of "real" effects. Using fractals, it is possible to produce images "of the world," as long as they are of an irregular nature: jagged coastlines, surfaces of planets, trees and forests, star and cloud systems. Computers and fractal equations, for example, were used to produce a complete five-minute sequence of *Star Trek II*, in which spectators witnessed the bombardment of a dead planet by a warhead full of a revolutionary regenerating product, followed by the rebirth of the planet and the emergence of ocean and land systems, islands, forests, and so on. Generally speaking, all modern science fiction films make use of a computerized fractal production of images, which are far more convincing than models created in the studio. In short, turbulence and irregularity govern the production of objects with an aesthetic function at practically all levels of sophistication, from the mass media to the more rarefied world of art galleries and concert halls.

Irregular Consumption

But there is a further fractal dimension in culture, that of consumption. I have referred to the concept of "productive consumption" a number of times in earlier parts of this book. If we base ourselves on the various sociological formulations available, "productive consumption" indicates a kind of consumption that does not remain passive but that, in the very act of consuming a cultural object, produces an interpretation that changes the nature of the object's content.[20] For example, a particularly playful consumption of so-called trash cinema (previously scorned as being below the level of genre films) can transform these films into another kind of entertainment. In Italy, this "neo-baroque" way of consuming popular culture has been linked to a particular cultural politics, sometimes referred to as "ephemeral." Since 1975 many events organized in Italy have been based on a consumption that is interpretive, or even aesthetic, rather than passive. Analogous examples exist elsewhere, however, in many cases at the level of popular cults. The most typical is the frequently cited *Rocky Horror Picture Show*, which has been all the rage for some years in several major cities (New York, London, Paris, Milan) and in which the real show is what happens, not on the screen, but in the cinema during projection. The live spectators break, splice, and fragment the flow of action on the screen by means of underscoring and repetition, parody and exhortation. Another example of the fragmentation of communicative flow, in this case both at the source and at consumption, occurred in a series of radio programs broadcast by the local Milan radio station Radio Popolare. The station broadcast a program called "Bar Sport," for the first time during the 1984 Los Angeles Olympics and then, more sensationally, during the Mexico World Cup. The game consisted in superimposing the radio program on the live broadcast on state television (RAI) by replacing the sound with an equally live commentary based either on the event itself or on the original television commentary. From the production viewpoint the program became an imitation of the kind of fragmented reception typical of a group of people in a bar. From the reception viewpoint, however, it invited the public (presumably a television public at the same time) to eliminate the RAI commentary in favor of that provided by the radio. Consumption became parodic, and the television image, comically insane.

In all cases, and quite beyond the examples which have just

been provided, irregular consumption seems to have become a constant feature of television viewing. This is particularly true in those countries that possess a large number of channels and, even more, in the case of private channels with frequent commercial breaks that disrupt programs. An extremely wide range of choices encourages the viewer to experiment with what has now been described as "zapping." Viewers no longer watch a program in a constant, unified way. They change obsessively from one channel to the next, reconstructing their own palimpsest from a variety of fragments of the images being broadcast. In this way they probably obtain a kind of consumption that no longer follows a linear interpretation of texts. The text obtained is completely different, functioning according to the occasional, rapid, and probably random meeting of images, rather than content. An irregular consumption of this type not only produces a collage of fragments, it can also become a kind of aesthetic behavior, endowing the mini-palimpsest that has been obtained with new meanings and values.

Intermittent communication (at the source, at the destination, and in the message conveyed) is thus based on general forms of turbulence, fractal dimensions, vortices, that disrupt the normal order of communication, and propose a new order for it. This "new order" of communication, however, functions on the condition that a kind of simultaneous change occurs in perception. Traditional static perception is no longer enough. We need an increase in perceptual dexterity and Gestalt-like speed. This might be why an aesthetic of this nature is more suitable for young people, physiologically endowed with the mechanism needed to realize and understand it. But this final observation takes us outside our field, even though we might consider whether changes in aesthetic values do not necessarily contain a generational element.

CHAPTER 7

The Knot and the Labyrinth

THE IMAGE OF COMPLEXITY

THERE IS A PASSAGE in the *Aleph* by Borges in which Joseph Cartaphilus, the main character, contrasts the labyrinth with chaos. Chaos appears to him to be endowed with sense, whereas the City of the Immortals, with its inextricable tangle of traffic, has no sense at all.[1] Borges is a connoisseur of labyrinths, and we should trust him. But on this occasion he is wrong. The labyrinth is simply one of the many forms taken by chaos, if, by chaos, we mean a complexity whose order is either complicated or concealed.

We might even say that the labyrinth is the most typical figurative representation of an *intelligent complexity*. All of the legends, myths, customs, and games that are based on the labyrinth have, in fact, two intellectual features: the pleasure of becoming lost when confronted by its inextricability (followed by fear) and the taste for solving something by the concentrated use of reason. One of the world's most famous labyrinthologists, Pierre Rosenstiehl, has drawn our attention to the fact that the English language still bears an obvious trace of the idea of "acuteness," as something intrinsic to the labyrinth.[2] The closest synonym, in fact, is *maze*, or "marvel." This is true of other figures that are related to the labyrinth, such as the knot, the curving line, and the braid. Once again we find the same principle: the loss of an overall vision of a rational path and, simultaneously, the opportunity to use our intelligence acutely in order to solve the riddle and, thus, rediscover order.

"Acuteness," "shrewdness," "marvel," "braid": these terms alone are enough to reveal how profoundly baroque the figures of the labyrinth and the knot really are. Very little proof is needed. We have only to recall certain operas of the historical baroque, based specifically on these key words. One of the most fascinating texts in baroque culture—a text that, not surprisingly, has recently returned to the limelight in a dramatic way—is called *Agudeza, y arte del ingenio*, the work of the Catalan Jesuit Balthasar Gracian. The greatest Italian baroque poet, Giambattista Marino, was inspired by the marvellous, while almost all seventeenth-century philosophers, even Vico, praised the virtues of ingenuity.

But the knot and the labyrinth are destined to emerge from a specific historical period, because they can be interpreted as signs of a more universal, metahistorical baroque. If we consider some of the most significant studies of the labyrinth, such as those by Paolo Santarcangeli and Hermann Kern, we notice that it appears most frequently during "baroque" periods: pre-classical antiquity, the late Latin epoch, the Alexandrine period, the late Middle Ages, the mannerist and baroque periods, and so on, up to certain baroque moments of the twentieth century.[3] In other words, wherever the spirit of loss of self, of shrewdness, of acuteness, raises its head, we find, inevitably, the labyrinth, and also the knot, if we are to believe Suzanne Allen's long article on the subject, revealing these motifs to us (closely linked to a sexual metaphor) at the most varied historical and geographical points in human culture.[4]

To say that knots and labyrinths are figures of complexity is not, however, sufficient. We need to specify what type of complexity they represent. Different types of complexity exist whose nature is quite different from that of knots or labyrinths. Chaotic natural forms, for example, are not necessarily labyrinthine. The chaos of the indefinite does not necessarily assume the figure of a knot. A systematic change within an order that, instead of moving toward equiprobability, is transformed into a different order does not become a maze. If we really consider the issue, we see that knots and labyrinths represent an *ambiguous* complexity. On the one hand (with the loss of an initial orientation), they deny the value of a global order, of a general topography. On the other hand, they challenge us to discover order once again, since they never induce the doubt that order itself might not exist. Let us look more closely at the challenge they represent. It begins with the pleasure of becoming lost and ends with the pleasure of discovering where we are.[5] Both these pleasures consist of substituting order by, in the first phase, annulment and, in the second, reconstruction. What is annulled is totality: we have no control over the topographical system, no maps that will guide us to the center of the labyrinth or help us to leave it, we are unable to distinguish one path from another or decide which thread should be unwound first. What is more, reconstruction is based on local inference. The labyrinth is overcome and the knot untied by deducing certain moves at each intersection. We are faced, in short, with a very special type of problem, defined by Rosenstiehl as "grid problems that can be solved myopically." The myopia he refers to is that of a calculation that progresses step by step, without making use of memory (the totality of the system). To be "myopic" does not mean "to see less"; it means seeing in a different way, "knowing that you don't see." The fundamental ambiguity of the problem stems from this: we continue to have recourse to some idea of totality, even though the solution of a single problem requires us to leave it to one side, or to annul the dominant formulation of totality, in order to enter the "myopia" of the specific. In other words, we are faced once again with instability. This is confirmed by another characteristic of the knot and labyrinth, that of being a *metaphor of movement*. If we look at the examples of Hermann Kern, all of which are *unicursal* (labyrinths, that is, without intersections and thus without the possibility of error), we shall see that the sense of enigma connected to contemporary labyrinths has been replaced by a conception of rhythmic movement rather than movement in a straight line.[6] And if we take some of the simpler knots, we shall see that the real problem is not to untie them but to understand how a single thread can be made to seem two. Once again we are faced with an opposition between stability and its contrary, transformation.

KNOTS AND LABYRINTHS AS FIGURES

A rediscovered passion for knots and labyrinths is evident from a series of greatly differing texts (in literature, mass media, art, and even music) that have been generated during the last decade, not to mention a parallel revival of research into the subject (by both historians and theoreticians). We shall now look at some well-known examples, bearing in mind that we are dealing only with those that have had the most success, and underscoring the fact that the knot and labyrinth appear in them primarily as *figurative motifs*.

Once again, as if to prove its intrinsically "neo-baroque" character, Umberto Eco's *The Name of the Rose* comes to our aid. As you will remember, Guglielmo and Adso, during their visit to the monastery library, find themselves in a labyrinth, from which they are able to escape thanks to the customary intellectual ability of the protagonist. Eco's labyrinth is a figure, but it is also a structure. It is, in fact, a genuine labyrinth, from which one escapes by following the famous rule, "turn right at every intersection" (a rule, nevertheless, that is either erroneous or naive). But the labyrinth clearly is also a metaphor for culture, since it is found in a library and its organization is based on an encyclopedic key. Furthermore, Eco's labyrinth derives from a medieval labyrinth, as we learn from an essay published after the novel had been drafted. Curiously, in the film version, by Jean-Jacques Annaud, a more recent form of labyrinth was chosen, based on the prisons of Piranesi and certain drawings of labyrinths by Escher. I say "curiously" because, since these labyrinth do not function on a single plane, the rule of turning right at every intersection is no longer applicable.

The figure of the labyrinth appears in two other famous contemporary films. The first appearance is in the final sequence of *The Shining* by Stanley Kubrick. The main character, Jack Torrance, pursues his son in order to kill him, and his son hides in the twists and turns of some tall bushes outside the snowbound hotel where Jack works as warden. Both characters possess the "shining," the ability to see into the past, present, and future. But Jack can only see what is just about to happen, whereas his son can see more profoundly into the future. Thus, in the labyrinth, Jack is unable to use his theoretical myopia and will remain trapped, whereas his son, endowed with a more than local knowledge, will be saved.[7] Another labyrinth appears in a film produced by George Lucas and directed by the inventor of the Muppets, Jim Henson, with the explicit title *Labyrinth*. Alice in Wonderland is transposed into a more modern world, and her journey is interpreted as a wandering among corridors and intersections until she reaches the final exit: a game, in other words, in which every intersection produces further obstacles and adventures. The labyrinth-as-game has been modernized and is now the basis of every video game on the market whose structure is that of a journey along the (often blind) alleys of a labyrinth. This labyrinth might be complete at the beginning of the game or, alternatively, constructed as the game proceeds, as in the famous *Digger*, in which a mole is pursued along dug-out corridors, which reproduce the classic Minoan maze, by monsters whose appearance is constantly changing. The most famous of these electronic labyrinths is *Tron*, produced to coincide with the film of the same name, which narrates the adventures of a hero who escapes from the labyrinth not only by finding the correct exits, but also by performing heroic feats and by identifying the right moves with increasing rapidity. The requisites of a labyrinth (getting lost, theoretical myopia, movement) are all respected.

Video games often contain the figure of the knot as well. As we know, electronic games are made up of a finite series of frames. The player enters a new frame after exhausting the possibilities of the preceding frame. The route that can be taken appears infinite. In fact, the various frames are connected to each other and the final frame is inevitably linked to the initial frame. The journey, which appears to move from one segment to another in a single line that begins at the beginning and ends at the end, is in fact circular, each frame representing a knot in the process of being unwound.

We also find a revived interest in the figures of the knot and the labyrinth in the field of the visual arts. It is no accident that, alongside the previously mentioned exhibition on classical unicursals by Hermann Kern, Milan put on an exhibition of modern art in 1981, organized by Achille Bonito Oliva. In this exhibition our figures were interpreted by the most significant artists of the twentieth century, including such famous names as Jackson Pollock, Giulio Paolini, Giacomo Balla, Giorgio De Chirico, Piet Mondrian, and so on up to the present day.[8] Kern himself, in an article entitled "Labyrinths: Tradition and Contemporary Works," refers to the number of analogous motifs in recent artistic production.[9] It is sufficient here to mention Adrian Fischer, who produced a plan for a labyrinth in Saint Alban's Cathedral in 1979; or Randall Coate, who, like Fischer, has constructed labyrinth-games as gifts at an industrial level, as well as having produced a garden labyrinth at Värmlands Säby in Sweden; or Richard Fleischer; or John Willenbecher. Among Italians I might quote from memory the labyrinthine figures of Enrico Pulsari and Antonio Passa, Marco Tirelli's knots, and the knots and labyrinths of Maria Grazia Braccati. We can even find "knots" in music, such as those invented by the composer d'Anglebert during the age of Louis XIV.[10] Or, for example, in the convolutions of someone like Branduardi in popular music; or in the knottings of Luciano Berio's scores, most obviously in the famous *Stripsody*, written for Kathy Berberian, with its interweaving of musical elements, noises, and figurative effects from comics.

The work of the most "knotty" and labyrinthine of modern

artists, Saul Steinberg, can also be seen as a combination of comic strips, illustration, and art. In an introduction to a catalogue of his work, Roland Barthes has pointed out that the labyrinth is an essential matrix in the activity of Steinberg.[11] And, at this point, another figurative element is superimposed on the motif that we are examining: the imaginary map. As soon as the "realistic" coordinates of a map are destroyed, it becomes a labyrinth. Alongside the work of Steinberg, therefore, we can place that of Alechinsky, the cartographical knots of Christian Tobas, the ideological maps of Oyvind Fahlström and the canceled maps of Emilio Isgrò.[12]

KNOTS AND LABYRINTHS AS STRUCTURES

Up to now we have examined how labyrinth and knots have been directly represented by certain authors. But the motif is not exhausted by this. Alongside the surface figure we can place the structural figure. Let us consider three examples: one from the world of academic research, one from the "creative" world, and one from the mass media. The first is the form chosen for the *Enciclopedia Einaudi*.[13] This is hardly surprising (the same publisher organized a seminar at Modena, Knowledge as a Grid of Models, later published as a book, in which the principles that we are now stating were explained).[14] The encyclopedia was not designed as a list of finite entries, nor as a closed block of essays, but as a geography of thematic *knots*, each represented by a condensation of interrelated themes placed eccentrically in the total system. Each entry thus refers to a knot, and the paths between entries constitute a labyrinth. Knot and labyrinth therefore become the structural image of knowledge itself: an open, interdisciplinary knowledge, in movement, and constantly at risk of becoming disoriented.

The second example is a novel by Gore Vidal, *Duluth*. We have already discussed its basic origin in an earlier chapter (Duluth is an image of America transformed into a single city, in which the heroes of every American television series live together). It is important to mention here that Vidal does not describe a linear series of events. His characters maintain their features even when they change their names and narrative situation. Thus the same actor might find himself projected into different plots if the narrative happens to have arrived at a point at which a number of stories branch out and intertwine. Quite simply, instead of following a linear path, the actor in question has entered a corridor that belongs to a different nature or dimension. The labyrinth thus becomes the general form of the work, with the knot as its instrument, rather than intersections on a single plane. In turn, however, the knot replaces the general labyrinthine form, as one of the basic themes of *Duluth* is that the plot offers neither an entry nor an exit. The reader-traveler is faced with the idea of a potentially infinite narration.[15]

A similar mechanism can often be observed in the model television series "Dallas" (obviously, since "Dallas" is Vidal's specific reference point). In "Dallas" too we are confronted by an interweaving of stories, from episode to episode, involving the same characters. There are three sets of characters in the series: an ever-present "older" generation; an irregularly present secondary generation; and a third generation whose members turn up only occasionally (by "generation" I mean a hierarchy of roles rather than a family tree). The viewer who attempts to read the series behaves exactly as he would in the labyrinth. Each episode is a section of the entire structure, which can be read and understood in isolation, but also in the context of the whole and, although it never arrives, of a potential end. Very simply, in this second case, it is a question of seeing how what is happening at the moment forms part of one of the three most important themes of the series: the economic theme (the ups and downs of the Ewing family), the sentimental theme (the loves of J.R. and of a small number of other characters), and the physical theme (the state of health of the characters). The immense length of the series, however, makes it practically impossible for all but the most faithful of viewers to establish their exact position at any particular point, since this would mean reconstructing the entire map of the edifice. In order to understand both the particular episode and the phase the series has reached, therefore, we need to become "myopic," depending on the specific local information that the labyrinth provides. The story tends to confirm this: none of its main characters seems to be supplied with a memory or the ability to learn from past experience. They also seem to move "myopically." Furthermore, in "Dallas," each episode is in accordance with the figure of the labyrinth and the knot. Every finale operates as an exit from the immediate story and as a prosecution, on another level, of a potentially infinite narration by means of the knotting together of events, exactly as we have seen in the analogous case of *Duluth*.

This is the paradox of the labyrinth and the modern knot, the most "baroque" of all precisely because of its constructed undecidability. An even more revealing example of this phenomenon can be found in a story by Robert Sheckley, the most scientific of modern science fiction writers. "The Emperor of the Last Days" tells the story of a duel between an emperor and someone who has been chosen by lot to kill him in order to take his place.[16] The emperor defends himself in his palace by a series of strategems, the most important of which is to make the palace into an enormous maze of rooms and corridors, with the emperor's residence at its center. Since every maze can be solved from outside, however, the emperor complicates the problem. He employs a group of bricklayers to knock down and rebuild the internal walls each day. A group of cartographers then produces a new map based on each new topography. Obviously, however, the map is *always false* and does nothing but confuse its potential owner. Thus the labyrinth must not only be beaten without memory or map, by means of myopic theory: it must be beaten by walking more quickly than the bricklayers are capable of working, thus annulling the only general rule of labyrinths, "never walk twice along the same corridor in the same direction." In other words, the only theorem that holds true is the one that Rosenstiehl has called "mad Ariadne": to go as rapidly as possible toward the solution by taking a new corridor at every intersection. The complementary theorem—"wise Ariadne"—cannot work, since there will never be any already discovered intersections where it is preferable to rewind the thread for the length of a corridor.[17]

THE PLEASURE OF LOSS AND ENIGMA

Sheckley's allegory seems quite clear. The most modern, "aesthetic" knots and labyrinths are those that, instead of offering the pleasure of their solution, satisfy a taste for loss and enigma. As Borges said, "The solution to the mystery is always inferior to the mystery itself. The mystery even partakes of the divine; the solution of a conjurer's trick."[18] In other words, what governs the modern knot and labyrinth is primarily the obvious pleasure of getting lost, of wandering, of renouncing that final principle of connection that is the key to the solution of the enigma.[19] This attitude has been analyzed in recent years, primarily by Gilles Deleuze and Félix Guattari. They have christened their structural model *rhizôme*. A rhizôme is a paradox of nature: an underground stem composed of segments that, rather than following a logic of connection to the tree, connect freely and unrestrictedly with one another. The famous six rhizomatic principles are revealing: multiple connectability at every point, heterogeneity of all components of the system, multiplicity without a generating unity, rupture without significance, cartographability, and transfer.[20]

From these principles we derive a phenomenal model that is not casual, natural-irrational, but "nomadic" or "vagabond," whose driving force is desire or, alternatively, a *constructed* asystemicity. Pleasure principle, aesthetic principle. It is thus no accident that a heterogeneous group of thinkers (scientists such as René Thom, critics such as René Huyghe, artists such as Pol

Bury, and many others) should have devoted themselves to *La création vagabonde*, a study of the nomadism that is an essential part of both scientific and artistic creation.[21] The aesthetic principle behind vagabond creation is not a search for the irrational, as in so many idealist aesthetics, but for the *suspension* or *undecidability* of all solutions in a system of knots or labyrinths; a system that, while necessarily implying an existing final horizon, either delays it or places it between brackets. Only the instrument of the rationality principle—the *local mind*, as Gregory Bateson calls it—is retained.[22] The reordering of the system (Borges's conjuring trick) is left in the air. All that remains is the sense of loss and challenge, all the more pleasant for knowing that somewhere or other a conclusion exists. In any case, the most entertaining enigma is that in which a solution can be imagined, but never reached. The "conjurers" Oedipus, Theseus, and Perseus have never been congenial to neo-baroque minds, who have always preferred the intellectual risk that preceded them.

Up to now we have seen how the same taste presides over not only the development (the term "development" is necessary because, as was the case with fractals, the official discovery dates back to 1926) of scientific theories of knots and labyrinths but also the elaboration of "motifs" and "structures" of their inner form. It would be wise to conclude this chapter, however, by specifying that the final characteristic of our figures (the pleasure to be derived from loss and enigma) resides in activities that have the appearance of being the most ordered and systematic imaginable. I am referring to a field that has been treated only sporadically in this work: that of the personal computer. Let us consider for a moment exactly what a computer is, for both the user and the programmer. It is, in fact, an "orderer" (as the French call it), even though it does not allow us to see, except at the most profound level, its elementary binary principles. The insertion of data takes place in a regulated but "blind" way. We send our material into a kind of "black hole." Each operation of manipulation and retrieval of data is

141

carried out as though we were following a thread along the curving paths of a labyrinth *without possessing a map of the entire maze*, but only the instructions for our movements. I have the impression that this kind of "blind flight" (in which a simple keyboard mistake can produce a "fatal error" or an interruption in the electricity supply cancel months of work) generates a kind of inebriation that evades the nature of the "stupid machine," as the computer has been called. In any case, a large anecdotal literature already exists on the intellectual accidents of the computer, just like the classical mythology of the labyrinth and the knot.[23]

Another "aestheticizing" element consists in the fact that the "stupid machine" is able to perform what appear to be enormously complex operations by starting out from absolutely elementary principles, just as in the mathematics of knots, where, given a single thread and a support, the number of possible knots is enormous, not to mention what happens when we have two, three, or even more threads. As Rosenstiehl has said, the amusing thing is that a limited and controlled number of elements, following limited rules of combination, can produce social chaos. A similar situation (in a quite implicit and unconscious way) has been simulated in order to produce a literary event and an explicit aesthetic effect. In 1985, during the course of a cultural festival at Avignon, a group of French publishers decided to see if seven French writers living abroad would be able to produce an "aleatory" novel by means of a network of computers and by following a fixed set of rules. The attempt was organized in the following way. Each writer had at his disposal an initial description and could put the first chapter of his work directly into the computer. After having read all seven first chapters, he had to choose one (excluding his own) to develop. At this point the number of possible stories could remain at seven or be reduced to two, which in turn could become seven once again. The end of the game came when an author was unable to produce a satisfactory ending. The game was complicated even further by the presence of three more authors in the role of *deus ex machina*. These authors could insert obligatory descriptions at any point in the story (such as, "it must rain at five o'clock this afternoon"). The final book was entitled *Marco Polo*, almost as if it were itself a voyage inside the activity of writing.

Clearly, this experiment does not move far beyond the literary tradition of the Oulipo group thirty years ago. It does, nevertheless, demonstrate the aesthetic potential of a blind use of the computer. Even in the simplest operations, in fact, the result is only visible locally. Only a final key ("print") ensures a result. In other words, what changes with the computer is not simply the speed of operation, the ability to store data, or (in the case of word processing) a technically perfect product. At most, these results provide us with the satisfaction of having exercised our rationality successfully. But what happens *before*? Before, there is the other pleasure of working without any control over the work, the pleasure of immersion into small blocks, areas, and zones, with no panoptic vision by one's creative intelligence. This might be why—as Eco stressed in a newspaper article—the computer influences our way of using, and thinking about, language and its applications, texts. Instead of a connected, paratactical construction, we think in "small pieces," hypotactically. The connections become logical *a posteriori*, rather than grammatically or syntactically. This is the only way we can protect ourselves from the possibility of "free-fall" when we enter, like Alice, the strange world of the computer.

CHAPTER 8

Complexity and Dissipation

DISSIPATIVE STRUCTURES: FROM SCIENCE
TO CULTURE

IN THE INTRODUCTION to *The New Alliance*, Ilya Prigogine and Isabelle Stenghers very clearly illustrate one of the great mutations (possibly the most important) to have occurred in contemporary science. Whereas from Newton to Boltzmann science searched for universal, eternal principles that sustained the functioning of nature, the present panorama is changing in a revolutionary way. The universe is no longer explained in terms of general, immutable laws. "[. . .] Only eternal laws seemed capable of expressing the rationality of science. Temporality was despised as being equivalent to illusion. This is no longer true. We have discovered that, far from being an illusion, irreversibility plays an essential role in nature and is at the origin of many spontaneous processes [. . .]. We find ourselves today in a world full of risks, a world in which reversibility and determinism are applied only to simple, limited cases, while irreversibility and indeterminism are the rule."[1]

In other words, while the project of describing and explaining nature as a concatenation of "behaviors" generated by a small number of repeated rules has failed, the idea of a fragmentary universe composed of local behaviors that differ in their quality has made its appearance. The general principle that resisted most stubbornly, and collapsed with the greatest uproar as a result, was the second principle of thermodynamics. As is well known, this principle consisted in the idea of the conservation of energy in a given system, and in the transformation of that energy toward a state of total equilibrium within the system, a state that was called "entropy." The concept of entropy contains not only the notion of equilibrium, but also that of the final evolution of any thermodynamic system (Clausius, the man who invented the term, and Boltzmann, who perfected it, based it on the Greek root *entropè*, meaning "evolution").[2] Entropy occurs in any microsystem, but it has also been theorized as being the general orientation of the universe, which would thus tend toward a final indifferentiation from the viewpoint of energy distribution.

And yet the discoveries made by Prigogine and other researchers are concerned precisely with this point. In systems that are still far from equilibrium, it is not necessarily the case that an evolution toward maximum entropy takes place. When a system is far from equilibrium it can transform itself by finding a different order from the one it had before. New dynamic states, in other words, can be originated by the system. These states depend on interaction with the environment that surrounds the system. Prigogine, paradoxically, has called these new structures *dissipative structures*. The paradox consists in the fact that while a system is *dissipating* energy, this dissipation does not lead toward entropy, but toward the formation of a new order, that is, of new structures. As a rule, dissipative structures are produced in a system into which instability has been introduced. Although, at a molecular level, the other existing structures behave traditionally, at a molar level the system begins to recall its fluctuating state. New structures are thus generated, and the system moves toward a new order. There is a touch of classicism in the image of this process, and Prigogine and Stenghers repeatedly cite the idea of *clinamen* from Lucretius: *clinamen* describes the behavior of atoms in space, random and yet responsible for the organized world. Obviously, dissipative structures appear primarily in highly complex systems, in which turbulence, fluctuation, and chaos can be found. Their appearance is governed by a series of laws: for example, the arrival of bifurcations, in the proximity of which a system begins to develop a capacity for "choosing its own future"; fluctuation around regions of instability; rupture

145

of symmetries (which actually appears to be responsible for the birth of living systems).

Our new image of the physical world can easily induce us to make comparisons with the social world. Human "systems," after all, appear to be highly complex systems, and it might be said that it is precisely within the ambit of human organizations that the law according to which systems tend toward equilibrium (i.e., toward chaos as the equiprobability of elements) must necessarily be proven true. And yet certain systems are maintained, while others are transformed. Might it not be possible to identify the existence of dissipative structures in the social world as well? Prigogine seems to be convinced that the answer is yes. In *The New Alliance* he makes the following statement: "Some people have wondered how it is that complex systems such as ecological systems or human organizations can preserve themselves. How do such systems avoid permanent chaos? It is probable that in very complex systems, in which species or individuals interact in a highly diversified way, diffusion—that is, communication between all points in the system—might be just as rapid [as in physical systems] [. . .]. In this sense, the maximum complexity that the organization of a system can achieve before becoming unstable would be determined by the speed of communication."[3] The clearest example is that concerning social innovation within any organized society. If the society is passing through a period of instability, even an innovation created by a small minority group might affect the entire system, as a result of the speed at which the innovation is communicated to each individual. If, however, the society in question is passing through a period of great stability, the innovation is lost as though it were simply anecdotal, precisely because of the high speed of communication within the system. The history of political avant-garde movements seems to reflect this perfectly.

Prigogine's remarks on the transferability of the notion of dissipative structures from the physical to the human world are limited to the fields of ideology and sociology. On the occasion of the 1985 exhibition *L'art et le temps*, however, Prigogine himself introduced the idea that a convergence was taking place between the figurative arts and the sciences of complexity, since both were occupied with time as duration, rather than as movement.[4] In this context he stressed the Bergsonian obsession with duration in all twentieth-century avant-garde movements.[5] It might be worth our while, however, to examine contemporary culture in an attempt to see whether aesthetic production (above all in the media) makes it possible to talk reasonably about the appearance of dissipative structures.

ENTROPY OR RE-CREATION?

In my opinion the metaphor would be neither banal nor farfetched. Take, for example, the traditional concept of "genres" in mass culture. Genres are generally interpreted as repetitive objects, whose form or content has been rendered inexpressive or desemanticized by use. Genres are sometimes even regarded as "degenerations" from an original that loses value as a result of being standardized or stereotyped.[6] In this sense genres might be regarded in two ways. First, as an orientation toward total entropy from the viewpoint of semantic or expressive power (the final stage of which would have to be annulment, or insignificance). Second, as a situation of extremely low entropy, since entropy is usually associated with information (as in the cybernetic theory of the same name).[7] The first way interests us directly. It is generally true that genres die when they reach a point of insignificance. It is, however, equally true that frequently genres not only fail to disappear, but undergo a process of revitalization from somewhere else. And this occurs, interestingly enough, in contemporary mass culture. I shall quote two examples from advertising, which seems to me to be the most suitable field since it ought to be, by definition, the point of arrival (and the tomb) of genres. The first example: the Elah candy commercial, which presents a series of versions of other advertising campaigns, but replaces the adult actors with children and the product with Elah candies. The individual commercials quoted (Lavazza coffee with Nino Manfredi, Bocchino grappa with Mike Bongiorno, Dash detergent with Paolo Villaggio) not only fail to die, as all commercials should after a certain period of use, but give rise to new commercials. The second example: the Annabella fur coat commercials directed by Zeffirelli, which were produced in two series. The first series announced the arrival of the commercial, like a cinema trailer; the second series was the actual commercial. In this way meta-advertising was able to reclassify an individual commercial as something other than a mere interruption of television "events." It became an event in its own right.

We begin to wonder at this point whether the "degenerative" rule has any real value; whether, that is, the principle of entropy is able to define certain contemporary phenomena that appear, on the contrary, to be constituted—albeit in a non-exclusive way—as *re-creation*. If we assume that this hypothesis is correct, we then have to ask ourselves how such a re-creation comes about. Let us see if some of the conditions governing the appearance of dissipative structures in the physical world are also to be found in the world of culture. At least two are relevant to our discussion. The first condition is that of distance from equilibrium. In effect, we can see that the system of genres in mass culture is necessarily held at a distance from equilibrium. Each repetition within a genre is generally accompanied by a desperate search for some element, even the smallest variation (as we saw in the second chapter), that makes it possible to *restrain* the product from reaching a state of entropy. The second condition is that of instability introduced into the system. Once more, we can see that in popular culture, and particularly in that of the television and cinema, there exists a massive production of *parodies* (almost immediately after the original genre product has been successful). But parody can quite easily be interpreted either as the final stage in the degeneration of genres (as a positivist critical position might sustain) or as the introduction of turbulence into the system of the particular genre. Surrounding phenomena of turbulence in a genre we find examples of genuine fluctuations that sometimes lead to the birth of new genres. A sensational example of this occurred recently on Italian television. One of Italy's most popular programs is "Fantastico," generally presented by Pippo Baudo. As is well known, Italy's most popular presenter has always produced his programs by maintaining maximum internal control in terms of direction. During the 1986 series, however, a number of episodes destabilized the world of Italian television variety. Some of these took place outside "Fantastico": multiple parodies in "Drive In," "L'altro varietà," and so on. Others occurred within the program itself: the comic trio Solenghi-Marchesini-Lopez, who incurred the wrath of the Ayatollah Khomeini; Beppe Grillo, whose joke about socialists had a similar effect on the Italian Socialist party. From that moment Baudo began to revolutionize his program. He introduced improvisation, sang at the top of his voice, and willingly made mistakes, thus changing radically (within his own terms, of course) his style of presentation.

I must apologize for the frivolous nature of this example. But I have specifically chosen something from the world of popular entertainment in order to make the point more clearly. Do not imagine that analogous phenomena are not having just as deep an effect at practically all cultural levels. The turbulence introduced into any creative system is not necessarily provoked by parody, but the result is the same.[8] Fluctuation, and the birth of dissipative structures, might also be caused by anomalous readings of a stabilized cultural product. This has happened recently in many artistic sectors as a result of the "disoriented" reading of a text by Jean-François Lyotard, *The Postmodern Condition*.[9] We have already seen that Lyotard refuses to recognize the vast number of "citationist" artistic texts as "postmodern." On the contrary, he has reaffirmed that the notion he baptized was never intended to liquidate the experimentalism of certain modern movements, such as the avant-garde. Nevertheless, a generalized reading based on an ironic stance toward modernism, the rediscovery of the past, of surfaces, and of decoration, has provoked not the development of a *critique*, but the birth of a genre of objects.

THE PRODUCTIVE CONSUMPTION OF CULTURE

This consideration of the pragmatic phenomenon of *aberrant readings*[10] helps us discover a variant in the origin of dissipative structures in the field of culture. Turbulence can in fact be introduced into an apparently stable, constant, and fluid cultural system by means of aberrant readings or, in any case, by readings that are not authorized by the texts themselves.

We have spoken in previous chapters of the notion of *productive consumption*, and I shall summarize it briefly once again. Whenever we enter into a relationship with any cultural object, we do not read it passively, but are enriched by it.[11] We argue with the text, we take sides, we cope with it, we understand only its surface, we prefer its worst aspect, and so on. Each reading, in short, produces culture, and this culture might be different from that of the text that is being read. This sociological interpretation, however, can be made more sophisticated by the addition of one or two further suggestions. For consumption to be "productive," we must deduce that a kind of conflict arises between the object "read" and the ability or attitude of the reader. As a corollary of this: the cultural conflict of the reader renders the object being read unstable insofar as it is "perceived." 'Perception" thus becomes unstable and, potentially, transformed. A single system of cultural objects can be read in a variety of different unauthorized or aberrant ways. When the number rises, sometimes to the point at which it begins to exceed that of authorized ways, we can say that the system begins to fluctuate. If an anomalous reading then gives rise to a stable and generally accepted "perception." we are in the presence of a new cultural order. And, paradoxically, new individual works that might previously have been regarded as part of the preceding order are produced under the banner of the order that has replaced it.

I have referred more than once to the neo-baroque character of the cultural attitude described as "ephemeral." Not surprisingly, this can be found in many ways of reading texts, as well as in the affirmation of aberrant readings of certain texts rather than others, and, finally, in the production of new texts appropriate to the affirmations of aberrant readings. I shall not repeat what has already been said, except to point out a specific example from cinema. Since the second half of the 1970s there has been a rereading of classic American cinema. This has not taken place because of nostalgia, but as a revival of the principle of pleasure on which such films were based. Cinema festivals throughout the world, television series, and critical studies in specialized reviews and the popular press have all been marked by their reevaluation of these films and the pleasure they produced. It had already become clear that American films from the 1950s and 1960s were no longer being regarded as instruments for the organization of consent. As soon as the potential poison had been expelled, a newly oriented reading was in a position to salvage the pleasure. But this (mass) critical behavior has provoked the birth of productions that recognize the presence of the new taste. A random selection: in *The Boxer and the Ballerina* Stanley Donen reconstructs the spectacular style of 1930s cinema, passing from the circus to vaudeville via scenes of war. In *Dead Men Don't Wear Plaid* we actually witness the reconstruction of an entire story from clips of some of the greatest film private eyes of the period, led by Humphrey Bogart. In Italy, Francesco Nuti has imitated Paul Newman in *Io, Chiara e lo Scuro*, and an equally mythical Bogart in *Casablanca, Casablanca*. Our thesis is confirmed. A genre that is "normally" projected toward insignificance is rendered unsta-

151

ble by an external, environmental intervention. And so we see the appearance of dissipative structures; structures, that is, that produce powerful new structures by accelerating their semantic consumption.

AT THE THEORETICAL POLES OF
AESTHETIC INFORMATION

We can now return to the double concept of entropy that we abandoned some time ago. Up to now we have shown that cultural systems are generated by *a certain form of entropy*, which levels out the signifying force and energy of a text. We have pointed out, however, that a second notion of entropy exists, which relates maximal equilibrium to maximal cybernetic information. As many people will recall, a large number of art theorists made use of this second notion during the 1950s and 1960s, and particularly those theorists involved in the avant-garde, such as, for example, Max Bense and Abraham Moles.[12] In their theories the production of entropy in an aesthetic text was a guarantee of its originality and self-awareness: the foundation of aesthetics itself. We can hardly fail to recognize that this concept is literally poles apart from what we have been examining up to now. But the reason for this seems clear. As in science, a *general principle* was sought for aesthetics, with constant and immutable laws. This was the mistake. It is even more curious when we think that the creative world has always been considered to possess a complexity that surpassed the expressible. Furthermore, theories of aesthetic information were also influenced by the desire to conform to the spirit of the avant-garde: originality as the basis of the work of art, and experimentation as its matrix.[13] These days artists have accustomed us to the fact that the work of art can continue to be generated by research into ambiguity, but that it can also derive from exhaustion and re-creation: from re-semanticization.

152

Three artistic examples, chosen, as usual, out of many, can be used to illustrate the concept. I have selected three architects who are also painters: Arduino Cantafora, Massimo Scolari, and Luigi Serafini. Their work is extremely varied. Cantafora depicts objects, most of which are architectural, with frequent references to the 1930s. Scolari refers explicitly to De Chirico, constructing mythical images such as the Tower of Babel or Noah's Ark, legendary edifices from a lost past. Serafini goes further back, to the watercolors of fantastic architecture that were in vogue at the end of the nineteenth century, eclectic and utopian at the same time. Nevertheless, the three artists have something in common: a tendency to *exhaust* (rather than merely cite) a style. But as they exhaust it, their contact with the contemporary environment transforms them into the bearers of a new order, of something that I would call "fantastic painting."

As we can see, aesthetic information is not very significant. We are confronted here by a very different matrix. But that is the point: the order of art is not unique or immutable, and its systems can be both irreversible and indeterminate. And, as we have seen, this is true for the order not only of art, but also of culture as a whole. The cultural universe presents itself to us as fragmented, generated by contradictory structures that coexist perfectly. Some obey the law of deviation from the norm, whereas others are produced by dissipation. This second group, however, is becoming more and more numerous and effectively distinguishes the spirit of our age.

The Approximate and the Inexpressible

THE PLEASURE OF IMPRECISION

IN HIS RECENT *Leçons d'à peu près*, the French mathematician Georges Guilbaud describes some important steps in the history of thought regarding approximation.[1] It is a history that covers twenty-four centuries of human activity. In doing so he rehabilitates the notion of "approximation." Regarded as a negative term in our vocabulary, which applies it to imprecise practices that contrast with the "exactitude" of science and, in particular, mathematics, approximation is in fact extremely valuable. According to Guilbaud, mathematics has always been concerned with approximate calculation, and in a fascinating way—but, even more significantly, in a *rigorous* way. If approximation is to be reevaluated, therefore, it must be done on the condition that we establish, on each occasion, *the type of approximation that is being adopted*, as well as the conditions in which it is to operate. Approximation, in fact, has different levels of meaning. *One*: the common level, in which it is used to mean "not completely true" when defining an object. *Two*: when an object is defined as "between two extreme thresholds." This is the level of collocation, which works by replacing a precise element with an interval.[2] *Three*: when approximation is defined in relation to the "level of precision required by the question being asked of the object." This is the criterion known as that of "successive approximations," according to which approximation can be arrested or advanced in relation to the pertinence of the question.[3] Calculus belongs to this type of approximation. *Four*: when the second level, also known as the "tolerance interval," is replaced by the so-called "faith interval." This is based on the hypothesis that an object can be approximated be-

tween two given thresholds, and on the belief that such a hypothesis has a good chance of being true.[4] Many new mathematical discoveries have been made as a result of this last general rule, such as those dealing with aleatory functions, fractal
dimensions, and even certain algorithms used by computers.

But does this mean that we are obliged to deduce, as did
Alexandre Koyré in his time, that the crescendo "approximate
value–tolerance interval–successive approximation–faith interval" depends on merely functional criteria?[5] Not at all. Guilbaud himself has pointed out that in the history of mathematics
a search for approximations has very frequently had nothing to
do with concrete needs. A striking example is that of the Baby-
lonian tables produced twenty-four centuries ago in order to
calculate square roots. These tables reached an accuracy to the
order of one-millionth, even though no technical need for such
precision existed at the time. This is clearly an example of pure
scientific "curiosity." The development of mathematics contains many analogous cases, in which the principle of discovery
was dictated by the pleasure to be derived from mathematical
marvels of this nature—a pleasure that we might define as a
cross between imprecision and the challenge of approximation,
a pleasure based on challenge, an aesthetic pleasure.

We can immediately see, however, that such pleasure has not
always been accepted, above all by advocates of a common-
sense approach. On the contrary, there have been periods during which the idea of a scientific rationalism permeated by
"exactitude," and the conviction that mathematics was able to
produce such exactitude, clearly prevailed. Mathematics is even
considered to symbolize the perfect order of measure. The opposition between order and disorder begins to represent an
opposition between precision and imprecision, fixed and oscil-
lating values. Consequently, it is influenced by those ethical,
aesthetic, physical, and passional categories that are already familiar to us from the beginning of this book. On the basis of
our argument, therefore, it is clearly not irrelevant to associate
with baroque taste the pleasure found in mathematical "mon-

sters" produced by approximation (a pleasure that, as Guilbaud suggests, even transforms exactitude into the "degree zero of approximation"), and with classical taste the desire for precision and order.

It is perfectly clear that the current "new science" is eagerly rediscovering the virtues of approximation. An indication of this interest is the splendid conference held at Urbino in the summer of 1986, during which mathematicians from the school of Guilbaud discussed approximation with psychologists, semiologists, historians, and art theorists, revealing both the extent of the concept and the fascination it exerts in all branches of human knowledge.[6] The universe of the imprecise, indefinite, and vague is shown to be powerfully seductive to our contemporary mentality. In this context, the French mathematician has always insisted that the growth of approximation is closely related to the appearance of a "mentality."

It is curious, however, that approximation should be so highly valued at the moment, precisely when technology has introduced instruments of precision that enable us to dominate, and describe, the universe more effectively than ever before. Liquid display calculators, quartz watches, electronic high-definition television, computers, automata, robots: despite the fact that these objects seem to have been constructed in order to provide exactitude in every area of knowledge, each one works by challenging, or rather by rigorously utilizing, approximation. An automatic calculator rounds up even at the eleventh figure. A quartz watch calculates time to a thousandth of a second, far below our perception threshold, yet the method it uses for measuring is imprecise. Although high-definition television produces a greater effect of reality, it does not reproduce it, but conventionally segments it even more than before. Algorithms in artificial intelligence often work by means of "randomization," that is, by the introduction of aleatoriness. Automata and robots simulate human labor, yet their precision is limited to the task at hand, and the simulation itself is generated by an ergonomic approximation.

This might be the reason why, in order to free ourselves from an "illusion of precision," we accentuate a taste for *constructed* or *controlled* approximation—a taste that, in the vast territories of creative (aesthetic) activity, sometimes assumes the connotation of a genuine plan of action.

A work of philosophy (not particularly recent, since the first draft dates from 1957) by Vladimir Jankélévitch represents this assumption perfectly. Its title is emblematic: *Le Je-ne-sais-quoi et le Presque-rien*. It was preceded some years before 1980 (the date the volume was revised) by a work entitled *Philosophie première: introduction à une philosophie du "Presque."*[7] "*Je ne sais quoi*" and "almost-nothing" become ethical principles on the basis of a series of reflections that (coincidences once again!) are themselves based on a large number of baroque philosophical works, beginning with Balthasar Gracian, who was better known than people realized, above all to specialists. Jankélévitch's philosophical intentions are clear from the first lines: he intends to deal with "something that might be said to be the wicked conscience of the good rationalist conscience and the final scruple of strong spirits; something that protests and 'murmurs more loudly' inside us against the success of reductionist enterprises. . . . "[8] In other words, that sense of malaise that we experience when we are confronted by incompleteness, the disquiet that we feel for anything that cannot be defined, explained, or made precise. It is a feeling that derives from the "leftovers" or "residue" of our activity of reduction, explanation, and control of knowledge.

It is easy to see this philosophy in the context of idealism or negativism. (This would, after all, be quite fair if we used the terms precisely.) Nevertheless, we can also look at the "modal" thought of Jankélévitch[9] as a series not of "feelings," but of practices aimed at the production of the inexpressible, the *je-ne-sais-quoi*: a controlled and, one might say, *rigorous* inexpressibility.

If we consider the significance of Jankélévitch's ideas, we realize that a specific theoretical practice has always existed (and especially during baroque periods): challenging the laws governing representation in an attempt to represent what cannot be represented, to express what cannot be expressed, to reveal what cannot be seen, and so on. At the moment, similar practices undoubtedly derive from a philosophical substratum. Simultaneously, however, they produce a taste, which they realize by means of an artificial use of language (in the most extended sense of the term). In other words, this substratum is a theory of signification that reveals its own paradoxes (representing the unrepresentable, and so on), and then induces us to challenge and to overcome them; it is within the language itself that we must seek the means for arriving at that *quid* (in the sense given the term by Jankélévitch) that will permit successive approximations. But as soon as the operation has been made into a "style," it can be inverted. It then becomes possible to *construct* approximation as an *aesthetic effect* by means of language.

Might this not be the reversible matrix of poetics based on vagueness, the indefinite, and the "almost-as-if"?[10] Might not stereotypical or genre-based operations such as the slogan used to advertise soap—"that certain something that goes to your head"—derive from this original poetic? In our apparently precise universe the increasing diffusion of artificial approximation obliges us to analyze the processes of ethical, aesthetic, physical, and passional valorization of, above all, approximation itself. But we also need to analyze the techniques of its discursive production, since it is precisely through this discourse that operations of style and taste are realized to the fullest.

Up to this point we have regarded the approximate and the inexpressible as united by a common spirit. It would be as well, however, to consider the relevant differences that exist between the two concepts. The taste for approximation that we have derived from mathematics is not the same as the taste for imprecision that we have seen in the last few examples. We shall consequently need to distinguish between the search for a *quasi-perfect representation*, which corresponds to the more "mathematical" sense of approximation, and the explicit search for a *quasi-representation*, which corresponds to the more philosophical sense of the indefinite, and which also includes, as its goal, the "rendering" of that which cannot be represented. The two effects must be regarded as divergent in terms of result, but as convergent in terms of motivation and matrix. Furthermore, the mechanisms by which they are realized in discourse are absolutely analogous.

Among discursive techniques, enunciation occupies a privileged position. Neither the approximate nor the inexpressible in fact is a property that belongs to the object represented in discourse. They both depend strictly on the subject, since they are concerned with the acts of hearing, speaking, seeing, listening, and perceiving: acts carried out by the subject in relation to the object. They concern, in other words, the definition of the object in space and time.[11] The approximation results from a partial "inability" to define the object on the part of a "weak" subject, in two different but concurrent ways. The subject is unable to focus on the object, or puts it deliberately out of focus; the subject is unable to grasp the contour, profile, or border of the object because the distance between subject and object is either mistaken or inadequate; the subject is unable to halt the duration of the object (and, in particular, its instantaneity), although this effect can also be constructed. In these three cases we have equated inability with lack, or defect. Inability, however, can also arise because of excess: it might be impossible to define the object because of an inability to discriminate between too many characteristics, or the lack of a discriminating criterion of relevance. The object might be too close. Its duration might be incalculable because of an excess of temporal detail. And so on.

There are very few cases, however, in which approximation depends on the nature of the object. Nevertheless, they exist, and they are transformed into figures of approximation, which are as easy to recognize in nature as they are to construct artificially. In nature, our perception of the sublime is always caused by an approximation of temporal and spatial perception, although this is inevitably combined with a passional aspect (which we shall see more clearly when we examine the inexpressible). Artificially we can create forms that are not clearly perceptible, either in a temporal or spatial sense: indistinct, amorphous, inextricable. They might be figures without contours, meaningless in relation to their background, or formless (that is to say, undecided among a number of representations, as we have seen in our discussion of monsters). There exists, in short, an iconography (and a chronography) of the indistinct, which ranges from Leonardo's shading to Turner's clouds, from the *ripetere sfumando* of classical music to free rhythm.

Inexpressibility, however, involves something else, something that Jankélévitch has called the "quoddity of the quiddity." Whereas in approximation we are confronted with a lack that might be evaluated as partial, more or less necessary, or more or less temporary, in the case of inexpressibility we are faced with a "residue" that is inexpressible. But this is accompanied by two facts that concern the subject: one, cognitive position; two, passional investment. The subject, in fact, *knows* of the existence of a residue in the definition of being, but *cannot* express it. And this disequilibrium generates passion. The subject is effectively *modalized* in a conflictual manner, or *suspended* within the tension created by two different modalities—for example, between *wanting to know* and *not being able to know*, or between *not wanting to know* and *having to know*, or any other modal couple that creates tension. We have already said that the sublime, at least in its most classical definition, consists in the passional realization of the tension to which the individual is subjected. It is no accident that the sublime has sometimes been regarded as the conflictual convergence of opposing passions, or as the irrational and immediate (instinctive) residue of any rational explanation. Once again we are confronted with a double typology: an inexpressibility resulting from lack, which we shall call an "almost-nothing" (as Jankélévitch did), that consists in a sense of the importance of a missing trifle in the overall vision of the object; and an inexpressibility resulting from excess, an "almost-all," that resides in the inability to capture detail because of an exaggeratedly panoptic vision of the object. Our perception of the inexpressible also presupposes a specific sensorial state, defined by Jankélévitch as *intravision*, a kind of vision "between" things and "within" the subject. On the one hand, inexpressibility requires the gift of intravision. On the other hand, it provokes it (once again, the inexpressible can be recognized or constructed—for example, by constructing a subject as passional subject).

OBSCURITY

Let us now rapidly examine some episodes of creativity drawn from a number of different fields, in which approximation and inexpressibility are constructed as discursive effects. We shall note, in passing, that although the search for this effect appears in disparate ways, it is a constant in current aesthetics, even from a statistical point of view. The first example of approximation and inexpressibility as a discursive figure, that of obscurity, might be entitled, in the jargon of the cinema, "fog-effect." Artificial fog, often produced in an orgy of special filmic effects, might even be regarded as its symbolic icon. We have only to think of the gravitational effect produced by fog in *Apocalypse Now*, in which Captain Willard's voyage in search of the mythical Colonel Kurz is rendered dense and passional not only by the imprecision of contours in the fog, but also by the large number of overlapping fade-ins and fade-outs, the superimposition of images, and limited lighting in the most important scenes. Furthermore, the point of Coppola's film is precisely that of a desperate search for a meaning that is constantly elusive (even to the director, who, as we know, made three different endings for the film). There is thus, in Coppola, a double fog: the enunciation, *of* fog (represented fog) and enunciation *as* fog (nebulous representation). And although we find represented fog as a special effect throughout fantasy and genre cinema (reaching an apex in *The Fog*, in which it becomes the protagonist), enunciational fogs are developed in two different ways. Either toward stereotype (a series of nuances, fade-ins, soft focus, and poorly lit scenes that finally produce a standardization of the inexpressible at the level of advertising) or toward creativity (the mistiness of Fellini's *Casanova*, episodes of "shining" in Kubrick's film of the same name, or the blinding flashes of *The Man Who Fell to Earth*).

"Obscurity" as a discursive effect can be achieved syntactically or semantically—for example, by subverting or subtracting connections between parts of the discourse, or by eliminating any evidence of common features between the semantic units. The result can emerge in a variety of ways. A comic effect might be created, as in many films by Woody Allen or in the "wacky" cinema that followed the success of John Belushi. The destruction of pertinence creates a kind of parodic obscurity, an "impertinence" (think of the senselessness of Woody Allen's monologues in *Love and Death*, *Annie Hall*, and *Manhattan*). Another effect is what Roland Barthes called "the babble of language": a stylistic and literary effect that has now made its entrance into the world of essay writing and philosophy. The texts of Jacques Derrida are a perfect example of this type of creative research, above all *The Truth of Painting* and *Letter to a Japanese Friend*. In other cases, finally, the destruction of syntactic or semantic links produces an obscurely mediumistic discourse (ranging from astrology to certain contemporary psychoanalytical practices), or a genuine sense of enigma. Greenaway's first two films, *The Draughtsman's Contract* and *A Zed and Two Noughts*, function by means of the immediate impossibility of connecting phrases and images into a logical sequence.

A great deal of irony (justified or not) has been expressed about obscure styles in literature, cinema, and art, as well as in philosophy, criticism, and methodology. In many cases there is no doubt that whenever obscurity becomes stereotypical it achieves an unintentional humor. But this is not the place to express value judgments on the loss of an *esprit de clarté*. It is the place, however, to stress once more the extent to which obscurity reflects a generalized aesthetic principle. It is no accident that we witnessed, a few years ago, the explicit claim made by critics of their intrinsic role in the creation of a work of art, alongside—and even in preference to—the role of the artist.[12] In this sense, the greatest credit for formulating what might be called a "neo-baroque criticism" goes to Achille Bonito Oliva, who, more than anyone else, has proclaimed the concept of the creative critic, and who has inaugurated behavior that befits such a concept, behavior based on exhibitionism and provocation.

VAGUE, INDEFINITE, INDISTINCT

It is not only obscurity, however, that produces aesthetic pleasure in discourses based on approximation and inexpressibility. We have already seen that it is possible to produce in such discourses not only enunciated figures, but also figures of enunciation in which the contours of the objects that are being represented disappear. In other words, the immediacy of *difference* is lost, while the *salience* of things in relation to each other and to their contours and backgrounds is partially canceled out in favor of their mere *potentiality*.[13] Our perception of discourse and of the objects represented in discourse becomes vague, indefinite, and indistinct. The concept "vague," for example, is worth considering. The adjective implies movement, a vagabond-like wandering that might refer to the object of the discourse, to its subject, or to the discourse itself, and that is manifested in a kind of roving around its own content. The result of this wandering discourse might be presented more clearly by means of an example. The most fashionable type of television program at the moment is based on improvisation and live transmission.[14] A number of people have noted that what counts in live television (and thus in the improvisation that gives it weight) is less the effect of reality or truth that is expressed, and more the aesthetic of risk: the risk of making a mistake, the risk of drying up, the risk of saying or doing something forbidden. The risk is inevitably increased by means of live effects, such as improvisation itself. When improvising, performers lose control of precision and exactitude and slide into a less definite and distinct flow. Some people are able to play with such effects. The highly acclaimed Italian program by Renzo Arbore "Quelli della notte" worked by producing imprecision, and then valorizing it as game, entertainment, pleasure. In particular, the most conspicuous effect was the "wandering" nature of the protagonists' discourse, apparently in the constant search for a subject (centered on the *salon*-like discussion of Catalano, Frassica, and colleagues).

This decline of difference, salience, and distinction, however, is not simply a phenomenon of popular culture (despite its extreme relevance in this context). We can see the same kind of thing in the world of art. If we consider some of the new generation of painters, for example, we find that a return to the easel is often accompanied by a voluntary and explicit abandoning of expressive precision. Groups such as the Nuovi-nuovi, baptized by Renato Barilli, tend toward a naive representation that is based not on ingenuousness but on naive imprecision as a sophisticated artistic effect. Among "citationist" artists we find painters such as Carlo Maria Mariani, who, while working in a neo-classicist style, "uglifies" his paintings in order to create an effect of provocative imprecision. In the United States we have the so-called bad painters, or dump art, which, in the work of Jan Borofsky, David Salle, or Julian Schnabel, for example, deliberately repeat in an "approximate" way the material of pop art, expressionism, hyperrealism, and so on. American graffiti artists can be traced back to the same origin. In their use of the environment (subways, sidewalks, public places) we can glimpse the idea of "live painting," based on the idea of rapidity, imprecision, and risk.[15]

Exactly the same phenomenon can be found in literature. If we look at the youngest generation of Italian novelists, for example, we discover an explicit taste for linguistic approximation, with the effect of producing a literary inexpressibility. An example of this is Aldo Busi's *Standard Life of a Temporary Pantyhose Salesman*, in which defects in grammar and syntax give added body to the text. These expressive choices are oriented toward irony in other authors, such as Enrico Palandri and Pier Vittorio Tondelli, who make use of adolescent slang. The same thing can be seen in poetry in the so-called wild poetry, for example, practiced by young authors who probably feel an affinity with certain rock groups, whose musical imprecision has the same sulfuric effect as their linguistic imprecision. The group Skiantos is possibly the most representative, although one might also mention the delightful example of the Neapolitan group Shampoo, who have managed to produce two records of Beatles songs in Neapolitan dialect, repeating "more or less" the diction of the English text and that "Beatles feel" that is so characteristic of 1960s music.

Remaining in the literary field—and frequently with excellent results—we can find experiments in theoretically untranslatable translations that do not seek imprecision, but attempt to realize the inexpressible. I am thinking of Umberto Eco's Italian version of Raymond Queneau's *Exercises de style*.[16] Since precision was impossible, Eco has attempted to reproduce the effect of the text analogously, creating his own Italian exercises in style. Two other examples of a similar enterprise can be given, one old and the other more recent. First, the Italian edition, published by Einaudi, of Anthony Burgess's *A Clockwork Orange*, which was obliged to invent an equivalent of the author's jargon.[17] And, more recently, the "insane" undertaking by Luigi Schenoni to translate *Finnegan's Wake* by James Joyce, a translation that inevitably involves the production of an autonomous work in Italian since our interest in the original text stems from the inventive delirium of its language, a delirium that cannot simply be transposed from one idiom into another.[18] In effect, these examples are not "translations" (the production of linguistic quasi-analogues), but re-creations of a spirit and aura: the *je-ne-sais-quoi* of the artist.

NEGATIVE VALUES: THE LANGUAGES OF APPROXIMATION AND THEIR USE OF IRONY

I said earlier that imprecision is particularly evident in the products of mass culture. The reason for this is obvious: only imprecision is able to give a routine sense of "naturalness" to a message that appears to be necessarily artificial. Once again, this concept is mannerist and baroque. In the *Cortegiano* Baldesar Castiglione called it "nonchalance"; Vasari described it as "naturalness" in his *Treatise on Painting*, and Torquato Accetto as "honest dissimulation" in his book on court life bearing the same name.[19] It is also true, however, that the imprecision deriving from the language of the media can be transformed into popular usage without any aesthetic purpose, but merely as a social characteristic. This fact has become widespread in recent years in Italy (and the same is true, I believe, in France and English-speaking countries) as a result of the mushrooming of private television. It is perfectly clear that a neo-language is becoming increasingly fashionable in Italy. Because of its characteristics, which we shall be examining, I suggest we refer to this new language as "squalorese," a term that describes its two essential features. *One*: the fact that it is a special language, or jargon, like "bureaucratese," "politicese," or "psychoanalese." *Two*: the fact that it nevertheless coincides with the national language. Squalorese does not coin new words for specific purposes; it simply renders the language of normal communication generic and imprecise. Squalorese can be found, however, in certain environments and not in others.

Squalorese is a collection of portions of the language, with no special or secret character. On the contrary, it tends to proliferate in all other areas of use. Let us look at a map of the fields it covers. The linguistic field that has been most clearly pillaged is that of commerce—not directly, but through the mediation of innumerable, exhausting television auctions. The emblem-word is the adjective *valid*, with its appropriate superlative—*extremely valid*. In this situation the word is not being used to define a new train ticket, but to indicate the value of a work of art, a design object, a financial investment, or an architectural plan. The adjective *special* with its superlative *extremely special* belongs to the same family. A "special" object is an "extremely valid" object, but one that might not appeal to everyone because of its unusual form. Something that receives the approval of everyone, on the other hand, is *really notable*, because it *responds* to all our *needs*. Something that responds to our needs without being "notable" is merely *correct*. I must also mention the squalorese verb *acquire*, which stands for verbs such as "take," "obtain," "conquer," or "buy," and the noun *proposal*, which is reduced to the rank of "offer," not necessarily in a commercial but also in a communicative sense (a painting "proposes" an artistic value). We should also notice another habit derived from the fact that television auctions are transmitted live: the same need to avoid pauses in discourse that one finds in traveling salesmen. Hence the existence of circumlocutions such as *a certain kind of*, *those that are*, and so on. A small group of words comes from the jargon of food—above all, rhetorical phrases combining different sensory sensations used in advertising ("the soft taste," "the fluted perfume"). Bureaucratic language has also played a part. Adjectives are fundamental: *propositional* is used to describe any conceptual message whatsoever; *negative* and *positive* are the two poles of any value judgment. The habit of talking about *situations* and *public opinion* both come from the world of politics. The mass media become *diffused culture* and the masses a *vast public*. Consumption is described by Catholics as *hedonistic culture* and by non-Catholics as *common sense*. The area of the social sciences is the final area to have been pillaged. *Sign* and *message* have been adopted from semiotics, without any technical content; psychology has provided *to manifest*, *to familiarize*, and *to realize oneself; consumer* and *deviant* have been taken from sociology. The all-purpose term *subject* has had enormous success in its semiotic, philosophical, psychoanalytical, and even slightly political sense.

I shall bring my list of examples of squalorese to a close here, since everyone is able to add to it from personal experience. The examples I have provided, however, make it possible for us to define two of its essential features. The first is impropriety: the terms become generic because they no longer correspond to their specific definitions. The second is a *vague* air of sophistication. In the conflict between these two features the criterion of squalorese becomes clear. Its starting point: a new social class takes shape that is no longer identified in traditional "class" terms, but according to its consumption, and, in this particular instance, to its cultural consumption. It is a class that has been molded entirely by mass communication. But in order to produce an identity (i.e., difference), this new class does not use common terms (not even in an improper way). It adopts a lexicon that is presented as "more elevated." But it is only superficially "more elevated," since the new class, deriving its identity from the mass media, is obliged to reconstruct the generic nature that makes those media available to the masses.

Although the characteristic of the language that I have just defined is approximation, quite independently of its aesthetic function, it is also the case that this very characteristic can be the starting point for creative activities. We can read the previously cited works of Woody Allen, or of Italy's Roberto Benigni, in this way as well. Irony based on squalorese in Italy has actually become an entertainment genre. Carlo Verdone and Nanni Moretti have both made use of the jargon of the 1977 youth movement. Nino Frassica imitates popular attempts to produce "high-flown" language. The comics of "Drive In" reproduce the deformations of young people's jargon, political circumlocutions, and the desemanticized language of advertising. The world of the media produces defects and immediately takes advantage of them.

168

Negative Values: "Quasi-Nothing"

In an entertaining essay entitled "In Praise of Nothingness," Carlo Ossola lists, and subtly comments on, the many writers who, in Italy alone, exalted nothingness during the seventeenth century.[20] This exaltation of Nothingness, it must be clear, can only partly be referred to a nihilistic philosophical matrix, since its other foundation is an exercise of style, a playfully inventive rhetoric on the theme of zero. The nothingness of writers such as Luigi Manzini, Marin Dall'Angelo, Giuseppe Castiglione, and Antonio Rocco goes hand in hand not only with the philosophy of *vanitas vanitatum*, but also with the thoughts of Pascal, the discoveries of Torricelli, and the scientific experimentalism of the academies during the period.

Nothingness has reappeared in the history of philosophical and aesthetic thought since the seventeenth century, and it has always maintained its baroque character. We have only to remember, as Ossola rightly points out, the Captain Nemo of Jules Verne. Currently we seem to be witnessing a new apogee not so much of Nothingness as of its more sophisticated baroque version, the so-called "annihilatio." Some examples of this can be found in the figurative arts, such as Christine Buci-Glucksmann in *The Madness of Seeing*.[21] Or, in particular, in the work of two German artists, Arnulf Reiner and Anselm Kiefer, whose neo-expressionist paintings clearly express a "reduction to nothingness" of the figures by means of cancellation, obliteration, and burning. It is not a case of eliminating the figure in favor of abstraction, a procedure that can be found in other forms of European experimentalism, but of actual annihilation: the figures are *disfigured*. Emilio Isgrò's work with cancellation might seem to be doing something similar in Italy, except that in his case the cancellation produces a new, though different, figure.

A reappearance of a certain type of Nothingness can also be seen in some avant-garde cinema from the early 1970s, when the camera was left without an operator in a variety of places, to film blindly the "nothingness" or "quasi-nothingness" that occurred. Something similar can be found more recently in both literature and cinema. The so-called American minimalists, quickly imitated in Europe, proceed by annulling narrative text, but without replacing it with experimentalism, as happened in the 1950s and 1960s. According to the reaction of critics, we can find the same phenomenon in a film like *Betty Blue* by Beineix, in which events are reduced to an absolute minimum.

Another manifestation of annihilation might be the "production" of silence. Many composers, from the 1970s on (from Cage to Cardini), have produced provocative silences. But perhaps in this case the concept is different, since what was being revealed was the *crisis of musical language*, rather than an exaltation of Nothingness. What seems to distinguish musical production at the moment (particularly light music) is Nothingness as sound. Indistinct, noisy, and unharmonious, it does not produce annulment, but simply nondistinction.

Is Nothingness in the sense of indefinition, then, another characteristic of the neo-baroque? The notion seems to be confirmed by Jean Baudrillard and Jean-François Lyotard. In *Amérique* Baudrillard insists on the figure of the desert as an emblem of America. Some time before, the same author had edited a special edition of the journal *Traverses*, dealing with the same theme. Baudrillard has also pointed out that, after the numerous sexual liberation movements (heterosexual, feminist, gay), we have now reached the point of "sexual indifference." Jean-François Lyotard, on the other hand, has organized an entire exhibition at the Beaubourg based on the theme *Les immateriewx*, as though to underscore the fact that the age of the calculator has brought with it the elimination of the very material of art: the aesthetic of Nothingness.[22]

Distortion and Perversion

A Non-Euclidean Geometry of Culture

In the preceding chapters I have tried to maintain my intention of naming the various branches of neo-baroque after categories borrowed from scientific disciplines. Even more deliberately, I have chosen those scientific disciplines that have been most massively influenced by what epistemologists now call the "new science." In this chapter, however, I shall make use of two nouns that are not necessarily scientific. There is a reason for this. Up to now I have tried to stress the formal and conceptual similarity that exists between the style of thinking of the "new science" and many aesthetic products in the age of mass communications. In this chapter, however, I should like to allow myself the pleasure of an inverse procedure. I should like to see whether both the objects of the "new science" and those analyzed by the human sciences can be identified by means of a common procedure. What, essentially, have we seen in the preceding pages? At least two fundamental principles. First, the "new science" encourages us not to produce exaggeratedly unified or simplified models. Neither the physical nor the human universe can be reduced to a unity. The universe is a fragmentary multiplicity, in which many models confront and compete with each other. The same phenomenon is being produced in the world of "creative" culture, even though few practitioners in the human sciences are aware of the change. Second, most phenomena in the universe cannot be attributed to stable models, but to an instability deriving from the fact that complex systems are more numerous than linear ones. Once again, as the century draws to a close, "creative" culture is offering us the end of all normative models and the production of unstable, complex, and polydimensional objects. The humanistic disciplines, however, hardly seem to have noticed.

In conclusion, we are witnessing a rupture that has something paradoxical about it. On the one hand, the "new science" and the aestheticism of cultural products show us this complexity in all its facets, while, on the other hand, the human sciences are revealing themselves to be inadequate, and unable to respond sufficiently quickly to the interpretation of complex phenomena. The "new science" and aesthetics are completely absorbed by problems arising from the *transformation* and *duration* of things, which inevitably leads to a concern with the nature of the change and a reevaluation of its *conflictual* origin. The human sciences, however, are either unaware of the question or, as they become aware of it, offer out-of-date solutions, such as those based on an outmoded idealism, an outmoded irrationalism, or an outmoded refusal of rigorous models. *Rigorous*, however, does not mean *unique* or *unified*. In other words, apart from a few exceptions (which I have frequently tried to illustrate, as it were, between the lines), the sciences of culture have remained at a stage that might be compared to that of classical physics. They are, that is, still anchored to a "Euclidean" vision of culture. Simultaneously, however, a non-Euclidean geometry of knowledge is being created. The terms used to entitle the preceding chapters in this book might be no more than metaphors. But I am ambitious enough to think that they help to illustrate the situation.

Leaving metaphors to one side, however, is it possible to indicate at least one characteristic that unites these intellectual products (scientific and aesthetic) that we have described as being under the banner of complexity, change, and instability? I shall attempt to name just one: the search for a different arrangement of *cultural space*. The terms used in the title of this chapter—distortion and perversion—derive from this. I have chosen to use distortion because the space in which culture is represented now seems to be subject to forces that bend and curve it, treating it as though it were elastic. I have adopted perversion because the order of things (in scientific models) and of discourse (in intellectual models) is not merely disordered, but rendered perverse. Instead of being overturned, or contrasted, these orders are changed in such a way that earlier logical systems are no longer even able to recognize them as being "other." The challenge now faced by the science of culture might be to find a new logic.

"NEO-BAROQUE" CITATION

In order to illustrate the concept of distortion and perversion more concretely, I shall now make use of an extremely restricted example. As is well known, many interpreters of "postmodern" have asserted that one of its main forms of expression is the citation.[1] There is something to be said for this. It is true, for example, that statistically citation is increasingly common. Nevertheless, the observation appears to me to be absolutely banal. Citation is a traditional way of constructing a text, and exists in every epoch and style. And the quantity of citations is not a good criterion for discrimination. Every classical epoch, for example, superabounds with citations, since classicism is based on principles of authority. It would hence be more revealing to discover *the type and nature of current citation*. Citation would be a relevant element only if it differed in some way from citation in the past.

Let us examine very quickly two cases in which the role played by citation appears to be fundamental, both from a quantitative viewpoint and (at least intuitively) from a qualitative one. The examples are—once more, alas—*The Name of the Rose* by Umberto Eco and *Raiders of the Lost Ark* by Steven Spielberg. The authors have admitted, and critics have demonstrated, that both the novel and the film are literally heaps of citations. Eco claims that not a word of the book is his own. Spielberg has crammed his film with approximately 350 references to other works, from both films and other sources.

173

There is, however, an initial problem involved in placing these two texts together. Whereas in a literary work it is relatively easy to recognize a citation (in its simplest form at least it is introduced by quotation marks or the indication of a different source), in a visual text nothing seems to correspond to quotation marks or their analogues.[2] The problem demands a kind of theoretical footnote concerning literary quotations, since, by extension, we might also ask ourselves whether a literary citation is isolated only by an extratextual indicator (in which case, what do we do with implicit citations?), or whether it is recognizable only by means of an encyclopedic knowledge on the part of the reader (in which case, how do we often recognize a citation when we know nothing of the work being cited?). In short, it is possible to claim that a citation is regarded as *a textual effect*, before its *truthfulness* is taken into consideration. This is easy to demonstrate: we sometimes use quotation marks when we are not citing but, for example, writing a phrase that is inappropriate, ambiguous, or intended for effect. We use the criterion of citation because we are citing *ourselves* for future use. Before producing a typology of citation, then, it might be well to clarify some aspects of its textual nature.

The simplest description of a citation is that it consists of a portion of text Y inserted into text X, with an indication of this insertion in text X.[3] How is the insertion indicated? By putting quotation marks around text Y, or by mentioning the name of the author. In both cases we are dealing with an act that operates at the level of enunciation. In both cases, in fact, a communicative simulacrum appears that is not identical to what is being enunciated from Y (*énoncé* Y). We obtain the following schema:

X		Y	
énoncé	enunciation	énoncé	enunciation
1	1	2	2

The relationship between X and Y is produced:

    a. by relating the two *énoncés* through the construction of an isotopy;

    b. by placing *énoncé* 2 *in relief*;

    c. by making apparent the instant of enunciation in text X;

    d. by indicating the otherness of *énoncé* 2;

    e. or by indicating the otherness of enunciation 2;

    f. or by indicating the otherness of the entire system Y.

Let us look at the schema again. The relationship between the two texts is constructed by means of an isotopy. This means that from a semantic viewpoint the two texts must be "made to agree." In other words, the citation will always be "evident" in relation to the *énoncé* into which it has been inserted. We should note that whereas it is necessary to create an isotopic level between the two *énoncés* in semantic terms, the opposite occurs from the viewpoint of expressive form. Here, in fact, a conflict between formal isotopies almost becomes necessary (but we are anticipating point d) if we are to recognize the quotation. The second shift means that an *embrayage* occurs in text X, that is, the appearance of the subject of the enunciation is stressed. This is because the quotation marks not only indicate the presence of the "voice" that has been inserted into the text; they also imply the "I-here-now" that supplies it. Obviously, a more complicated example could be given in which the quotation is pronounced by a character in text X, in which case we would have an enunciated enunciation. The principle, however, would remain the same. The fourth shift has analogies with the second. We are dealing, in fact, with an indicator that differentiates the *énoncé*. This can be produced by means of conflicting isotopies of expression (formal relief), or by simply marking *énoncé* 2 as other than *énoncé* 1 (an imprecise citation, summarized, and without quotation marks). Alternatively, or simultaneously, the otherness of enunciation 2 is indicated (e.g., when the name of the author of the citation is cited, or when the quotation marks reveal his "voice"). Otherness can naturally occur at the level of both *énoncé* and enunciation.

This, very roughly, describes a "normal" citation. The mechanism is still not exhausted, however. There are still two more essential principles in the functioning of a citation. They are both pragmatic principles, that is, principles concerning the relation between text and reader that are implicit in the text. The first is related to the way in which the cited *énoncé* is placed in relief. Alongside semantic, enunciative, and expressive relief there must be a way of persuading the reader that the citation is *true* (e.g., when bibliographical references are supplied in order to check the citation), and of making it *relevant* (because, otherwise, what point would there be in citing someone?). The second characteristic becomes especially important when some of the textual rules mentioned above are lacking, that is, when the citation is concealed. The mere relevance of an insertion can produce the effect of citation even when no citation is indicated.

Truthfulness also influences the *énoncé* by means of the so-called *epistemic modalities*.[4] Let us examine the structure in which they are articulated:

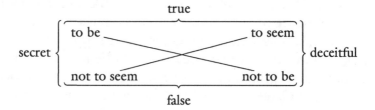

Citations are affected by the upper part of the square or, at most, by the part on the left. A "normal" citation can never, by definition, be false or deceitful. It should be noted, however, that the language foresees this possibility, and we shall be looking at it later.

Relevance, on the other hand, concerns another square, which we have already examined in the chapter dealing with details and fragments. It is the square of singularity:

176

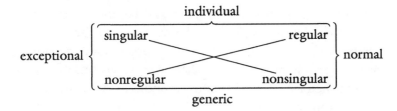

Once again, citations are affected by the upper part of the square, by the left pole, or by the part on the left (in most cases). It should be noted, however, that, as was the case with the epistemic modalities, the language also foresees the opposite possibility.

Now let us come to what I have called "neo-baroque citation" and to the two examples I promised to examine. Let us limit ourselves, for the sake of brevity, to the introduction to Eco's novel. You will remember its claim that the work is the rediscovery of a book "by a certain Abbot Vallet," itself translated from a seventeenth-century edition by J. Mabillon, the copyist of Adso of Melk's manuscript. It also states that the book has been lost, with nothing left but the author's Italian translation on notebooks from the Papeterie Gibert. A thorough search has failed to come up with other copies of Vallet's book, or the edition of Mabillon that contains the manuscript. Furthermore, a work by Milo Temesvar contains citations from Aldo attributed to Father Kircher, the fanciful seventeenth-century Jesuit. Finally, as regards the style to be adopted for publication, the author declares himself to be in a state of absolute doubt as to the authenticity of his source, which appears to be a complete mixture of reworkings, Aldo's cultural background, and a series of manipulations carried out by earlier copyists and translators. In other words, the introduction provides us with one of the most powerful (and, curiously, least analyzed by critics) keys to the novel "of the rose." This key is the doubt cast upon the authenticity or falsification of the truth. The work of the writer is in fact to "write out of pure love of writing," "for sheer narrative pleasure," which leaves *in doubt* any distinction between truth and falsehood. "In short I am full of doubt," says Eco. Shortly before, he advances the hypothesis (naturally sustained by unspecified citations): "There are magic moments . . . that produce visions of people known in the past . . . and visions of books as yet unwritten."[5] Eco's citations are always ambiguous. They produce an effect of truthfulness, but are impossible to check. Alternatively, they produce a falsifying effect, and yet induce us to verify their falsity. Or, finally, they are true, but all traces of their status as citation have been eliminated. Everything becomes extremely *undecidable*. Each block of *énoncé* (throughout the entire novel) that appears to be a citation will be influenced neither by the "normal" values of our preceding squares nor by their opposites. The citation will be *suspended* or, alternatively, *distorted and perverted*. The most striking case might be the episode in which William of Baskerville solves the minor mystery of the black horse near the abbey. It appears to be a normal narrative digression. In fact, we are dealing with a citation from Voltaire's novella *Zadig*, in which the horse is white. Not only that: there is also an autocitation from an essay by Eco, about the novella, which discusses searching for clues.[6] Everything, however, has been seasoned with undecidability, a hypothetical notion of historic time, and a suspension of ownership of the text that is being cited.

In *Raiders of the Lost Ark* we can find analogous phenomena. As I have already said, the film contains at least 350 extracts taken in various ways from other texts. Sometimes the citation is almost explicit (the opening sequence's use of *King Solomon's Mines*, for example); at other times, less so. Nevertheless, in almost every image we have the sensation, the effect, of citation, even in those cases where no citation exists (such as the duel between Indiana Jones and the Muslim with the scimitar). Certain passages are treated as if they were to become citations in the future (the duel, in fact, will be referred to once again in *Indiana Jones and the Temple of Doom*). We are hardly ever able to decide anything specific about a textual portion that emerges from the text of the film. The key to the poetic of perverted authenticity, however, can be found in an exemplary form in a scene from *E.T.* At a certain point in the story, the children take E.T. out of the house at Halloween, when everyone is disguised as a monster. E.T. sees a child dressed up as Yoda (a character from *The Empire Strikes Back*). Assuming him to be the real thing, he hurries to embrace him. The opposite situation occurs in the same film. E.T. hides in the children's wardrobe, which is filled with stuffed animals. The children's mother opens the door, but does not realize that E.T. is a living creature. The two situations are complementary. The former plays with the relation between true and false by citing E.T.'s filmic "cousin," whereas the second plays with the relation between false and true (E.T. is assumed to be false) by citing the Muppets and other cinematic puppets.

DYSTOPIAS OF THE PAST

These two examples have also introduced us to a very important aspect of citation: the fact that it is an instrument for rewriting the past. In effect, all periods rewrite their past, since, as Himmelmann so clearly said, to speak of the past inevitably means to create a "utopia of the past."[7] Each epoch draws the past back within its own culture, reformulating it in terms of a system of understanding in which all aspects of knowledge coexist. There are many different ways of drawing the past back to us, however: the historian reconstructs it, the critic interprets it, the popularizer explains it, and people generally do all these things simultaneously. The artist, however, does more than this: he or she "renews" the past. This has nothing to do with reproducing it. On the contrary, by working with the forms and contents of the past, scattered as though in a kind of warehouse, the artist restores ambiguity, density, and opaqueness, relating its aspects and significations to the present.

We might refer to this operation as a kind of "shifting." It consists in endowing an element from the past with a modern meaning or, alternatively, endowing a contemporary element with a meaning from the past. Citation plays a part in both operations. Citation can authorize an interpretation of the present (the past has authority), and it can do the reverse (valorizing the present by a reformulation of the past). In both cases, however, two different results can be produced. The first consists in using the shift to *stabilize* an idea, either of the past or of the present. For example, I can resort to the past in order to recollect values and models that seem to have been lost; alternatively, I can use a present that is regarded as stable in order to "normalize" our understanding of the past (by trying to "unravel its mysteries"). The second, on the other hand, consists in destabilizing the past or present. I can adventurously adopt an uncertain element from the past in order to produce an anomalous present interpretation; alternatively, I can make use of an improbable contemporary theory in order to produce a fanciful idea of the past. I can provide an example by drawing on the material regarding the Etruscans that has overwhelmed us during the 1985 celebrations devoted to this ancient people.[8] The use in advertising of Etruscan characters in order to exploit the "genius loci" in Tuscany can be regarded as a formal element that stands for the entire Etruscan culture, which is thus stabilized and reduced to stereotype. The work of the historian equally can be considered as a process of stabilization at the level of both content and form, since it seeks to *establish* what authentically belonged to the Etruscans. An artist's work based on Etruscan architecture, on the other hand, is an activity of formal destabilization, since it reelaborates and renders ambiguous a stylistic element, just as another artist's work based on the Etruscan idea of death might destabilize at the level of content.

Similar phenomena recur throughout the history of culture, which thus appears to be a succession (neither cyclical nor causal) of processes of stabilization and destabilization carried out on its own sources. Is this what is happening at the moment? I have the impression that the mechanism has become too distorted and perverse for us to continue to use the same terminology. What we have just described is in fact a phenomenon of *inversion* of categories (stabilization and destabilization). At the moment, however, we seem to be witnessing an actual implosion of these categories. Our epoch—as has often been said—is above all one of simulacra rather than documents. The past, the notion of tradition, turn out to be explicitly fictional products. Furthermore, the modern world appears to have rendered everything contemporaneous by means of its "total visualization" of the imagination. We have only to think of a single day's television. Images from different periods are placed beside one another and hence emerge as contemporary. Their subject might be any time, period, or style. *Everything is absolutely synchronous*. The "'past" no longer exists, except as a discursive form.

This does not occur only in the media. We have already seen how many modern artists make use of material deriving from a tradition that is conceived as a formal warehouse for a new "palette." This is true not only of "citationists," in the sense that they have given to themselves; it is also true of the constructors of the "strada novissima" at the 1979 Venice Biennale, and they are not even "anachronists," as Calvesi called them during the 1984 Biennale.[9] On the contrary, those artists who most closely correspond to citationism and anachronism are probably the least "modern" in the contemporary scene. They are simply eclectics suffering from regressive nostalgia, something that has occurred in many previous epochs, as we have seen. The most modern artists are those who create a *dystopia* from the past, by adopting a reckless, improbable use of the past, devoted to its cancellation rather than to its reevaluation. They pervert the connecting vectors of history, and eliminate the conjunctions of temporal indicators (cause-effect, reconstruction, nostalgia). They devote themselves to the most modern of all attempts: the improbable connection, and ahistorical syntax, eliminating the value of chrono-logy in favor of

181

the unity of the parts of knowledge. But this is implicit in the mechanism of "shifting," which we have already evoked. Neo-baroque "shifting" has the sense of drift, not in terms of meaning, as some French philosophers insist, but in terms of history. Neo-baroque objects, or objects that have been reinterpreted from a neo-baroque viewpoint, give the impression of having "always been here." "Here," in this sense, comprises history in its entirety, and without distinction; it consists in a *modernity* conceived as the concurrence of all epochs and even as the co-existence of the possible with the real. The sense of *duration* becomes increasingly subjective, as Bergson suggested, particularly in Deleuze's rereading of the term. Duration within history, in fact, depends on collocation in a contemporaneity that has been determined by a present subject. This is hardly surprising. The age of mass communication has almost necessarily created this effect. If we think that *current* affairs, in the journalistic sense, have begun to determine our entire vision of the world, it is not difficult to understand how history can be conceived in terms of its relation to the hub of it all, that is, the present. Anything that is recuperated from the past is valorized only if it connects with the present. This is why it might be said that history is either *finished*, as some people seem to want, or adrift and in search of a new meaning for itself.[10]

Some Like It Classical

DOES A "CLASSICAL FORM" EXIST?

I N THE CHAPTER devoted to instability and metamorphosis
I suggested that a mechanism of formal turbulence is appear-
ing, which is probably responsible for a change in "mentality."
Stable, ordered, regular, and symmetrical forms are being replaced by unstable, disordered, irregular, and asymmetrical
forms. This is happening because the dominant system of values is being influenced by phenomena of fluctuation, which
destabilize it. We should not, however, imagine that instability
is the only characteristic of our contemporary cultural universe.
On the contrary, even though the processes we have already
examined are encouraged by a movement away from equilibrium, most of our cultural universe is still composed of highly
traditional, stable, and ordered subsystems. There is thus a
competition between irregular and effectively super-stable
forms, just as there is between their figurative manifestations.
On the other hand, is this not the universal characteristic of
thought? The appearance of one of its specific forms must not
encourage us to believe that alternative, competitive forms do
not exist. On the contrary, it becomes interesting to observe
how different competing forms are structured, not only in
themselves, but in relation to "other" forms. Throughout this
volume we have seen how a hypothetical "neo-baroque" system
functions, both intrinsically and in terms of its opposite pole,
an equally hypothetical "classical" system. Now, the only possible conclusion is to see very rapidly whether the opposite exists: a representation, that is, of "classical" taste produced by
the existence of a "neo-baroque" universe.

Let us specify more clearly exactly what is meant by the term
"classical." I do not mean simply the repetition of figures from

the ancient Greek and Roman world, nor the Renaissance, nor the eighteenth century. Exactly as writers such as Wölfflin, Focillon, and D'Ors have claimed, talking about "classicism" is not a question of discovering iconographical reappearances of objects from an ideal past. It consists in the appearance of certain underlying morphologies in phenomena endowed with order, stability, and symmetry; and, as I have tried to argue in the course of this book, in a coherence of value judgments made about these phenomena. The various forms of classicism are never simple returns to the past, as we saw in the preceding chapter. Each classicism is a new form of order, which rereads antique classicism in order to transform it into an idealized component of contemporary culture. As a result of this, each classicism can be constituted not only of figures that belong directly to the past, but also of those that have no apparent relation to it. The internal morphology and the structure of value judgments ordered in a coherent manner according to positive and negative categorical poles remain identical. That which conforms to a physical ideal is necessarily also good, euphoric, and beautiful; that which is deformed is evil, dysphoric, and ugly. A "classical" system conceived in this way is, in general, rigorously normative and prescriptive. Anticlassical or baroque systems, on the other hand, are generated by a break in symmetry and by the appearance of fluctuations within categorial orders, as a result of which they are far less regulated. In the case of our own "neo-baroque" not even a rigid opposition to the classical exists any longer: instability is produced by a total suspension of categories.

Some Like It Classical

A further distinction must be made between the terms "classical" and "traditional." I have already argued that classicism does not necessarily imply a return to the past. Many people before me have observed, in fact, that any classicism worthy of the name avoids problems connected to the history of cultural facts.[1] The reevaluation of the past (in archaeology, for example) is frequently sustained by a process of idealization, even when the archaeologist insists that he or she intends to "restore" an ancient civilization to contemporary understanding. In short, classicism does not necessarily comprise conservative or nostalgic drives, even though most forms of classicism have ended up by embracing a rejection of the new in favor of a return to preexistent principles. This is simply a question of consequences, however. If the fundamental concept is the universal nature of the classic, the desire to ratify it by reference to an earlier existence is very frequent. I mention this because, in the next few paragraphs, we shall be looking at some classical forms that have entered contemporary culture, and some readers might be startled to see such apparently discordant objects being placed side by side: the Bronzes of Riace and their success, the physical model of Stallone-Norris-Schwarzenegger, the activity of bodybuilding. It is difficult to unite these phenomena historically. It is unlikely that Rambo's physique derives from that of the two bronze warriors, when other models, such as the Samson, Hercules, and Maciste of 1950s cinema, are nearer at hand to explain its iconography. Precedents for bodybuilding can also be found in the American tradition of concern with health and physical culture. Nevertheless, analogies exist at an underlying morphological level. In all three cases we are dealing with the rediscovery or constitution of a classical subgenre: *the idealization of the heroic body*. This is, furthermore, in line with that characteristically classical ordering system that we discussed at the beginning of the chapter. We are, in fact, confronted by an extremely prescriptive canon, modeled according to rules of proportion, by which every other real body can be measured. All this agrees perfectly with other proposals of order that are increasingly present in our society: from the success of books containing rules of etiquette (works on "manners," the precepts of Count Nuvoletti, popular magazines dealing with psychology and love, manuals on

185

behavior, "do-it-yourself" books) to the obsession with popu-
larizing that can be found among publishers, on television, in
the schools, and even at universities.

Not only, therefore, does there exist a classical form, but that
form attracts certain people, in contraposition to those irregular and unstable morphologies that we have called "neo-
baroque." We might wonder why this form is so successful,
since it is hardly feasible to attribute it simply to an organized
consensus on the part of those in power. There is only one possible answer: that movement away from equilibrium that favors
the appearance of irregular forms inevitably provokes a parallel
desire for stability, not because stability is "better" than instability (this is determined *a posteriori* by a system of value categories), but because it is far more economical. Stability allows
us to make simpler predictions, and hence to behave with a
greater sense of security. Society behaves in essentially the same
way as the stock exchange, which reacts well to political tran-
quility, even though the economic forces might not love the
governments in power, and penalizes any kind of institutional
revolt. We probably need to recognize that the "social exchange," however much it might appreciate certain upheavals
within the system, unconsciously desires its stabilization and
continuity.

A Brief Phenomenology of the Bronze

The first classical objects to be closely examined are the Bronzes
of Riace; not, obviously, as archaeological or artistic findings,
but as a collective phenomenon. The story of art has rarely seen
the kind of mass reaction to a "masterpiece" that greeted the
discovery of the Bronzes. This indicates that the beauty of the
two statues is not enough to explain their critical and public
success. There is evidence, in fact, to believe that the opposite
is true. The exhibition devoted to the Etruscans in Florence in
1985 was almost a failure in terms of public response, despite

the presence of not one but many masterpieces; and the discovery of an entire Etruscan ship off the coast of Tuscany has failed to excite the mass media to the same extent. There must be other reasons, therefore, for the Bronzes' rise to power in the contemporary imagination, reasons that are concealed in the symbolic capacity of their form. Let us see if we can identify them, in the spirit of someone making an inventory. Immediately we notice something familiar about their appearance. The two warriors are *nude*. Like most Greek sculpture, you might say. Certainly. But the Greek nude has always exercised an extraordinarily seductive power over us, as Francis Haskell has revealed in his examination of the way in which classical statuary has been revived through the centuries because of the ideal character it attributes to the human body.[2] It is even possible to classify the abstract types of Greek nude.[3] There is Apollo, or the narcissism of the perfect form. There is Venus, in her Platonic terrestrial and celestial variants (the senses and the spirit). There is the heroic-energetic nude, in two other variants: athlete or warrior. There is the pathetic nude, languid and abandoned. There is, finally, the ecstatic nude, transported by passion. It is clear that the Bronzes belong essentially to the category of the energetic nude, representing both the athlete and the warrior. However, they exhibit none of the torsion lines that, typically, represent movement in the heroic nude. There is neither the "heroic diagonal" nor the "heroic spiral." The Bronzes do not unleash an idea of strength, then, but express an energy that is waiting to explode, a potential, contained, and measured energy. At the same time, their pose is somewhat Apollonian: perfectly proportioned and coherent, immobile, hieratic in front of the eyes of their admirers. Heroic and Apollonian, perfectly idealized in their microcosm as reference to, or metaphor of, the macrocosm, they are the perfect prototype of the idea of spectacle in the etymological sense: objects to be seen, pictures in an exhibition. They are hence universal objects, because they demand to be regarded as models. This is obviously the reaction they excited when they were exhibited to the public. The spirit in which Greece produced its works of art was certainly not the same as ours is today. The sense of admiration then was probably oriented toward the ideal content of perfection. These days the spectacle obviously does not summon up the abstract measure of the universe, but the more prosaic construction of a fetish. We might say that this is the way in which the present has transformed the past: from a measure of the universal into its totem.

At this point the external history of the Bronzes intervenes to enhance their fetishized universality. The Bronzes reappear adventurously after twenty-five centuries (give or take a century) *from the depths of the abyss*. The narrative value of the event is clear. Let us break it up into two equally important sequences. First sequence: "after twenty-five centuries." The form of the Bronzes has resisted the ravages of time, the discontinuity of history, the degeneration of events. The Bronzes thus express a *duration* that lasts far longer than the lives of men and their everyday artifacts. Second sequence: "from the depths of the abyss." The form reemerges despite its cancellation, despite the extent of its fall, despite the nothingness into which it has sunk. Hence the Bronzes also express *indestructibility*. They resist any notion of the present, since all contact with the reality in which they were created was lost at the very moment they sank into the abyss. We know nothing about them—who made them, who owned them, where they came from, where they were going, the name that defined their meaning. They are *nameless*, that is to say, *propertyless*. They have the same appearance as a miracle, or legend. The proof of this can be seen in the fact that many critics have made references to mythical sculptors, such as Phidias. In doing so they have told the tale of the two heroes in the same way that classical authors, such as Pliny, narrated their ideal anecdotes. The Bronzes have become, in short, a myth of origin.[4]

Universal, ideal, eternal, miraculous. These attributes of the Bronzes of Riace are enhanced as much by their substantial form as by their modern narrative form. But let us see what happens when a universal symbol takes on a concrete physical form. The physical form becomes, more than anything else, a canon of conformism, beauty, morality, and euphoria. Never, in fact, have so many exaggerated judgments based on an aesthetic value been made as in this case. Furthermore, stories about an assumed ethical role have sprung up around the Bronzes. For example, it has been suggested that they fulfilled a ritual role in a city in Magna Grecia, or that they represented foundation divinities, or even that they symbolized the power of the "new world" (as Italy was seen in the eyes of the Greeks). On a popular level—in comic books and magazines about the supernatural, UFOs, and so on—the Bronzes have appeared in stories involving fatal love affairs, pagan sacrifices, and mediumistic revelations. As far as emotional reactions are concerned, it is easy to see what the Bronzes have provoked. They have excited a generalized passion, evident in the collective delirium of the exhibitions in Florence and Rome after their restoration, as well as in the innumerable requests for loans from all over the world, beginning with that of the Los Angeles Olympics in 1984.

Rambo and His Brothers

In the 1950s, and before, a number of Mr. Universes entered the film world. The most famous was probably Steve Reeves, who played Maciste and Samson. But these muscular types, and their less well known cousins, did not represent a classical ideal, despite their bulging biceps and enormous torsos. They were closer to savages: immersed in jungles, or a barbaric mythological past, or a cruel and bloody ancient tale. They were excessive, exotic, and quite removed from the classical notion of the hero and his athletic feats. It might be pointed out that Rambo also ends up in a jungle to combat Vietnamese "savages." Or that Chuck Norris interprets an invincible fighter against the Red Hordes invading America. More subtly, one might say

189

that Schwarzenegger plays exactly the same figure in *Commando* as he does in *Conan the Barbarian* or *Terminator*, in which he is almost a monster. Clearly, there is an element of continuity with 1950s cinema that should not be undervalued. Nevertheless, although it was difficult to fall in love with Hercules and his colleagues, because a man in a leopard skin is nothing more than a circus phenomenon, Rambo can be regarded as a phenomenon of civilization. It is acceptable, in other words, to turn him into a *model*. It is impossible to deny that, whereas the Hercules of the 1950s were flesh and pasteboard, our modern heroes have an absorbed manner that is typical of the admired object, utopian and idealized. It is hard to imagine Eisenhower receiving Reeves at the White House. It is "normal" to see Stallone shaking hands with Reagan. Rambo is a "real" statue, a "real" monument. Maciste is a farmyard turkey.

We can see further differences at the level of image. During the 1950s actors like Reeves were never treated as stars, unlike Rambo. An interpretation of Rambo as "classical" might be objected to on the grounds that his films are excessive, and can thus be categorized as "neo-baroque" according to the criteria that have already been described. But we need to understand exactly what we mean. Although it is true that some phenomena exceed regulated and ordered systems, precipitating them toward transformation, it is also the case that certain forms of simple exaggeration, or hyperbole, corroborate the system in its struggle against turbulence. Let us continue. The American hero, cousin to the Bronzes, is undoubtedly a statuesque character. Hercules and Maciste were simple swelling torsos with an animal-skin G-string. Our new heroes are something else. Their physique emerges, powerful and well proportioned, from whatever garment they put on. They are capable of becoming icons. Rambo might have on a cartridge belt and bazooka, a sweatband tied around his forehead, a military shirt and backpack, or boxing shorts. But his body always expresses a kind of "tension," whether in movement or poised on the brink of explosion. Hercules was a bodybuilder or weight lifter. Rambo could be provided with a pedestal.

Finally, the temporal dimension has changed. Hercules could only live in a specific period (however fantastic it might have been). "Rambo" is timeless. He can appear in a neo-gothic, metaphysical fantasy as Conan, a possible present as Rambo, a medievalized future as Terminator. As a result, he becomes universal, independently of the figure being por-trayed. Like the Bronzes, he possesses duration and hence in-destructibility. Like them, he comes from an abyss: in *Conan* the abyss of memory, in *Terminator*, of the possible.

BRAZEN FACES

Bodybuilding is the third element in play in our revived ideal of the heroic body. We shall not relate it to the Bronzes or to Rambo by banal iconographical analogy, but, once again, be-cause of an underlying morphology. Bodybuilding is not a re-vival of physical culture. Physical culture was a "poor" concept: pumping up the body was a strictly quantitative activity, and thus extremely material. Proof of this can be found in the way in which physical culture has always been promoted. We find it in the small ads of comic books and popular magazines. We see it as a substitute for sexual identity, or as a surrogate for personality. Bodybuilding, on the other hand, is fashionable, classy, and healthy—to such an extent that it has been extended to include the female body. We must assume, therefore, that it is sustained by some kind of ideal, however weak or counterfeit it might be. And that, in fact, is what we find. If the classicism of the Bronzes moves essentially from an aesthetic ideal (mea-sure) to which physical ideals (canon), ethical ideals (perfec-tion), and passional ideals (admiration) all correspond, and if the classicism of Rambo moves from an ethical ideal (purity) to which physical ideals (canon, once again), aesthetic ideals (se-duction), and passional ideals (identification) all correspond,

191

then the ideal bodybuilder moves from a physical ideal (well-being) to which the usual ethical ideals (health), aesthetic ideals (seduction), and passional (admiration, once more) all, inevitably, correspond. Bodybuilding is also classical in the sense of being normative and labeling. In order to build the perfect body, one must carry out a series of exercises; but these exercises depend on a kind of interior philosophy. Finally, the term "bodybuilding" is, itself, classical. The body is *built* as it would be in architecture, thus satisfying the classical idea of the physique as a metaphor for the perfection of every artifact, from the smallest to the most immense, nature itself. Physical culture never possessed such a concept of universal harmony, now underscored by the fact that modern gymnastics are generally accompanied by music and choreography. Physical culture was exaggerated, whereas bodybuilding is well proportioned and harmonious. The physical canon is thus transmuted into an aesthetic ideal. The notion of variable beauty is eliminated, and physical beauty is standardized. Clearly this issues from the gym and becomes a social norm, indirectly propagandized by television programs portraying young couples, by cosmetics advertising, by films such as *Nine and a Half Weeks*, and by the aestheticizing style of Armani publicity shots.

I have used the adjective "aestheticizing." I consider it appropriate to the situation we are examining. It is inevitable, in fact, that the proposal of an ideal canon be translated into aesthetic idealization, replacing the idea of beauty as a product of a number of physical and moral elements with the notion that a superficial material beauty indicates moral beauty as well.

SOME CAUTIOUS CONCLUSIONS: EVERYTHING AND ITS OPPOSITE

After this observation, I feel that I can move on to make a few final remarks. What does this desire to rediscover an aesthetic, physical, passional, and ethical canon in the surface of things, rather than in other combinations, mean? What significance does the search for universality and duration in phenomena have? In my opinion, we need to recover a basic philosophical position in our model of classicism (whatever one might think of the type of examples that have been adopted here). Whereas an irregular system of value judgments exalts the subjectivity and relativity of the judges, classical value systems tend to minimize the role of the judging subject, and to search for an objective *quid* in the things themselves. If this objective *quid* exists, the entire value system becomes organic; it no longer requires invention on the part of the subject, but only that the subject adapt to external principles. The value system is thus entirely self-regulating and functional, with a built-in tendency to eliminate turbulence and fluctuation. Crisis, doubt, and experiment are features of the baroque. Certainty is classical.

It might be possible to explain why classicism naturally tends toward conservatism in this way. But the conclusion would be anything but final, since it is not required and would probably be an oversimplification. It is interesting however, to consider the fact that authoritarian regimes have generally expressed themselves in favor of classical art rather than of anticlassical experimentalism. Both the Nazi regime and Stalin considered the avant-garde as "degenerate art." If we disregard for a moment the pejorative connotation that Hitler and Stalin gave the expression, we can see that its meaning is surprisingly accurate in a morphological sense. From our point of view, in fact, all "baroque" phenomena are produced by a process of "degeneration" (or rather, "destabilization") in an ordered system, whereas "classical" phenomena result from the maintenance of the system when confronted by minor disturbances. Thus, whereas at times the baroque effectively "degenerates," the classical produces genres: the inevitable result of a canon.

The final conclusion to be drawn concerns the relation between classical and baroque. As we have seen, this relation has been reduced here to one of *morphological models*, based on *forms of taste*. The two categories have thus been abstracted from any temporal setting, and examined solely in terms of their formal functioning. However, since a formal definition demands the construction of an interdefining categorical system, it seems clear that classical and baroque define each other to an equal extent—at least from an analytical viewpoint. One cannot exist without the other. Even more, one necessarily *posits* the other in an implicit (or even explicit) manner. Classical and baroque, in any case, do not succeed one another historically. They coexist. History is, finally, the field in which a *prevalence*, whether qualitative or quantitative, is expressed. Observing it, we produce a history of forms. Describing its foundation, we produce a theory of forms. In this book I have cautiously tried to do both, with the inevitable defects that result from excessive ambition. It might be possible to produce a history of forms in another way without, however, touching upon the social problem of prevalence. One could simply concentrate on a single frozen historical *moment*, decided upon and localized, in which to examine the inevitably conflictual presence of contrast between the systems, revealed in a series of precise, specific, and *dated* figures.[5] A history and theory of culture could be composed in this way, since cultural forms exist, compete, and are defined by their relation to one another.

We have seen the *way* in which objects that correspond in terms of taste and value intertwine and compete within society. The problem of *judgment*, however, remains open. From the introduction on, I have stressed that it is not a question here of constructing hierarchies and tables. In other words, we need to describe before we can evaluate. Even more importantly, values themselves need to be described in terms of their cultural production. My main aim was to capture the "spirit of the time," and to articulate the areas in which it is expressed. This does not mean, however, that many of the phenomena examined are not "better" than others. The problem is to define them without adopting predetermined criteria, with a constant awareness of the subjectivity of judgment. In the value category system that I have been proposing since the first chapter of this book there is, perhaps, an interesting feature. The judgments that made up a categorical matrix were conceived as *built-in valori-*

zations, already contained within the texts being examined. They could therefore be associated with those mechanisms that governed the functioning of the texts. This does not mean, however, that we need to *accept* the matrix, or the judgments implicitly built into the text. After all, any phenomenon can be proposed as a perfect example of the spirit of the time and then inserted into one poetic rather than another. What we need to do is see how effectively the suggestion made by the text produces a value.

Throughout the book we have seen how the constitutive principles of the "neo-baroque" have been revealed in production, works, and receptive behavior. This *describes* the creation of a poetic in terms of how to use it and, particularly in our case, reveals the way in which the neo-baroque poetic emerges from the diffusion of mass communications. Nevertheless, we have seen in each chapter that the texts examined operate at *different levels of intensity*. In the section devoted to limit and excess, for example, we noted the way in which the two categories are frequently represented ambiguously, with one simulating the other. This means that some kind of differentiating principle exists within a general "taste": for example, the observation of the extent of *real intellectual risk* involved in a poetic based on breaking limits, or excessiveness. In the chapter on instability and metamorphosis we glimpsed a second neo-baroque characteristic. But once again there existed the possibility of difference between objects. It appears, in fact, that the more normal it becomes to invert categories of value in new systems of correspondence, the more arduous it is to suspend them, since this implies a greater strain on the system, a conflict of *acceptability*. In another part of the book we stressed that a new formal principle might be offered in a simple and direct way or, alternatively, in a complex and conscious manner. This is yet another way of judging the intensity of a transformation.

As you can see, what I am basically proposing is no longer a hermeneutical interpretive key, but an evaluative one. And this time I am doing it in a personal sense, quite beyond the criteria

195

that compose this book. The three key expressions that I have just used are, in fact, *intellectual risk, conflict of acceptability,* and *working upon aesthetic material.* But if my own system of preferences operates according to these three rules, and assuming that they are not derived mechanically from my method of analyzing phenomena, it might still be said that a relation with that method exists. Otherwise, how could *my* judgments be formulated, if not on the basis of a satisfactory description and interpretation of phenomena? How could I begin to apply a criterion of quality if I did not already have a criterion that enabled me to *discriminate* and thus to *recognize* the characteristics of the objects being examined? Only the existence of this criterion allows me to accept one work rather than another, to *criticize* it. Just as it is only the existence of this criterion that allows me to surmount the threshold of prefabricated judgments, which would be nothing more than a photocopy of a system of value that had already been constituted. I firmly believe that all critical activity must be based on interpretation. Interpretation restores a sense of liberty and independence to value judgments, a sense of the search for unprejudiced quality, and a sense of the adventure of aesthetic ideas.

❖ Notes ❖

FOREWORD

1. In my case I don't hope so, I know. See my essay "Innovation and Repetition: Between Modern and Post-Modern Aesthetics," *Daedalus* 114 (Fall 1985), which draws upon some Italian essays written in the previous two years. The essay was also inspired by some essays by Calabrese, and it might be seen that my reaction to the problem that he poses is somewhat different, precisely because I had written *The Open Work* twenty years before. Essentially, however, the essay explains how I would write the second volume of my first work today.

2. For a possibly oversimplified distinction between "open" and "closed" works, see my introduction to *The Role of the Reader* (Bloomington: Indiana University Press, 1979).

3. In this sense my position was different—and still is—from that taken by "radical deconstructionism." Cf. "Intentio Lectoris," *Differentia: Review of Italian Thought* 2 (Spring 1988).

CHAPTER 1
TASTE AND METHOD

1. Periodization is frequently a central element of debate among historians. If we look at "general" works (e.g., Nicola Tranfaglia's *Storia contemporanea*, Feltrinelli, or the *Storia d'Italia*, various authors, Einaudi) we find ample discussion devoted to the way in which events are divided up and partitioned. And even though obvious warnings about the conventional nature of these partitions are made, it is interesting to observe the *criterion* that is adopted. Sometimes an event is assumed to be a symbolic discriminator between two politicoeconomic totalities. At other times it is regarded as a social emblem. Alternatively, an event is chosen because it operates as a hub for a cultural change, or a change in attitudes. In this sense, for example, the Congress of Vienna, the American Revolution, and the discovery of America, despite all three of them being "macro-events," are extremely different types of historical signs.

2. In other words, two concepts of history are being opposed: history as continuity and history as fracture. But the opposition is less

197

rigid than I am suggesting here. Historical "continuity" is not simply deterministic, just as historical "discontinuity" belongs to a large number of widely differing trends of thought. In any case, for an orientation on history as fracture, see Louis Althusser, *Lire le Capital* (Paris, 1965), and Michel Foucault, *Les mots et les choses* (Paris: Gallimard, 1966). In Althusser we rediscover the concept of "coupure," which separates the great moments of history by starting from the notion of class, and in Foucault the concept of "epistemic fracture."

3. Semiotics in fact has recently begun to be concerned with the way in which "historical discourse" is produced. It is within the context of this discourse that the coherence, verisimilitude, and reciprocal pertinence of phenomena are constructed. See, among others, Algirdas J. Greimas, "Sur l'histoire événementielle et l'histoire fondamentale," in *Sémiotique et sciences sociales* (Paris: Seuil, 1976).

4. Here I have merely simplified and adopted Jean-François Lyotard's analysis of how Kant regarded the "signs of progress in history." Kant believed that one of these signs was *enthusiasm*, understood not as the passion felt by the protagonists of history, but as the emotion of spectators who were not directly involved. See Jean-François Lyotard, *L'enthousiasme* (Paris: Editions Galilée, 1986).

5. "Bonne distance" is a concept invented by Lévi-Strauss *(Anthropologie structurale* [Paris: Plon, 1958]). It means that an analyzed object needs to be at a certain distance from the observer. Not all distances are equal, however. There is usually one that is most adapted to a "perspicuous" observation by the analyst. See also what can be deduced at the level of language in Jean-Claude Coquet, "La bonne distance," *Actes Sémiotiques (Documents)* 55 (1984).

6. The idea that culture is a system that resembles the living system is an old one. We find it, for example, in Kant's *Kritik der Urteilskraft*, 1790. More recently, an analogous concept has pervaded the so-called general theory of systems. In particular, one of its founders, Ludwig von Bertalanffy, has tried to transfer an "organismic" conception from biology to all fields of knowledge and reality. See Ludwig von Bertalanffy, *Das biologische Weltbild* (Bern: Franke, 1949) or, by the same author, *General System Theory* (New York: Braziller, 1968). Extreme biologism is generally refuted now, but the culture-biology metaphor remains part of a common language. For a discussion of the growth of the idea of "system," see Tomàs Maldonado, "Politica e scienza delle decisioni: nuovi sviluppi della ricerca sistemica," *Prob-*

lemi della transizione 5 (1980); and Giacomo Marramao, *L'ordine disincantato* (Rome: Editori Riuniti, 1985).

7. By "encyclopedia" I mean a model of socialized competencies in a specific historical moment, something that a dictionary (a model of the ideal competencies of an ideal speaker) is absolutely unable to explain. See Umberto Eco, *Trattato di semiotica generale* (Milan: Bompiani, 1975).

8. On the relation between the "globality" and "locality" of knowledge, see Jean Petitot, "Locale/globale," in *Enciclopedia* (Turin: Einaudi, 1979), vol. 8.

9. For the concept of the grid applied to cultural phenomena, see Marc Augé et al., *Il sapere come rete di modelli* (Modena: Edizioni Panini, 1981); and Pierre Rosenstiehl, "Rete," in *Enciclopedia* (Turin: Einaudi, 1980), vol. 11.

10. I refer primarily to three essays by Foucault: *Les mots et les choses* (cited above), *L'archéologie du savoir* (Paris: Gallimard, 1969), and *Nietzsche, la généalogie, l'histoire*, in *Hommage à Jean Hyppolite* (Paris: Gallimard, 1971). For microhistory I must obviously refer in general to the school of the "Annales." In particular, however, see Paul Veyne, *Comment on écrit l'histoire* (Paris, 1971); Jacques Le Goff et al., *Faire l'histoire* (Paris, 1974); Manfredo Tafuri, *La sfera e il labirinto* (Turin: Einaudi, 1980) and *L'armonia e i conflitti* (Turin: Einaudi, 1983); and Carlo Ginzburg, *Il formaggio e i vermi* (Turin: Einaudi, 1976).

11. This, in fact, is the criticism leveled in the most recent writing on Foucault, above all by the "philosophers for a return to order," who contest the preceding *"pensée 68."* See Gilles Deleuze's reply to this trend in his *Foucault* (Paris: Minuit, 1986).

12. Eugenio Battisti, *L'antirinascimento* (Milan: Feltrinelli, 1962).

13. Federico Zeri, "Rinascimento e pseudorinascimento," in *Storia dell'arte italiana* (Turin: Einaudi, 1983), vol. 5.

14. For a survey of "historical" criticism, see, once again, Ginzburg, *Il formaggio e i vermi*.

15. In the field of art theory this has been happening for some time, above all in the group of Histoire et Théorie de l'Art of the Ecole des Hautes Etudes in Paris, composed of Hubert Damisch and Louis Marin, and many much younger scholars, such as Maurice Brock, Georges Didi-Huberman, Jean-Claude Bonne, Philippe Morel, Daniel Arasse, and others.

16. Atomic weight is a consistent method, but it is chosen by the analyst according to convention and thus depends on his "subjective" criterion. It does not belong in an immanent way to the objects being analyzed, which is the only condition by which something can be defined "objective." On the matter see Ilya Prigogine and Isabelle Stenghers, "Sistema," in *Enciclopedia* (Turin: Einaudi, 1981), vol. 12.

17. Even a semiotics of the author and the reader, but in terms of that which is inscribed in the text, of the abstract models of the authorial "voice," and of the reader's cooperation in the deciphering of the text. See, in this context, Umberto Eco, *Lector in fabula* (Milan: Bompiani, 1979).

18. This is the title of a book by Angelo Trimarco, *L'inconscio dell'opera* (Rome: Officina, 1974), in which the term has a more restricted meaning than that given here.

19. Severo Sarduy, *Barrocco* (Paris: Seuil, 1975).

20. Statistically this might even be the case: the invention of gunpowder, printing, gravitational theory, the heliocentric planetary system, and so on might be responsible for changes in attitude. Nonetheless, we must not understand by "origin" merely the point of departure of a *genesis* but, as Walter Benjamin said, "a vortex in the flow of being," a "creative character" ("Ursprung des deutschen Trauerspiels," in *Erkenntniskritische Vorrede* [Berlin, 1925]).

21. By "axiological categories" I mean categories concerning values, rather like those that began to assert themselves at the beginning of this century with the so-called philosophies of values, to which the success of the term is due (see, e.g., Eduard von Hartmann, *Grundriss der Axiologie* [Leipzig, 1908]). But see below, in Chapter 4.

22. This idea has gained ground recently in the fields of sociology and philosophy: in the work of Michel Maffesoli and Gianni Vattimo, for example. But not everyone is in agreement, including some of those considered to be "fellow travelers," such as Mario Perniola. In this context see the debate conducted in the magazine *Alfabeta* throughout 1985–1986 and, in particular, the following works: Gianni Vattimo and Pier Aldo Rovatti, eds., *Il pensiero debole* (Milan: Feltrinelli, 1985); Michel Maffesoli, *L'ombre de Dyoniss: Contribution à une sociologie de l'orge* (Paris: Librairie des Méridiens, 1982) and, by the same author, *La connaissance ordinaire* (Paris: Librairie des Méridiens, 1985); Mario Perniola, *Transiti* (Bologna: Cappelli, 1986).

23. See Paolo Carravetta and Paolo Spedicato, eds., *Postmoderno e*

letteratura (Milan: Bompiani, 1984), and also Maurizio Ferraris, *La svolta testuale* (Milan: Unicopli, 1986).

24. Jean-François Lyotard, *La condition postmoderne* (Paris: Minuit, 1979).

25. The American sociologists are Derek Bell, *The Coming of Post-Industrial Society* (New York, 1973); Ihab Hassan, *The Dismemberment of Orpheus: Toward a Post Modern Literature* (New York: Oxford University Press, 1971); M. Benamou and C. Caramello, eds., *Performance in Post-Modern Culture* (Wisconsin: Center for XXth Century Studies, 1977); and so on.

26. Lyotard, *La conditione postmoderne*, p. 5.

27. Paolo Portoghesi, *Postmodern* (Milan: Electa, 1979).

28. Jean-François Lyotard, *Le postmoderne expliquè aux enfants* (Paris: Editions Galilée, 1986).

29. See Tomàs Maldonado, *Il discorso moderno e il termine "post-,"* in *Il futuro della modernità* (Milan: Feltrinelli, 1987).

30. I have the impression, at least as regards postmodernism in architecture, that the original philosophical idea has been radically rewritten in the context of a different, and earlier, ideological project. Anyhow, many trends that have since been recognized as postmodern appeared on the scene long before the label. Think of the controversy surrounding "pop" architecture in the 1960s, or "radical architecture" in Italy during the 1970s. See, in this context, the controversy that enlivened Tomàs Maldonado's *La speranza progettuale* (Turin: Einaudi, 1970), involving Americans on the one hand (Bob Venturi, Denyse Scott Brown, Charles Jencks, and others) and Italians on the other (Alessandro Mendini, Aldo Rossi, and, later, Paolo Portoghesi).

31. Sarduy, *Barrocco*, who naturally picks up the formalist tradition of Wölfflin and D'Ors. See also Claude-Gilbert Dubois, *Le Baroque: Profondeurs de l'apparence* (Paris: Larousse, 1973); Gérard de Cortanze, *Le baroque* (Paris: M. A. Editions, 1987); and Christine Genci-Glucksmann, *La raison baroque* (Paris: Editions Galilée, 1984) and, by the same author, *La folie du voir* (Paris: Editions Galilée, 1986).

32. Gillo Dorfles, *Architetture ambigue* (Bari: Dedalo, 1985), in which a short book by Dorfles dating from 1951, *Barocco nell'architettura moderna*, is reprinted with additions and updatings; and above all his *Elogio della disarmonia* (Milan: Garzanti, 1986). The term is

also accepted by Pierluigi Cervellati, "Aria di neo-barocco," *L'informazione bibliografica* 1 (1986).

33. This is obviously not a new idea. We find it, for example, in Maurice Blanchot, *L'espace littéraire* (Paris: Gallimard, 1968). But think how explicit it has become in the literary and artistic neo-avant-garde. The title of a famous book by Lamberto Pignotti, *Istruzioni per l'uso degli ultimi modelli di poesia* (Milan: Lerici, 1967), is emblematic.

34. Heinrich Wölfflin, *Kunstgeschichtliche Grundbegriffe* (Munich, 1915), p. 59.

35. I am translating—legitimately I hope—one of Wölfflin's concepts into somewhat "linguistic" terms: "figures" are in fact the way in which the text is manifested in concrete terms, independently of the more abstract structures that regulate the mechanism of their appearance. Thus one can say that a style appears historically with forms that are simultaneously connected not only to the historic *moment* but also to an abstract figurative *type*.

36. Kant's idea of the "organic" nature of human productions, expressed in his *Kritik der Urteilskraft*, has been gaining ground ever since the end of the last century. In 1886, for example, Arsène Darmesteter applies a biological metaphor to language in *La vie des mots* (reprinted by Librairie Delagrave in 1950).

37. Henri Focillon, *La vie des formes* (Paris: Flammarion, 1934).

38. Eugenio D'Ors, *Lo Barrocco* (Madrid, 1933).

39. Ibid., in the chapter "Species of baroque."

40. Luciano Anceschi, *L'idea del barocco* (Bologna: Nuova Alfa Editoriale, 1984), containing Anceschi's studies of the baroque from 1945 to 1966, and, in particular, beginning with *Rapporto sull'idea del barocco*, originally the introduction to the Italian edition of D'Ors and the first authoritative voice to be raised in Italy against Croce's view of the style.

41. Pierre Francastel, *Limites chronologiques, limites géographiques et limites sociales du Baroque*, in Enrico Castelli, ed., *Retorica e Barocco* (Rome, 1955). René Wellek, *Il concetto di Barocco nella cultura letteraria*, cited by Anceschi, *L'idea del barocco*.

42. In other words, any cultural fact has its own specific, concrete manifestation, which is its "form" in the traditional and generic sense of the term; but cultural facts also have underlying "forms" that are far more abstract, evading the ways in which single facts "appear" in specific epochs. In this sense we can assume that, in different times

but also simultaneously, "forms" appear that differ from one another in that they belong to a single logical entity, of which they are the categorization. An example of this can be found in the work of James Sacré on mannerism and the baroque. Sacré provides formal definitions (mannerism: a poetic of conflictual categorizations; baroque: a poetic of suspended oppositions) that are simultaneously general and concrete. See James Sacré, "Pour une définition sémiotique du maniérisme et du baroque," *Actes semiotiques (Documents)* 4 (1979) and, by the same author, *Un rang maniériste* (Neuchâtel: A la Baconnière, 1977); see also the proceedings of the international symposium of the University of Chicago, "Baroque: Models and Concepts," 1978 (mimeo).

43. Aristotle, *Categoriae*, ed. L. Minio-Paluello (Oxford: Oxford University Press, 1949); Immanuel Kant, *Kritik der reinen Vernunft*, 1781; Karl Rosenkranz, *Aesthetik des Hässlichen* (Königsberg, 1853); Robert Blanché, *Les catégories esthétiques* (Paris: Vrin, 1979). See also Jean Lacoste, *L'idée de beau* (Paris: Bordas, 1986); Murielle Gagnebin, *Fascination de la laideur* (Lausanne: L'Age d'Homme, 1978).

44. Aristotle, *Categoriae*, 16 25 and following.

45. The semiotic square is a logical schema composed of four positions, arranged according to two axes of contrary terms (horizontal), two axes of contradictory terms (diagonal), and two axes of implications (vertical), as we can see in the diagram:

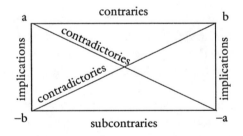

This square is particularly useful if we want to "expand" the articulation of an opposition. The schema allows us to "see" simultaneously both semantic and grammatical oppositions expressed by means either of lexical negation ("black" negates "white") or of grammatical negation ("nonwhite" negates "white"). It also renders visible implications (the assertion "*x* is black" implies that "*x* is nonwhite"), as well as combinations along the contrary axes (complex: "*x* is black

203

and white"; neutral: "*x* is nonwhite *and* nonblack") and the axes representing implication ("*x* is white and nonblack"; "*x* is black and nonwhite").

46. "Appreciative" categories presuppose a judging subject who expresses a preference; "constative" categories imply the simple recognition of a quality.

47. In other words, any predicate of an object that is a predicate of value consists of an adjective. The adjective is the result of a combination of semantic traits, whose totality is governed by categories, by their logical articulation into stages, by the intersection of different categories, and by interaction with other semantic traits that belong to the context in which the adjective is placed. The linguistic and logical source for a formulation of this type is obvious. We need only remember that Algirdas J. Greimas's *Sémantique structurale* (Paris: Larousse, 1966) operates in a similar fashion.

48. "Isomorphism" indicates an analogy at a deep formal level between objects belonging to different systems. In linguistics, we speak of "isomorphism" when structures are identical at the level of expression and of content. See Luis Hjelmslev, *Omkring sprogteoriens grundlaeggelse* (Copenhagen: Ejnar Munksgaard, 1943). Michel Serres has used a similar concept, that of "isomorphy," in order to describe morphological analogies between objects that have apparently differing forms. (See Michel Serres, *Esthétiques sur Carpaccio* [Paris: Hermann, 1975].)

49. It is possible, in fact, to interpret the articulation of a category from both a semantic viewpoint (value as a meaning attributed to an object) and a syntactical one (value as the *position* of a term in relation to others). See, for example, Claude Zilberberg, *Les modalités tensives* (Brussels: Benjamin, 1979).

50. The transformation of "a common sense of decency" is a typical example. Although it is true that "decency" is a common social trait, the facts that characterize it change according to the way in which society valorizes them.

CHAPTER 2
RHYTHM AND REPETITION

1. This is Benedetto Croce's well-known aesthetic position, as expressed in *Estetica come scienza dell'espressione e linguistica generale* (Bari: Laterza, 1928). Even though Croce's idealism has been super-

seded in modern times, some traces can still be found in contemporary criticism. Even in the semiotics of art it is generally admitted that the verbal description of a work of art does not "express" the work, and that there is a difference between what is "visible" and "sayable" in it. See Louis Marin et al., "La description de l'image," *Communications* 15 (1970). But the caution of semiologists has given rise to wrong interpretations and controversy concerning the very legitimacy of semiotic studies of art and literature, involving the "dusting-off" of quarrels last heard during the 1960s. See Alberto Berardinelli, *Il mestiere di critico* (Milan: Il Saggiatore, 1983); Franco Brioschi, *La carta dell'impero* (Milan: Il saggiatore, 1983); Donald Shattuck, "L'interpretazione letteraria," *Comunita* 2 (1982).

2. For a clearer picture of standardization, one need only read Henry Ford's *La mia vita* (Bologna, 1925) (scattered essays collected only in an Italian edition). A penetrating commentary can be found in Mario Tronti's *Operai e Capitale* (Turin: Einaudi, 1973). The classical texts dealing with intellectual standardization are Edgar Morin, *Le loisir* (Paris: Seuil, 1962), and Jean Baudrillard, *Le système des objets* (Paris: Gallimard, 1968). More recently: Alberto Abruzzese, *Sociologia del lavoro intellettuale* (Venice: Marsilio, 1980); Omar Calabrese, *Le comunicazioni di massa fra informazione e organizzazione del consenso*, in Nicola Tranfaglia, ed., *La storia* (Turin: Utet).

3. For a brief examination of the notions of "uniqueness" and "variation" in a scientific sense see Fernando Gil, in *Enciclopedia* (Turin: Einaudi, 1979), vol. 6 (under *identità* and *differenza*). In a philosophical sense see Gilles Deleuze, *Différence et répétition* (Paris: Presses Universitaires de France, 1968). A scheme of reference that helps us to understand the crisis of this notion can be found in Maurizio Ferraris, *Differenze* (Milan: Multhipla, 1982). See also Claude Lévi-Strauss, ed., *L'identité* (Paris: Presses Universitaires de France, 1977).

4. Using different terminology, but with the same content, see Fausto Colombo, "Déjà vu," in Francesco Casetti, ed., *Un'altra volta ancora* (Rome: Eri, 1984).

5. See Stefan Amsterdamski, "Ripetizione," in *Enciclopedia* (Turin: Einaudi, 1980), vol. 12; Fernando Gil, "Classificazione," in ibid., vol. 2.

6. Emile Benveniste, *Problèmes de linguistique générale* (Paris: Gallimard, 1966).

7. My definition of rhythm in a musical sense is taken from Gino

Barratta, "Ritmo," in *Enciclopedia* (Turin: Einaudi, 1981), vol. 12; Jean-Jacques Nattiez, "Ritmo/Metro," in ibid. The notion of rhythm has, in any case, been studied at length in linguistics and semiotics. See, for example: Henri Meschonnic, *Le rythme* (Paris: Klincksieck, 1980); Meschonnic et al., *Le rythme* (Albi: Colloque d'Albi, 1983); Marco Jacquemet, *Materiels pour une définition du rythme* (Albi: Colloque d'Albi, 1983); Ivan Faragy, *La ripetizione creativa* (Bari: Dedalo, 1982).

8. See the formal analyses of Focillon, *La vie des formes*; Wölfflin, *Kunstgeschichtliche Grundbegriffe*, and, more recently, George Kubler, *The Shape of Time* (New Haven: Yale University Press, 1967).

9. This has been emphasized well by Jean Petitot in "Sémiotique et théorie des catastrophes," *Actes sémiotiques (Documents)* 47–48 (1983).

10. Umberto Eco, *Trattato di semiotica generale* (Milan: Bompiani, 1975).

11. Umberto Eco, *La struttura assente* (Milan: Bompiani, 1969).

12. Semiologists will recognize in the generic terminology adopted here some concepts that correspond to more precise semiotic notions. When I speak of thematic level and surface narrative structures I allude to Greimas's theory of "generative paths," according to which each manifestation presents a discursive surface, under which lie superficial semionarrative structures and, beneath these, deep structures. Furthermore, each level is constituted by a syntactic and semantic component. Thematization belongs to the semantic component of the discursive level. See Algirdas J. Greimas and Joseph Courtés, *Sémiotique: Dictionnaire raisonné de la théorie du langage* (Paris: Hachette, 1979); Joseph Courtés, *Introduction à la sémiotique narrative et discoursive* (Paris: Hachette, 1977). I shall refer later to the static and dynamic aspect of structures. I am in fact hiding behind this implicitly vague terminology a reference to the concept of a "dynamic of systems," such as that proposed by René Thom, *Stabilité structurelle et morphogénèse* (Paris: Denöel-Gonthier, 1978).

13. Sarduy, *Barroco*, pp. 41–45.

14. Ernst Cassirer, *Philosophie der symbolischen Formen* (Oxford: Cassirer, 1923); Northrop Frye, *Anatomy of Criticism* (Princeton: Princeton University Press, 1957).

15. Mikhail Bakhtin, *Estetica e romanzo* (Turin: Einaudi, 1979). The "crarotype" of modern aesthetics might be *frenzy*, as René Payant suggests in "La frénésie de l'image: Vers une esthétique de la vidéo," *Revue d'Esthétique* 10 (1986).

16. I have already expressed the convention that an awareness of the need to rewrite the fantastic originated in the nineteenth century, in *Garibaldi* (Milan: Electa, 1982). I pointed out that certain "places" in the action of the novel (and also in the "real" action of life) necessarily became encyclopedic "places," set scenes, with the ability to establish a kind of enunciative contract with the reader by constructing a system of narrative expectations.

17. Eco makes explicit mention of this in his "Postille al Nome della rosa," *Alfabeta* 49 (1983). Even though he does not use the term "neo-baroque," and gives no more than a knowing nod to literary expressions of "postmodern aesthetics," he seems to have advanced a considerable way along the path indicated here. See also Daniel Arasse et al., *L'imitation: aliénation ou source de liberté?* (Paris: La documentation francaise, 1984); Jacques Ruffié et al., "Répétition et variation," *Corps écrit* 15 (1985); René Passeron, ed., *Création et répétition* (Paris: Clancier-Guenaud, 1982).

18. Gaston Bachelard, *La poétique de l'espace* (Paris: Seuil, 1962).

Chapter 3
Limit and Excess

1. Iuri Lotman, *La semiosfera* (Venice: Marsilio, 1985).

2. Ibid., pp. 58–63.

3. Rudolph Arnheim, *The Power of the Center* (Berkeley and Los Angeles: University of California Press, 1982).

4. Nicholas Bourbaki, *Elements d'histoire des mathématiques* (Paris: Hermann, 1960).

5. See Jurgis Baltrusaitis, *Anamorphoses* (Paris: Seuil, 1972).

6. See Omar Calabrese, *La macchina della pittura* (Rome-Bari: Laterza, 1985).

7. In other words, the entire history of adventure stories, up to their finest hour, Haggard's *King Solomon's Mines*.

8. Lotman, *La semiosfera*, p. 62.

9. See Lucio Lombardo Radice and Lina Mancini Proia, *Il metodo matematico* (Milan: Principato, 1979), pp. 68–94.

10. Honoré de Balzac, *Théorie de la démarche* (Paris: Gallimard, 1978).

11. Francesco Alberoni et al., *Psicologia del vestire* (Milan: Bompiani, 1972).

12. See Lévi-Strauss, *L'identité*.

13. In 1984 the magazine *Panorama Mese* devoted an entire issue to the notion of gratuitous risk as life-style. In the cases examined by the magazine, risk was transformed into an aesthetic of behavior: pure *depense*.

14. Lotman, *La semiosfera*, p. 59.

15. I have preferred to describe the notions of "limit," "eccentricity," and "excess" in spatial terms, and only by means of a group of isolated lemmas. This is not really correct. In the first place because, according to the techniques used elsewhere in this work, terms are chosen because they can be interdefined by means of oppositions. In the second place because, alongside spatiality (in Greimas's terms, one of the moments of *aspectualization*, along with temporality) there exists the problem of *quantification* (when excess, for example, is opposed to insufficiency or defect in expressions such as "too much," "too little," "a little," "a lot," "not at all," and so on). François Bastide, "Les logiques de l'excés et de l'insuffisance," *Actes sémiotiques (Documents)* 79–80 (1986), has examined this semantic area in terms of quantification and aspectualization, and readers are directed to his essay for an excellent discussion of the problem. A complementary issue not touched on by Bastide is that of the topological aspect of the question, and of the lemmas that express it.

16. Rosencranz, *Aesthetik des Hässlichen*, has recently been the object of studies of aesthetics, for example at Palermo's Centro internazionale di estetica, where the Italian translation was made in 1984.

17. Gigantism has recently been studied in a special issue of the journal *Communications* (n. 42, 1984), proving that practices and theories are frequently subject to the same taste and spirit of the time.

18. A monographic issue of the journal *Traverses* (n. 37, 1984) has examined the fin de siècle.

CHAPTER 4
DETAIL AND FRAGMENT

1. See Fernando Gil and Jean Petitot, "Uno/molti," in *Enciclopedia* (Turin: Einaudi, 1982), vol. 14.

2. I mean by "enunciation" that simulacrum of communication that appears in a text, initially as a relation between work and reader (or between "author" and "reader"), and secondly as any kind of communicative relation (e.g., a dialogue in a story is an enunciated enun-

ciation). On the theory of enunciation see Benveniste, *Problèmes*; Greimas, *Sémiotique*; and Oswald Ducrot, "Enunciazione," in *Enciclopedia* (Turin: Einaudi, 1979), vol. 3, and, by the same author, *Dire et ne pas dire* (Paris: Hermann, 1972).

3. See Chapter 6.

4. That is, when an apparently fragmentary work is presented as though it were a whole. In this case its reference points are missing and the "fragment" presupposes nothing beyond itself, recalling its purely phenomenological state.

5. See Giovanni Careri, "Il dettaglio patetico," *Metafore* 1 (1986), in which the author shows how details of a painting can become autonomous works. But this depends on the nature of the analysis. It is based, in fact, on the presupposition that the part shown says "more" about the system to which it belongs simply because both detail and whole share at every point the same "sense."

6. Omar Calabrese, *Il linguaggio dell'arte* (Milan: Bompiani, 1985).

7. I mean by "abduction" the choice of a hypothesis that can help to explain empirical facts; proof based on these facts is then transformed into a law. See Eco, *Trattato*; Charles Sanders Peirce, *Collected Papers* (Cambridge: Harvard University Press, 1931–1936).

8. Umberto Eco and Thomas Sebeok, eds., *Il segno dei tre* (Milan: Bompiani, 1985).

9. Carlo Ginzburg, "Spie," in Aldo Gargani, ed., *Crisi della ragione* (Turin: Einaudi, 1979); now also in Carlo Ginzburg, *Miti, emblemi, spie* (Turin: Einaudi, 1986).

10. Sigmund Freud, *Die Traumdeutung*, 1915.

11. The work, in short, is read fragmentarily, as though it were being observed from a partial, singular, and local hypothetical point. Its production and consumption are subject to chance. This, effectively, is the theory of Anne Cauquelin, *Court traité du fragment* (Paris: Aubier, 1986).

12. For an overview of the historical school deriving from the group of the journal *Annales*, see, among others, Georges Duby, *Le rêve de l'histoire* (Paris, 1983).

13. For a less superficial examination of problems relating to singularity, see Thom, *Stabilité*. Some of the problems that have been considered here in a metaphorical sense can be traced back to problems surrounding the generic/nongeneric. In geometry a "nongeneric

point" is a point that changes its internal order if subjected to the slightest disturbance, whereas a "generic point" does not change the form of a configuration even when subjected to more substantial disturbance. See the marginal note to Thomas Martone by Jean Petitot in Omar Calabrese, ed., *Piero teorico dell'arte* (Rome: Gangemi, 1986).

14. For the notion of "semiotic square" see Chapter 1, note 45.

15. On this theme see Tzvetan Todorov, *I formalisti russi* (Turin: Einaudi, 1964); Victor Shklovsky, *Teoria della prosa* (Turin: Einaudi, 1980); and Roman Jakobson, *Saggi di linguistica generale* (Milan: Feltrinelli, 1966).

16. John Summerson, *The Classical Language of Architecture* (London: Methuen & Co., 1963); Bruno Zevi, *Il linguaggio moderno dell'architettura* (Turin: Einaudi, 1973).

17. The idea of the pure conception of an architectonic language as deviation has been debated in a special edition of the journal *Casabella* (n. 430, 1978) devoted to architecture as language.

18. See on this theme Umberto Eco et al., "Semiotica della ricezione," *Carte semiotiche* 2 (1986); and, naturally, Hans Robert Jauss, *Pour une esthétique de la reception* (Paris: Gallimard, 1978).

19. Maurizio Calvesi, *Arte allo specchio* (Milan: Electa, 1984).

20. Roland Barthes, *Fragments d'un discours amoureux* (Paris: Seuil, 1979); *Barthes par lui même* (Paris: Seuil, 1977).

CHAPTER 5
INSTABILITY AND METAMORPHOSIS

1. Gilbert Lascault, *Le monstre dans l'art occidentale* (Paris: Klincksieck, 1976).

2. This citation is secondhand. I have taken it from Blanché, *Les catégories*.

3. See Corrado Bologna, "Mostro," in *Enciclopedia* (Turin: Einaudi, 1980), vol. 9.

4. There is no criterion behind choosing this rather than other categories, apart from the fact that ethics, beauty, form, and emotion are more or less, according to contemporary common sense, sufficiently homogeneous parameters when judging phenomena. It would have been possible to add the category "truth" and the situation would have been more or less identical; but judgments of truth are more

complicated than of the other four categories, which more clearly correspond to one another.

5. See also Omar Calabrese, "Zelig l'uomo nessuno," *Panorama mese* 14 (1983).

6. Renato Giovannoli, "La sintassi dell'alieno," in *La scienza della fantascienza* (Rome: Espresso Strumenti, 1983).

7. The mechanics behind the spatial construction of the spectator are obviously more complicated, and I am simplifying a much more articulated and profound observation made by Francesco Casetti, *Dietro lo sguardo* (Milan: Bompiani, 1986).

8. Out-of-field does not operate as "something that isn't there" but as something implicit. To understand how the implicit works, see Ducrot, *Dire et ne pas dire*, and Catherine Kerbrat-Orecchioni, *L'implicite* (Paris: Colin, 1985). For the functioning of the visual implicit, see Francesco Casetti, "I bordi dell'immagine," *Versus* 29 (1981), later reelaborated in *Dentro lo sguardo*.

9. It has often been noticed that heroic video games are very "Japanese" precisely because the player has to assume the position of a technologically revamped samurai, a solitary warrior against a universe of foes. This is why, despite possessing a "cycle" of successive frames, heroic video games never allow the player to complete the circle, since the speed of the "enemies" constantly increases. Further material on this subject can be found in a series of "reviews" of video games that I wrote with Renato Giovannoli in *Linus*, 1980. See also Alberto Abruzzese et al., *Videogames: storia e struttura* (Rome: Basaia Editore, 1982).

10. Italo Calvino, *Se una notte d'inverno un viaggiatore* (Turin: Einaudi, 1979); Umberto Eco, *Il nome della rosa* (Milan: Bompiani, 1981); Gore Vidal, *Duluth* (London: Heinemann, 1983).

11. Carlo Ossola, "'La rosa profunda': Metamorfosi e variazioni sul *Nome della rosa*," in Giuseppe Barbieri and Paolo Vidali, eds., *Metamorfosi: Dalla verità al senso della verità* (Rome-Bari: Laterza, 1986).

12. As can be seen from Italo Calvino, "Comment j'ai écrit un de mes livres," *Actes sémiotiques (Documents)* 51 (1984).

13. On the theme of performance, see Lea Vergine, *Il corpo come linguaggio* (Milan: Prearo, 1974); and Renato Barilli, *Informale, oggetto, comportamento* (Milan: Feltrinelli, 1979).

14. Sterling's case is emblematic: the modern art section is on only

two floors, with a connecting elevator. The elevator would normally be used by people moving heavy weights or by those who are unable to walk up the stairs. But in this case the elevator is so "artistic," so similar to a "celibate machine," that museum visitors gather around it. The elevator acquires an aesthetic as well as a functional role, with people tending to use it obsessively.

15. See John L. Cloudsley-Thompson's excellent book, *Tooth and Claw: Defensive Strategies in the Animal World* (London: Dent & Sons, 1980).

16. Sarduy, *Barrocco*.

17. Eco has expressed this concept by using the technical term "encyclopedia." In this sense the term describes a model of competence realized at a given historical moment, which the dictionary (a model of the ideal competence of an ideal speaker) cannot explain in any way. Eco, *Trattato*, p. 43.

18. I refer to the by now classical debate between the descriptive and explicative functions of scientific models. In "catastrophe theory" this discussion has been resumed in a variety of positions. René Thom, for example, is in favor of a descriptive function, whereas Jean Petitot insists that the novelty of the theory lies in its ability to explain phenomena.

19. The thesis is this: whereas the scientific model for the description/explanation of phenomena is often completely extrinsic to the phenomena themselves (e.g., statistics has nothing to do with the behavior of voters, whose average it calculates), the catastrophic model is *immanent* to phenomena, in the sense that catastrophic geometries *are* the geometries of those phenomena. But this means that this type of model can be applied not only to phenomena but also to itself. See Giulio Giorello, "Thom e la nozione di spiegazione, ovvero cosa i filosofi della scienza possono imparare dalla teoria delle catastrofi," *Prometheus* 1 (1985).

20. I am applying here one of the seven elementary catastrophes, the so-called cusp catastrophe, the second in terms of complexity, which can be represented in a three-dimensional space. Naturally there are more complex catastrophes requiring more dimensions. See Thom, *Stabilité*.

21. Thom refers explicitly to these in *Stabilité* when discussing the work of artists like Escher and Magritte. See also Omar Calabrese and

Renato Giovannoli, "Geometrie della paura," *Alfabeta* 43 (1982); Omar Calabrese, "Catastrofi e teoria dell'arte," *Lectures* 15 (1984).

22. Apart from the texts cited above, see Tito Tonietti, *Catastrofi* (Bari: Dedalo, 1983); and Piero Meldini, ed., *Katastrofe'* (Bologna: Cappelli, 1984).

23. Cloudsley-Thompson, *Tooth and Claw*, chaps. 1–4.

24. Desmond Morris, *Manwatching: A Field Guide to Human Behavior* (London: Elsevier, 1977).

CHAPTER 6
DISORDER AND CHAOS

1. Giorgio Careri, *Ordine e disordine nella materia* (Rome-Bari: Laterza, 1983).

2. Benoit Mandelbrot, *Les objets fractals* (Paris: Flammarion, 1977); by the same author, "Des monstres de Cantor et de Peano à la géomètrie fractale de la nature," in François Guénard and Gilbert Lelièvre, eds., *Penser les mathématiques* (Paris: Seuil, 1982).

3. Ilya Prigogine and Isabelle Stenghers, *La nouvelle alliance* (Paris: Gallimard, 1979).

4. Reinhardt Breuer, "Das Chaos," *Geo* 7 (1985); Heinz G. Schuster, *Deterministic Chaos: An Introduction* (Weinheim: Physik Verlag, 1982); Robert May, "Simple Mathematical Models with Very Complicated Dynamics," *Nature* 21 (1976); James Crutchfield et al., "Il caos," *Le Scienze* 222 (1987).

5. This well-chosen phrase was the name given to the proceedings of a seminar, *La sfida della complessita* (Milan: Feltrinelli, 1985). Luhmann's theories, rather than "grading" complexity, are oriented toward the problem of reducing it, sometimes drastically. See Niklas Luhmann, *Gesellschaft und Semantik* (Frankfurt: Suhrkamp, 1980).

6. For an overview of these themes, see Ferraris, *La svolta testuale*; and Pier Aldo Rovatti and Gianni Vattimo, eds., *Il pensiero debole* (Milan: Feltrinelli, 1983).

7. The analogy consists in the first place in identifying the phenomenon of complexity, and in conceiving it as the product of instability, polydimensionality, and conflict. The difference lies in (a) the existence of privileged models for the extension of all forms of complexity (for Prigogine the physical thermodynamic model, for Thom

a mathematical model, for Mandelbrot a geometrical model, and so on); (b) a privileged level of articulation for the analysis of phenomena (Thom examines deep structure, Mandelbrot surface structure, Prigogine the systematic aspect that provokes the phenomenon).

8. Mandelbrot, *Les objets fractals*, p. 9.

9. Ibid., p. 7.

10. Mandelbrot, in fact, has "invented" nothing. He has, however, proposed a reformulation of certain preexistent mathematical problems as a model for the construction of an *ad hoc* mathematics for certain real phenomena.

11. Reproduced in Jacques Cavaillès, *Philosophie mathématique* (Paris: Hermann, 1962).

12. For Peano the phenomenon was the famous "curve" that fills a plane. Peano describes the paradoxical case of a series of polygons that fill a square so densely that their perimeter touches every point of the square. Von Koch also constructed a "monstrous" curve by inserting an aleatory datum into the function of the curve. In simpler terms, Koch's curve is a closed curve that resembles a snowflake or an island with a jagged coastline.

13. Some examples: in meteorology, the American scientist Edward Lorenz of the Massachusetts Institute of Technology has been studying atmospheric turbulence mechanisms since the 1960s. He has reached the conclusion that although turbulence is unpredictable and chaotic, it follows a "certain method"; the transitional phase leading to chaos is created by the fact that, unlike systems directed toward stable or fixed states, the atmospheric system is too complex to be "attracted" to specific points; Lorenz has thus hypothesized the existence of a "bizarre attractor"; in aeronautical engineering, designers exploit this principle in order to simulate certain paradoxes, such as "unstable vortices." A vortex is, in fact, an extremely regular form that can, however, become irregular in the atmosphere, as jet pilots know: the design of wings and hulls must therefore take into account the sudden transition from regular to chaotic states. In ethology, Robert May of Princeton University has studied sudden changes in the population density of certain insects in the presence of control parameters based on food quantities and present population size by means of "transition chaos thresholds." In medicine, a physicist from the Massachussetts Institute of Technology, Richard Cohen, has been able to explain the apparent chaos of cardiac fibrillation, by means of a com-

puter simulation of a large number of disturbances that cause the phenomenon. Other physicists and mathematicians, such as the American Mitchell Feigenbaum at Los Alamos and the Italian Valter Franceschini, have discovered a series of numerical thresholds that constitute the equations for the transition to chaos. In mathematics, an American, Joseph Ford of Atlanta University, a Russian, Boris Chirikov, and an Italian, Giulio Casati, have set up interdisciplinary research programs at Como, where two important conferences dealing with the theme were held in 1977 and 1983. Although not all applications make use of the theory of fractals, the discovery of the "laws of chaos" has confirmed to some extent the extendable nature of the mathematical notion reelaborated by Mandelbrot. See, among others, May, "Simple Mathematical Models."

14. Heinz-Otto Peitgen and Peter Hans Richter, eds., *The Beauty of Fractals* (Berlin: Springer, 1986).

15. Herbert Marcuse, *One-Dimensional Man* (Boston: Beacon Press, 1964).

16. See Breuer, "Das Chaos."

17. See Franke's text in Peitgen and Richter, *The Beauty of Fractals*, and the work of Devaney, a mathematician at Boston University, in Gary Taubes, "C'é troppo caos, facciamo ordine," *Genius* 2 (1984).

18. For example, a young American mathematician, Peter Oppenheimer, nephew of the famous physicist Robert, has begun to produce fractal works that are used as a mixed form between art and decoration. Oppenheimer has produced, for example, a gigantic fractal video clip for New York's most luxurious discotheque, the Palladium.

19. On the theme see *Vidéo-Vidéo*, a special number of *Revue d'Esthétique* 10 (1986) and, in particular, the article by Robert Allezaud, "Images primaires, images fractales."

20. See, among others, Alberto Abruzzese, *La grande scimmia* (Rome: Napoleone, 1979). Gillo Dorfles's recent *Elogio della disarmonia* (Milan: Garzanti, 1986), uses a different language to discuss the same theme, without restricting itself to consumption.

Chapter 7
The Knot and the Labyrinth

1. Jorge Luis Borges, *El Aleph* (Buenos Aires: Editorial Losada, 1952).

2. Pierre Rosenstiehl, "Labirinto," in *Enciclopedia* (Turin: Einaudi, 1979), vol. 8. See also Jearl Walker, "Expériences d'amateur," *Science* 112 (1987).

3. Paolo Santarcangeli, *Il libro dei labirinti* (Milan: Frassinelli, 1984); Hermann Kern, *Labirinti* (Milan: Feltrinelli, 1981).

4. Suzanne Allen, "Petit traité du noeud," in Jean-Marie Benoist, *Figures du baroque* (Paris: Presses Universitaires de France, 1983) (but only the proceedings of the 1976 Cerisy conference). See also Pierre Rosenstiehl, "I nodi immateriali," *Materiali filosofici* 1 (1983).

5. See Rosenstiehl, "I nodi immateriali"; and Georges Perec, *Espèces d'espaces* (Paris: Denoël-Gonthier, 1974).

6. Kern, *Labirinti*, p. 9.

7. See Omar Calabrese, "Il linguaggio del cinema," *Prometeo* 16 (1986).

8. Achille Bonito-Oliva, *Luoghi del silenzio imparziale* (Milan: Feltrinelli, 1981).

9. Hermann Kern, "Labyrinths: Tradition and Contemporary Works," *Artforum* 9 (1981).

10. Ibid., p. 251.

11. Roland Barthes and Saul Steinberg, *All Except You* (Paris: Repère Editions d'Art, 1983).

12. Omar Calabrese, Pierluigi Cerri, Renato Giovannoli, and Isabella Pezzini, *Hic sunt leones* (Milan: Electa, 1983).

13. This is even made explicit, at least if we look at the structure of the entries in volume 16, *Sistema*, which is designed to reveal the thematic "paths" within the work. Einaudi also organized a seminar specifically to discuss the gridlike "form" of the encyclopedia, later published as *Il sapere come rete di modelli*.

14. The following entries, in particular, relate to the conference: Fernando Gil, "Sistematica," vol. 12 (1981); Fernando Gil and Jean Petitot, "Uno/molti," vol. 14 (1982); Giulio Giorello, "Modello," vol. 9 (1980); Pierre Rosenstiehl, "Rete," vol. 11 (1980).

15. I reprint a passage by Vidal in its entirety, which clearly reveals the author's awareness of this principle, suggesting a familiarity with Eco and his theories of narration: "Like most absolute laws, the fictive law of absolute uniqueness is relative. Although each character in any fiction—as in any life or nonfiction—is absolutely unique (even if you cannot tell one character from the other), the actual truth of the matter is more complex.

"When a fictive character dies or drops out of a narrative, he will then—promptly—reappear in a new narrative, as there are just so many characters—and plots—available at any given time. Contrary to the relative fictive law of absolute uniqueness is the *simultaneity effect*, which is to fiction what Miriam Heisenberg's law is to physics. It means that any character can appear, simultaneously, in as many fictions as the random may require. This corollary is unsettling and need not concern us other than to note, in passing, that each reader, like each writer, is, from different angles and at different times, in a finite number of different narratives where he is always the same yet always different. We call this *après* poststructuralism. The many studies that are currently being made of the *simultaneity effect* vividly demonstrate—as if demonstration were necessary!—that although the English language may decline and dwindle, English studies are more complex and rewarding than ever.

"The law of absolute uniqueness requires—except in those cases where it does not—the total loss of memory on the part of the character who has died or made only a brief appearance in a fictive narrative. Naturally, when the writing of the book is finished, all the characters who are alive at the end are available to other writers for reentries, as it were. Sometimes this is called plagiarism, but that is a harsh word when one considers how very little there is in the way of character and plot to go around. Ultimately, plagiarism is simply——in the words of Rosemary Klein Kantor herself—*creation by other means*.

"The characters that are in any given book—though abandoned by their author when he writes *finis* to his *opus*—will still continue to go through their paces for anyone who happens to read the book. Hence the proof—or a proof—of the *simultaneity effect*. Once this particular true fiction or fictive truth is concluded by the present author . . . [the characters] . . . will drift off to new assignments, unknown to them or him. They will forget him. He will not recognize them—except in those cases of outright plagiarism when civil law will scrutinize the truth of a fictive text with a thoroughness unknown even at busy Yale." Vidal, *Duluth*, pp. 20–21.

16. Robert Sheckley, "The Emperor of the Last Days."

17. See Rosenstiehl, "Labirinto," and "Labirinti," in Paolo Fabbri and Isabella Pezzini, eds., *Mitologie di Roland Barthes* (Parma: Pratiche, 1986).

18. Borges, *El Aleph*, p. 86.

19. On the relation between labyrinth and enigma see, once again, Rosenstiehl, "Rete," and Kern, "Labyrinth."

20. Gilles Deleuze and Felix Guattari, *Rhizôme* (Paris: Minuit, 1976); and also Gilles Deleuze and Félix Guattari, eds., *Nomades et vagabonds* (Paris: Christian Bourgois, 1976).

21. Jacques-Louis Binet, ed., *La création vagabonde* (Paris: Hermann, 1986).

22. Gregory Bateson, "A Theory of Play and Phantasy," *Psychiatric Research Report* 2 (1955).

23. Rosenstiehl, *I nodi immateriali*.

CHAPTER 8
COMPLEXITY AND DISSIPATION

1. Prigogine and Stenghers, *La nouvelle alliance*.

2. Ibid., pp. 109–33.

3. Ibid., p. 175. The debate surrounding the image of complexity and its transference to social systems has become even broader recently. See, for example, the proceedings of the Montpellier conference, *Science et pratique de la complexité*, 1984, with contributions from, among others, Edgar Morin, Niklas Luhmann, Ilya Prigogine, Henri Laborit, the fourth part of which was devoted to social problems: complex human systems, management, spontaneous social orders, democracy and government, and political forecasting; and the analogous conference *La sfida della complessità*.

4. Michel Baudson, ed., *L'art et le temps* (Brussels: Societe des Expositions de Palais des Beaux-Arts, 1984). The catalog contains an essay by Ilya Prigogine and Serge Pahaut called "Redécouvrir le temps."

5. Prigogine and Pahaut, "Redécouvrir le temps," p. 24. See directly Henri Bergson *Life and Consciousness*, Huxley Memorial Lecture, London, 1911; reprinted in the centenary volume *Oeuvres* (Paris: Presses Universitaires de France, 1970).

6. Gérard Genette and Tzvetan Todorov, eds., *Théories des Genres* (Paris: Seuil, 1986); Tzvetan Todorov, *Les Genres du discours* (Paris: Seuil, 1978); Maria Corti, *Principi della comunicazione letteraria* (Milan: Bompiani, 1972); Cesare Segre, "Generi," in *Enciclopedia* (Turin: Einaudi, 1979), vol. 6; Gianfranco Bettetini et al., *Contributi bibliografici ad un progetto di ricerca sui generi televisivi*, special issue of *Appunto del Servizio Opinioni*, no. 299, Rai, Rome, 1977.

7. Rudolph Arnheim, *Entropy and Art* (Berkeley: The Regents of the University of California, 1971); Abraham Moles, *Théorie de l'information et perception esthétique* (Paris: Flammarion, 1958); Umberto Eco, ed., *Estetica e teoria dell'informazione* (Milan: Bompiani, 1972); Ugo Volli, ed., *La scienza e l'arte* (Milan: Mazzotta, 1972); Umberto Eco, *La struttura assente* (Milan: Bompiani, 1968); for the mathematical aspect of information theory see C. E. Shannon and W. Weaver, *The Mathematical Theory of Communication* (Urbana: University of Illinois Press, 1949), and Colin Cherry, *On Human Communication* (New York: Wiley, 1961); for the physical aspect of entropy see Prigogine and Stenghers, *La nouvelle alliance*.

8. For an examination of parody as a fluctuation in the citation system see Antoine Compagnon, *La seconde main* (Paris: Seuil, 1979).

9. Lyotard, *La condition postmoderne*; see also his reflections in *Le postmoderne* and the comment by Tomàs Maldonado, *Il futuro della modernità* (Milan: Feltrinelli, 1987).

10. On this Phenomenon see Umberto Eco, *Lector in fabula* (Milan: Bompiani, 1979); "Postille al nome della rosa," *Alfabeta* 49 (1983); "Appunti sulla semiotica della ricezione," *Carte semiotiche* 2 (1986).

11. See Chapter 6, note 19.

12. Moles, *Théorie de l'information*; Max Bense, *Aesthetik* (Baden-Baden: Agis Verlag, 1965).

13. This shares the same basic matrix as the theory of "deviation from the norm", created by the Russian formalists and later expounded in many aesthetic theories based on notions of information and structure. See Umberto Eco, *Opera aperta* (Milan: Bompiani, 1962); by the same author, *La definizione dell'arte* (Milan: Mursia, 1968).

CHAPTER 9
THE APPROXIMATE AND THE INEXPRESSIBLE

1. Georges Guilbaud, *Leçons d'à-peu-près* (Paris: Christian Bourgois, 1986).

2. We use it in everyday life, when we make an appointment, for example, "between eight and ten past eight."

3. This criterion consists in stopping at a sufficient quantity, and defining the approximation; for example, halting division at a certain number after the decimal point.

4. For example, when we try to define the apparent age of a person who "must be between thirty and thirty-five."

5. Alexandre Koyré, *Etudes d'histoire de la pensée philosophique* (Paris: Max Leclerc & C. 1961).

6. Centro Internazionale di Semiotica e Lingoistica *Il pressapoco*. The conference included papers by, among others, Eco, Fabbri, Le Goff, Marin, Petitot, Rosenstiehl, and Desclés.

7. Vladimir Jankélévitch, *Le Je-ne-sais-quoi et le Presque-rien* (Paris: Seuil, 1980); and *Philosophie premiere: introduction à une philosophie du "Presque"* (Paris: Presses Universitaires de France, 1960).

8. Jankélévitch, *Le Je-ne-sais-quoi*, p. 11.

9. Jankélévitch himself has used this term to describe his philosophy, since it is based on reflections upon "modalities" (to want, to have to, to be able to, to know, to be, to do).

10. Guido Almansi and Guido Fink, *Quasi come* (Milan: Bompiani, 1976).

11. Or: the grammatical expression of the subject ("I"), his temporal expression ("here"), and his spatial expression ("now"). For a complex vision of the problems associated with the subject in discourse see Jean-Claude Coquet, *Le discours et son sujet* (Paris: Klincksieck, 1985).

12. Traces of this can be found in the theories of Achille Bonito Oliva. See, for example, *Manuale di volo* (Milan: Feltrinelli, 1982).

13. Renè Thom, "I contorni in pittura," *Alfabeta* 44 (1981).

14. Jordi Prat, Nora Rizzi, Patrizia Violi, and Mauro Wolf, "La ripresa diretta," *Dati per la verifica dei programmi trasmessi* 52 (1984).

15. For an overview of contemporary art see Renato Barilli, *L'arte contemporanea* (Milan: Feltrinelli, 1984).

16. Raymond Queneau, *Esercizi di stile* (Turin: Einaudi, 1984).

17. Anthony Burgess, *Un'arancia a orologeria* (Turin: Einaudi, 1972).

18. James Joyce, *Finnegan's Wake* (Milan: Mondadori, 1982).

19. Torquato Accetto, *Della dissimulazione onesta* (Genoa: Costa & Nolan, 1984).

20. Carlo Ossola, "Elogio del Nulla," in Gigliola Nocera, ed., *Il segno barocco* (Rome: Bulzoni, 1983).

21. Buci-Glucksmann, *La folie du voir*.

22. Jean-François Lyotard, *Les immaterieux* (Paris: Centre Pompidou, 1984); Jean Baudrillard, *Amérique* (Paris, 1986).

CHAPTER 10
DISTORTION AND PERVERSION

1. See, for example, the lengthy debate in *Alfabeta* dating from 1983 in which, alongside a strictly philosophical dimension, this type of interpretation was clearly being made by art and literary critics.

2. Practically nothing exists on the theme of visual citation, apart from Renato Barilli's reflections on Lichtenstein the "citationist" in *Informale, oggetto, comportamento* (Milan: Feltrinelli, 1976); on "absence" as a way of resuming the past in *Fra presenza e assenza* (Milan: Bompiani, 1974); and on literary citation in *L'azione e l'estasi* (Milan: Feltrinelli, 1967).

3. On the same theme see the schema of Compagnon, *La seconde main*. His schema, however, is used for a more complicated procedure involving a theoretical "mixture" of Greimas's and Peirce's semiotics.

4. According to Algirdas J. Greimas and Joseph Courtés, *Sémiotique: Dictionnaire raisonné de la théorie du langage* (Paris: Hachette, 1979), epistemic modalities are the expression and expansion of the modal categories *to believe* or *to know that one is*, which give rise to belief and truthfulness.

5. Umberto Eco, *Il nome della rosa*, p. 12.

6. Umberto Eco, "Il cane e il cavallo: un testo visivo e alcuni equivoci verbali," *Versus* 25 (1980).

7. Nikolaus Himmelmann, *Utopia del passato* (Bari: De Donato, 1981).

8. Omar Calabrese, ed., "L'Etrusco immaginario," in Franco Borsi, ed., *Fortuna degli Etruschi* (Milan: Electa, 1985).

9. Calvesi, ed., *Arte allo specchio*.

10. See, for example, the articles in *Politique fin-de-siècle*, a special issue of *Traverses*, 33–34 (1985).

CHAPTER 11
SOME LIKE IT CLASSICAL

1. See Wölfflin himself, *Kunstgeschichtliche Grundbegriffe*.

2. Francis Haskell and Nicholas Penny, *Taste and the Antique* (New Haven: Yale University Press, 1981).

3. Kenneth Clark, *The Nude* (Washington, D.C.: National Gallery, 1953).

4. On myths of origin see Charles Morazé, "Saint Georges, une expérience allégorique," *Connaissance des Arts* 1 (1970); Albert Van Gennep, *Les rites de passage* (Paris: Emile Nourry, 1900); and Victor Turner, *The Forest of Symbols* (Ithaca: Cornell University Press, 1977.)

5. This position is held, for example, by an art historian such as Kubler (*The Shape of Time*).

❖ *Index of Names* ❖